Praise for **INVISIBLE TARGET**

"*Invisible Target* is an important book. It is an honest and compelling memoir that takes the reader inside the mind of a young girl who was molested by her teacher and vividly describes the psychological and physical trauma she overcame to tell her story. It embodies the triumph of the human spirit.

"In the past, most targets of educator abuse have been unable to tell their stories. Some were convinced they were at fault or would not be believed. Others were unable to talk about the horror they experienced. Andrea describes how her teacher groomed her, how the abuse began, and how she found the courage to share her story. *Invisible Target* will help other youngsters in similar situations know they are not alone.

"Tragically, Andrea's story is not an aberration. Hundreds of teachers are molesting hundreds of children on a daily basis in our nation's schools. Although the topic is obviously very disturbing and disheartening, Andrea's story is one of hope."

—Robert J. Shoop, Ph.D., Professor Emeritus, Kansas State University,
    former director of the Cargill Center for Ethical Leadership,
    founder of Kansas State University's School of Leadership Studies
    Dr. Shoop has served as a forensic expert in over one hundred educator abuse cases.

"*Invisible Target* is a compelling story from a very courageous woman, Andrea Clemens. This is a story of survival and victory over a great many adversities that came from people who held positions of sacred trust . . . the trust of caring for and protecting a child and later a young woman.

"*Invisible Target* cries out to be read. Andrea's story gives readers an intimate view into the epidemic of educator sexual abuse. Andrea is not alone in her story. This story is one of several thousand—past, present, and regrettably the future.

"It is a painful view—one that will cause the readers to cringe, especially classroom teachers. How is it possible that a state-licensed teacher chooses to cross professional boundaries to 'groom,' abuse, and rape an innocent student?

"Andrea speaks to the reader about things 'unspeakable,' but things all students, parents, and educators should and need to hear. As it took great courage for Andrea to write her story, so it shall take courage to read this book. Being aware, acknowledging, and understanding educator sexual abuse is the only way to prevent and stop it.

"As a lifelong educator, veteran classroom teacher, and vice president of S.E.S.A.M.E., I highly recommend *Invisible Target* to be read and discussed in every school community in the country. In doing so, many students can be protected from the heinous crimes of educators who prey on our children.

"Thank you, Andrea, for having such great courage to tell us your story."

—John M. Seryak, M.Ed., Vice President of S.E.S.A.M.E.:
    Stop Educator Sexual Abuse, Misconduct, and Exploitation

"Andrea Clemens has written a courageously honest book about her experience of being the target of a teacher sexual predator. She lets the reader see how predators work and shares the often contradictory emotions and responses that those who are abused experience. But more than that, she takes us through her journey of awareness, anger, and empowerment. We see how hard it is and we see her triumph. Hers is not a rare story. What is rare is that Ms. Clemens is willing to tell it without holding back or simplifying the complexity of emotions and responses. This book can help students identify predators, parents to support their children, and educators to prevent abuse."

—Charol Shakeshaft, Ph.D., Professor, School of Education,
    Virginia Commonwealth University

INVISIBLE TARGET

Breaking the Cycle of Educator Sexual Abuse

ANDREA CLEMENS

Chris,
Thank you for making
this book a reality!

Andrea Clemens

HICKORY NUT
PUBLISHING
CLERMONT, FLORIDA

Published by:
Hickory Nut Publishing
Clermont, FL

ISBN: 978-0-69239-219-5

Cover and interior design: Gary A. Rosenberg • www.thebookcouple.com
Cover photograph: Shauna Hundeby • East Coast Photography

Printed in the United States of America

Contents

———◄○►———

To the voices that refuse to be silenced,
to the helpers who refuse to look the other way,
and to the adults who trust their instincts
and protect our children

Acknowledgments

———◄○►———

A book like this would not be possible without the help and support of others. I'm fortunate to have many people who have supported me, not only in the process of writing this book, but also in helping me to become the woman I am today.

I want to thank God and all His angels for protecting me throughout the years. Although I questioned God's presence at various dark times in my life, it is now crystal clear to me that He was right by my side, providing me with a greater purpose than the immediate pain I was experiencing.

I can say with absolute certainty that this book could not have been written without the assistance of my partner William Vaughan. One of the greatest blessings I have ever received was the day I met him. Not only has he brought me great joy and complete acceptance, but also he literally helped me write this book. I had been intermittently writing it for about eight years and had little accomplished. Once William got involved, the real work began. He helped me organize my thoughts, my paragraphs, and my chapters. He encouraged me when I was frustrated, and he soothed me when I was anxious. He pushed me when I was too timid or tentative to write the real truth, and he slowed me down when the real truth got too mean. I will be forever grateful for William's influence on my life and on this book.

I want to offer special thanks to my favorite Book Couple, Carol and Gary Rosenberg. Gary's involvement with the book's layout and cover created the exact look and feel I desired, and he did this effortlessly. Carol spent many hours editing these pages with the utmost care and intuitive attention. The blend of her understanding of the importance in my message with her years of expertise in publishing made *Invisible Target* the book I wanted it to be.

Shauna Hundeby from East Coast Photography did a superb job in capturing my vision for the front cover of *Invisible Target*. We met at predawn and carried an old school desk for what felt like miles through paths and fields. I silently questioned, "What could possibly warrant this early hour and this arduous trek to make a picture look so good?" I quickly found my answer. I wanted the cover of this book to evoke an emotional reaction, and Shauna certainly delivered.

Many others shared their support and expertise to help this book come to its fruition. Some of the folks who graciously provided their time, thoughts, and experience were Jodie Beckstine, Casey Brown, Laura Brown, Michelle Corbin, Dr. Charles Hobson, Heather Honekamp, Matt Killian, David Maldonado, Nancy Foley McCafferty, Terri Miller, Dr. Charol Shakeshaft, John Seryak, and Dr. Robert Shoop.

I consulted multiple people through emails, Facebook, personal meetings, phone calls, and other ways to gather facts, compare notes, bounce ideas, or simply to ask for cheerleader support throughout the writing of these chapters. Some of these wonderful supporters include Debbie Badamo, Linda Baker, Chris Barber, Casey Brown, Laura Brown, Kelli Bryant, Linda Cieri, Paul Cieri, Ron Cieri Jr., Cheryl Clemens, Karen Cote, Jill DeBlasio, Marcia DiMaria, Vicky Ferguson, John Ferrari, Laura Grohe, Deborah Hirschland, Denise Kiley, Andrew Kral, Lynn Lypsey, Jennifer Martin, Joan McNamara, Joe Paras, Brian Petrie, Alvin Pollard, Sherri Smith, Kristin Stone, April Troiani, Ashley Varnum, and Paul Vasington.

There is no way I would have been able to arrive at the place of healing I have had it not been for the love and support of so many warm people throughout the years. Some I see every day, while others I have not spoken with in decades. I hope they all know that their impact on my life and in my healing was vital for me to be able to share my story in a way that can hopefully help others. I would love to list everyone here, but the list would look like another book altogether. Thank you for all your valuable influence.

I want to thank my family for loving me, even during the times when they had no idea who I was or what I was going through.

I have a very special thank-you saved for my son, Zachary Clemens. Zach has shown me what true innocence is all about and how it should be protected. He helped me become a stronger parent and woman just by being himself. One of my many prayers for Zach is that he may always know his boundaries and be able to speak the truth, no matter how frightening that may be.

I made the decision to independently publish *Invisible Target* and decided to launch a Kickstarter campaign to raise the necessary funds to get this book out into the public. Kickstarter is a crowd-funding platform that helps people generate funds to create a project. Publishing this book is a dream come true for me, but it would never have been possible without the phenomenal, generous support of so many people who share my determination in educating people about this epidemic. The following is a list of the names of wonderful people who took time out of their busy lives to watch and read my campaign, pledge their hard-earned money, and share my project with countless others. My gratitude is endless.

Sally Friedman Berenzweig, Katrina Levensaler Pytel, William Vaughan, Jon Gress, Saham Ali, Erum Ali, Aaron Juntunen, Angel Gonzalez, Steve Porter, Lauren Dottley, Kevin Nations, Caleb Cover, Linda Baker, Deborah Hirschland, Mary Kate DiNisio, Linda Schiller, Vicky Ferguson, Kristen Croke, Bob Shoop, James Sutton, Kirsten Raymond, Michelle Corbin, Rocco Tartamella, Lee, Susan Zeichner, Trevor O'Hare, Michael Keith, Stephen Grocer, Florian "Spelaea" Hirt, Joslyn Cardin, Amy Chen, Bill Westwood, Susan H., Christine and Myanna Carbin- O'Brien, Laura Brown, Lisa Caudle, Chrissy McDonald, Susan Krupski, Amy, Kay and Bob Blaha, Jude Ierardi, Elaine LeFave, Stephen and Donna McDonald, Catherine Connor-Moen, Kevin and Maggie O'Connell, Jeff and Anne Scheetz, Kristina, James Yuenger, Debra Kral, Tom Bremer, Sarah Sanders, Colin Eggers, Jean MacFarland, Jennifer Lake, Chocolate Soop, Kristin Cieri, Chris Molonea, Steph Carse, Kelli Bryant, Sharon Osborn, Eileen Ewashko, Donna Hobbs, Cheryl Clemens, Charles Mitchell, Linda Cieri, Laura West, Donna Sullivan,

Ron Cieri, Jr., Casey Brown, Jennifer Martin, Dan and Sue Slowe, Debbie Badamo, Rita Liza, Adrienne Sanders, Dave West, Tom, Marvin Miller, Mary Baker, Leni Gross Young, Michelle McKinley, Cherie Benjoseph, Thomas Nassar, Michael Russer, Maria Doyle, Bethany McGonnigal, Susan Baker O'Connor, Tony Stranges, Wendy Johnson Sharon, Amy Nerdig, Amy Rose, Tammy and Michael Wiggins, Scott Frank, Tony Stranges, Tammy Lewis, Randy Congdon, Heather Vaughan, Jen Koch, Paul Vasington, Raquel Paz, Dennis Folan, Kurt, John Ricci, Lois Folan, Barbara Kornack, Lisa Sheridan, Gil Perez, Kim Lilja, Dorine S. Russo, Sheila Downing-Ruth, Cheryl Knox, Susanne Maher, Bob Martin, Maureen Sullivan, Kimberly, John Nee, John Seryak, Tammy Daughtry, Nancy Bilotta Scavotto, Carol Benanti-Nowlin, Evan Dimov, Maureen Jacobson, Mary McElroy, Lynn Lipsey, Mariann Bradley, Jill DeBlasio, Kristin and Matt, Donna Meschke, Matthew and Jodie Killian, April Troiani, Chuck Baenen, Denise Kiley, Allison Mahan Manis, Laurie, Edith McGee, Jeanne Lesperance and Frank Collins, Dana Mosley Sieben, Sue Rodman, Jim Delbou, Christine Holton, Lauren and Clint Bierman, Christine Norton Sheehan, Joe DiMaria, Ashley Brent, Terri Miller, Chevonne, Karen Cote, Destry Holmes, John Cieri, Cathy Shachoy, The Meehan family, Melodie Bissell, Ashli T., Sheila Brown, Mike, Joe Paras, Nora Crouch, Donna Feola, Mark Davis, Shauna Hundeby, Danielle Cooper, Renee Maloof, Jill Cannon-Dadmun, Joan Ball Scanlon, William and Sandra Discepolo, Shannon and Bill Novick, Heather Severson, Author of *Trust Me: Lessons I Should Not Have Learned in School*, Christine Farrell-Riley, Tim and Taryen Shannon, Karen Donahue, Robin A. Greiner, Chris O'Riley, Cathie Green Twiraga, Yvette Lugo, Laurie Baker, KiloMarie Granda, Tim DeMarco, Michelle Hopkins Hallock, Margot Napoli Bryant, David Maldonado, The McKenney family, Mike Patterson, Henry Grau, Andrea Bonner, Ponce Adult Family Care, Arianne Adamson, Marcia DiMaria, and Karla Van Horn.

And finally, I want to thank you for reading this book. Please share any lessons you learn from my story. Let's work together to keep our children safe.

Foreword

———◀◯▶———

Educator sexual misconduct—what's in a name? *Epidemic, ignorance, shame, anguish, stolen innocence, despair, betrayal, trauma, humiliation, fear, broken relationships, chaos, confusion, lifelong suffering, mental illness, physical illness, suicide.* One would think with all these severe symptoms that we as a society would come together to help and demand justice. Sadly that is not the case. Year after year, thousands of children are suffering the effects of sexual abuse at the hands of educators and school staff.

Nearly 1 in 10 children between kindergarten and twelfth grade will experience some form of educator sexual misconduct. One in 7 children will experience physical sexual abuse by an entrusted educator. Every year hundreds of teachers/coaches/ancillary staff are arrested for sexual crimes against students. In 2014, over 450 teachers made the headlines with arrests for sexual crimes against their students.

The Los Angeles Unified School District settled lawsuits with multiple victims on one elementary school teacher's sexual abuse case, for nearly $170 million. Millions of children's lives are irrevocably changed, decade after decade. Again, one would think this problem is a no-brainer to fix and that school administrators, legislators, and community leaders would be scrambling to correct and extricate the offenders with swift and sure action to protect our children, but, sadly, that is not the case. Victims are disbelieved and vilified, parents become exasperated trying to seek justice, perpetrators are given a pass with quiet resignations or full-pension retirements, and administrators would rather save face and money than save a child. In other words, child protection is clearly not a high priority in school systems.

Over thirty years ago, I was informed about the inappropriate behavior of a high school teacher in the small town where I was raising my family, Pahrump, Nevada. In 1983, after the aerobics class I was taking ended, my instructor asked me if I would take over the weekly class and keep it going. She told me she was divorcing her husband and leaving town. She was a math teacher at the high school, and her husband was a teacher and coach. She said she had found him in bed with a high school student.

I had just had my third child and my oldest daughter was four years old. This information was especially disturbing because my children would one day attend that school. I called the principal the next morning to report what I had been told. He told me that without a victim coming forward, there was nothing he could do.

Those words would stick with me for the next thirteen years. I continued to make complaints and inquiries to any local official who would listen. It was abundantly clear that I was up against a system that was more concerned about the reputation of its award-winning championship coach than it was about children being sexually abused by him.

I made attempts to bring in trainers to educate the students about sexual harassment in the hopes one of them would report, but the school principal refused to approve the training event. When my eldest daughter reached high school age, I forbade her from taking any classes or participating in any activities that the teacher taught or supervised. I filed a formal complaint under Title IX, in 1993, specifically asking for a formal investigation of the teacher, hoping that enough evidence would be found so the school board would have grounds to terminate him.

By this time, the teacher had married and divorced the student he had been caught in bed with ten years earlier, rendering her into a state of single motherhood. He already had his next victim in his clutches and married her in the midst of the investigation. Even though the investigation found ample grounds for the investigator to make a recommendation to terminate, the school board only suspended the child predator for five days without pay.

After the teacher threatened to sue the district if they didn't remove the findings from his file and reimburse him his pay, the school district settled with him. That same year the teacher started his campaign for a seat on the school board. With defeat weighing heavy on me, I tenaciously and vigorously pursued an investigation to identify the victims.

After he won the primary election, I began my quest to find the victims and encourage them to come forward. I spent countless hours, with the help of a handful of friends to help me find them. In the end, the teacher was elected to the school board, but two weeks later, he was arrested on three counts of sexual assault against his most recent victim, a 1994 graduate. She had the assurance that sixty-five victim/witnesses would be supporting her case. In the spring of 1996, the teacher finally pled an Alford Plea to one count of sexual assault and was sentenced that summer to five years to life in prison. He served sixteen years and is a registered sex offender for life.

Unfathomably, my story is not unique. Many victims, their families, and school faculty have similar struggles in ridding their schools of sexual predators. I always find it incredulous that extricating a child predator from a school becomes an exasperating battle. It just shouldn't be that hard.

In my own case, the principal could have easily called his own employee in to question her (the math teacher) about finding her husband (the teacher/coach) in bed with one of his students. That should have been enough for him to take swift and sure action to protect the children in my community. This case and many other incidents of sexual offense against children in our local high school uncovered the need for policy change and laws to prohibit sexual abuse of students. Thus, my advocacy work began.

In 1996, after my story went out on the AP wire, I was contacted by S.E.S.A.M.E. (then known as Survivors of Educator Sexual Abuse and Misconduct Emerge) to become a member. I was asked periodically to share my experience with others going through similar struggles. I appeared on national news programs and in a number of articles. I lobbied the Nevada Legislature to criminalize sexual conduct between educators and students who were over the age of consent, in 1997. I filed Title IX complaints together that resulted in a complete compliance review of the school district's policies and procedures on handling sexual harassment and discrimination complaints.

All of these experiences equipped me to become the advocate I am today. In 2001, I took up the leadership role as President of S.E.S.A.M.E. at the behest of our founder, Mary Ann Werner. Our board of directors decided we needed a more proactive name. Stop Educator Sexual Abuse, Misconduct & Exploitation began its evolution to become the leading national voice to protect students from sexual abuse by educators and other school staff.

Serving as S.E.S.A.M.E's leading advocate, I met Andrea Clemens. She is a rare survivor in that she has remained in contact for over ten years. I have had the privilege to serve her and support her throughout her ordeals and victories. I have always been in awe of Andrea's ability to articulate her experience in such an elegant and composed manner. I have watched her grow from a reserved survivor to a self-assured outspoken advocate and activist.

There is no more persuasive voice than that of one who has suffered and survived. S.E.S.A.M.E. has always given survivors like Andrea and others a platform to elevate their voice and to advocate for one another. Andrea has truly been dependably supportive to countless survivors who are forever grateful for her wise words of encouragement and heartfelt empathy. She has made a huge impact in legislative change and public awareness. I am so fortunate to have had the experience of raising our mighty voices together in perfect harmony to make real change in our communities and our country.

Invisible Target is a masterfully written account of Andrea's experience that illuminates the complexities of succumbing to methodical grooming techniques, emotional manipulations, calculated physical intrusion, and mind-controlling coercion. She has thoughtfully written this book with prevention as the hallmark of her arduous writing endeavor. It's not just an autobiography; it is a training tool to instruct all stakeholders within educational environments, not just schools but any facility or extracurricular activity where children and adults interact.

Andrea's comprehension of the importance of bringing awareness to the epidemic of educator sexual abuse and misconduct is a giant leap forward in the battle to protect America's school children. Her understanding of the complexities of victimization and survivor recovery is so vitally important in educating school staff, students, parents, and all community stakeholders. Without knowledge, there is no change. Training is the key to prevention and intervention.

Andrea is determined to make change. She is able and ready to deploy her mighty voice in support of legislative overhaul. With Andrea's support in 2014, Pennsylvania was the first state to pass the Stop Educator Sexual Abuse, Misconduct & Exploitation Bill. She has given her all to help support this legislation that criminalizes educator sexual misconduct with students and prohibits the insidious practice of what is known as "passing the trash"—the troubling act of allowing abusive teachers to quietly resign and move to other school districts.

This legislation also mandates annual training. The Protecting Students from Sexual and Violent Predators Act—a federal bill that will mandate states to conduct comprehensive and uniform background checks on all school personnel, including ancillary staff and prohibit "passing the trash" from state to state—is also supported by S.E.S.A.M.E. together with the amazing Andrea.

In closing, I just want to say—Andrea, I am honored to have served you, I am privileged to know you and to have become your friend, I am inspired by you, and I am blessed to be witness to all your triumphant success. *Invisible Target*—you did it and you did it well. You are not invisible anymore!

—Terri L. Miller, President of Stop Educator Sexual Abuse,
Misconduct & Exploitation (S.E.S.A.M.E., Inc.)

Introduction

————◄○►————

When I decided to take on the task of writing a memoir about the abuse I suffered, I had few illusions about the challenges ahead of me. The topic of educator sexual abuse alone can evoke strong feelings in almost anyone. But what exactly does this term mean?

When I refer to *educator sexual abuse,* I am referring to the alarmingly inappropriate actions of school employees who abuse their positions of power and manipulate children for their own pleasure and other selfish, misguided reasons. We have all heard stories in the media in which someone who has been teaching for many years suddenly gets caught having an "affair" with a student, and the whole community is shocked. "He was such a well-respected, popular teacher," they say. "How could this be true?"

People tend to think these stories are rare incidents, when in fact 39 million people in the United States are victims of childhood sexual abuse, according to the *Journal of Interpersonal Violence.* When the Penn State child sex abuse scandal erupted in 2011, a country's attention was focused on the horrors assistant football coach Jerry Sandusky had inflicted upon numerous boys for many years. We also learned that various administrators and coaches had turned a blind eye to this horrific behavior, permitting the torment and abuse to continue.

Sadly, this is only one of thousands, perhaps millions of stories like it. For every story the media covers, countless others are hidden away, silenced. Many stories remain untold.

I decided it was time to tell my story.

The exact moment I made this decision eludes me. However, as I got older, the voice inside me that had once been silenced grew louder and stronger. I first saw this book as an opportunity to document a harrowing and painful experience and my subsequent survival. I knew that, as difficult as the task would be, a written account would be important for my overall well-being. That is truly why I embarked on this writing journey.

As my manuscript progressed, however, I found a greater purpose in my story. As I typed, I could feel what I can only describe as a warm energy surrounding me, and I felt somehow protected as the words flowed onto the page. I had a "knowing" that my work was no longer simply self-serving.

Throughout this book, many lessons ring loud and clear. Much of the time, it didn't feel like these messages came from me, but rather it felt as if they came *through* me. I have a strong, deep belief that the reason I endured the abuse I share in this book is precisely because I am someone who *can* share my story and the lessons learned to help others. **I have always been amazed that the people who seem to be the deepest and most empathic are those who have suffered the greatest. I am now one of them.**

The difficult challenges I faced during this process presented themselves on several levels. First, while I have written papers for graduate school and I have composed several songs for my own and my friends' enjoyment, I never considered myself a writer. An undertaking such as writing a book—a real book with the intention that others would actually read it—was a daunting thought.

Second, while my story is beautiful at times, it is also ugly. To write "ugly" in an honest manner was more challenging than I had expected. I anticipate that many readers will not understand some of the actions I took or, in some cases, my inaction. I don't expect everyone who reads this to approve of, or agree with, some of the decisions I made. Being a perpetual people-pleaser, I found this particularly difficult to work through. Conversely, writing the beautiful parts was not easy either. I had become accustomed to negative self-talk, so presenting any part of myself as strong, whole, and confident challenged me to my core.

Third, to write some of these chapters, I had to revisit feelings and events that frankly were not my favorite places to visit. As a result, I had some really tough days and nights throughout this process with occasional flashbacks and panic attacks. I would become frightened, anxious, and angry with myself, feeling like I had lost my momentum. The consistent and gentle reassurance of wonderful friends who reminded me that judging the process would get me nowhere kept me moving forward.

Finally, I was worried about how certain people would react to this book. Growing up in a climate of silence, I was trained to protect other people's secrets and shame. However, for readers to grasp and recognize the nature of the abuse, certain events had to be included—regardless of how tough it was for me to write or how tough it may be for someone to read. I have moved to a place of true acceptance and forgiveness in my life, and I have no desire to "bash" anyone. Please understand that I have written this book in the spirit of truth and understanding. Each person involved in my story has helped to create the woman I am today, and, for that, I am grateful.

So why write a book if all these challenges are so painful?

I had no choice but to write it. This book is not about making myself or others feel comfortable. Throughout the process I kept telling myself, "This book *must* be written." According to the U.S. Department of Education's *Educator Sexual Misconduct: A Synthesis of Existing Literature* by Charol Shakeshaft, nearly one in ten children will experience some form of sexual misconduct by a school employee by his or her senior year. One in ten! That's 4.5 million kids! This is clearly a very troubling epidemic. How could I possibly keep this story to myself? I wish someone had handed me this book during my years of abuse—or, better yet, before the abuse began.

So, ultimately, I wrote this book to raise awareness of educator sexual abuse. Who better to weigh in and illustrate the inner workings of these crimes than someone who experienced the abuse directly?

I want *Invisible Target* to cause teachers to scratch their heads and say, "Hmm, why is 'Mr. White' spending so much time with 'Susie'? Something just doesn't seem right. I had better look into it."

I want this book to cause administrators to say, "I must report this allegation to the police, or countless other students could be harmed."

I want this book to cause parents to say, "I should speak to my child about the time she is spending with her teacher outside of school."

I want this book to cause girls to say, "What if 'Mr. Powers' is only showing me special attention so that he can take advantage of me?"

Although I tend to use feminine pronouns when referring to the student, I want boys to see themselves in these pages as well. I want *all* children to understand the difference between a sincere interest in their well-being and inappropriate attention from a teacher.

Can this book alone put an end to educator sexual abuse? No. However, if it can raise awareness, if some schools become safer, or if even one student is spared the horrors of abuse from a school employee, then this book has done its job.

Why did I choose the title *Invisible Target*? I believe this title reflects a good understanding of the complicated nature of this type of abuse. Many targets of educator sexual abuse are kids who feel they are invisible. They are in need of attention, love, and care. They are lost and looking for guidance and acceptance. Abusive teachers have an uncanny ability to hone in on the kids in the back of the pack, those who are lost and straggling behind. The "invisible" part of the abuse equation is a vital one.

For years I believed my story was bizarre and unique. After all my research, I came to realize that my experiences presented a textbook case of abuse. I recognized the personal things that happened to me in virtually everything I read on the topic. To see identical accounts of my painful experiences discussed in writing was both jarring and comforting. Therefore, this book is more than just a memoir. I am presenting it as a case study.

Please keep in mind that I did not sugarcoat any of the material in this book. At times I found it necessary to speak in a fairly graphic nature about what happened to me. I write about body parts, sexual acts, and raw thoughts and feelings. While the majority of this book is not graphic in nature, I found it crucial to explain the circumstances as honestly and authentically as possible to accurately depict the abuse I endured.

WHO SHOULD READ THIS BOOK?

The audience for this book includes students, parents, teachers, administrators, and survivors. At the end of each chapter, I ask a series of questions for the reader's consideration from the viewpoint of each group in the target audience or generally. My hope is that these questions will create dialogue among parents, children, administrators, teachers, and other school staff. To begin, I ask some important questions below that I hope you will answer for yourself as you embark on my cautionary, eye-opening story:

Students—This book is geared for middle and high school students who can handle some of the more graphic details. Students can be the first line of defense in protecting themselves and one another from educator sexual abuse. They are the pulse of the school and generally know every rumor and incident that takes place on and off campus. Students should ask themselves the following questions:

- *What would I do if my favorite teacher told me he or she had strong feelings for me?*

- *What if that teacher wanted to take me to the mall or out to my favorite restaurant?*

- *What if he bought me a gift to let me know how special I am?*

- *What if my best friend was spending more time with my teacher and less time with me?*

- *What would I do if my friend confided in me about her secret relationship with a special teacher of hers?*

- *What if I heard rumors about some teacher sleeping with a student? What would I do?*

These are not easy questions, but they are important ones, so I encourage students to talk to others about these questions and their answers. An active dialogue with other students, friends, parents, teachers, and administrators is the first step in creating a safe learning environment.

Parents—Parents have the toughest jobs in the world. Keeping our children safe is no small feat, especially in today's world. The more awareness and understanding parents have of the environment that surrounds their children, the more they can arm their kids with the proper tools for surviving and thriving. Parents should ask themselves the following questions:

- *Can my child really talk to me about everything?*

- *Does my child have a clear concept of her personal boundaries?*

- *How would I rate my child's self-esteem?*

- *How would she respond to special attention from her teacher?*

- *What would I do if my child tells me she feels like she "fits in" because her teacher spends extra time with her?*

- *How would I respond if my child's friends joked that a certain teacher is a pervert?*

Considering these questions and related scenarios can help parents start important discussions with their children about the dangers and realities of educator sexual abuse.

Teachers—I have the utmost respect for the many dedicated men and women who teach our children. They are faced with countless situations in any given school year in which judgment calls have to be made. By reading my story, teachers can be better equipped to pay attention to their instincts if something seems awry. They can gain insight into the behaviors of predatory educators as well as learn appropriate means of responding to concerns. Teachers should ask themselves the following questions:

- *What would I do if I saw a colleague spending extra time with students outside the classroom?*

- *What would I do if I saw another teacher giving a student a ride home after school?*

- *How would I handle a student telling me that a certain educator gives her the creeps?*

- *How would I respond to rumors about a well-respected coach having a sexual relationship with one of his athletes?*

- *What if one of my students told me that the educator recently voted teacher of the year had touched her hair in a way that made her feel uncomfortable?*

The more teachers consider their answers to these questions and discuss them with one another, the more aware and prepared they will be to adequately address the threat of educator sexual abuse.

Administrators—In addition to their responsibility to provide safe environments for both students and teachers, administrators should be aware that school districts and administrators could be held liable for failing to report allegations of educator sexual abuse to the proper authorities. Administrators should ask themselves the following questions:

- *What training, if any, is in place for educating the staff about educator sexual abuse?*

- *How often is this training conducted?*

- *Is the training adequate to provide clear and concise protocols for every staff member to know how to proceed in the event of a concern about misconduct?*

Administrators must adequately address the threat of educator sexual abuse with their staff and make every effort to keep the children in their care safe from predators within their own school walls.

Survivors—I have told my story to many people over the years, and I am always surprised by the number of people who share with me that they have had similar experiences. There are *many* survivors out there. As this book goes to publication, I personally know eight people who experienced some form of sexual misconduct by a school employee during their childhoods.

My hope for survivors who read this book is twofold. First, I hope that by sharing the account of my abuse, survivors can gain a sense of peace in knowing that they are not alone so that additional healing can take place. Second, I hope that my message of speaking out and breaking the silence around sexual abuse can be fully grasped and appreciated. **There are many dangers in remaining silent. Silence can perpetuate the shame that is often wrongly integrated by the survivor. Even more dangerous is the potential for the abuse to be thrust upon others.** Survivors reading this book should answer these questions:

- *Did I ever tell anyone about the abuse?*

- *Is the teacher who abused me still teaching?*

- *Does any administrator know about the abuse?*

- *Were the police notified?*

- *Did the teacher get reassigned to another school district?*

- *What might happen if I continue to keep this abuse to myself?*

- *What if I heard that this same teacher abused more students after me?*

- *What if the teacher abused students prior to me, and no one told anybody?*

- *How would that make me feel?*

- *If I have children of my own, how would I feel knowing my child was sitting in a classroom with a teacher who has abused students in the past?*

I know firsthand how difficult and painful it is to examine these questions. Unfortunately, I also know the greater pain that comes from leaving the questions unexamined. Please consider your answers to these questions and the issues surrounding them while reading my story.

* * *

Educator sexual abuse is clearly an epidemic that needs heightened awareness. Although this book may be difficult for many to read, my hope is that by sharing my story, I can help empower others to see warning signs and help prevent this abuse. Please take the lessons you learn here and share them with others.

CHAPTER ONE

The Child I Was

———◀○▶———

Only after a look back at my childhood can we fully understand the complicated layers of my story. One thing is certain to me:
  A target does not simply appear.
  It is created.

What is childhood supposed to look like? Have I met anyone who actually had an ideal childhood? Maybe. However, many people have told me over the years that their childhoods were far less than ideal or that they were *unique,* to say the least. I think many of us still hold an ideal of what childhood is supposed to look like in our minds. Perhaps this notion of an ideal childhood got created from watching television shows like *The Brady Bunch* or *The Cosby Show* or the countless others that have presented the template we've embedded in our minds, showing us that, at its core, the idea behind this ideal is a feeling of comfort—a comfort that is just out of reach for many of us.

Or maybe it is not that programmed. Maybe the uncertainty we feel about what an ideal childhood should be stems from being an outsider looking in through an ephemeral veil of happiness, while the lives being lived are the exact opposite of what we suppose. Many people seem to wear this veil of happiness, either individually or as a family, when in reality they are struggling in pain . . . and the veil is actually quite brittle.

When I think of what childhood is supposed to be like, I envision innocence, safety, trust, limits, boundaries, education, friends, sports, play, love, fun, hope, faith, religion. I could easily list a hundred more qualities. Ask any psychologist, and he or she will tell you that a child's foundation is critical in shaping the way the child walks through this world—how she makes decisions, how she views herself, how she forms relationships, how she functions in school and work, and so on. It defines who she will become as an adult. The family in which a child is raised is critical in the development of all these factors. Although my childhood was not completely void of all these qualities, it did lack many of them.

Why am I mentioning all this? Because if you are going to understand how a child can be targeted and manipulated by a teacher, or how this abusive "relationship" can last for years following high school, you need to understand the makeup of the child—of me. It's time to explore why I became the perfect invisible target.

An Ideal Childhood

By all appearances, I lived in a safe environment. I spent my entire childhood in one home in a small suburban town close to Boston. My neighborhood was an old-fashioned type where everyone knew one another. On Halloween, when we went trick or treating, we went to every single house, and parents who opened their doors knew who our parents were. I was able to walk to and from school, as it was located right at the end of my street. Since my mother was a stay-at-home mom, I even walked home for lunch. My paternal grandparents lived up at the top of the neighborhood. Their sons, my uncles, lived right down the street. In my early years, I was surrounded by cousins of all ages. Holidays were always spent together as a family at one house or another.

When I was young, we had pool parties and birthday parties. There was the normal amount of drinking and partying, but nothing excessive. To everyone else, we were a regular family—hardworking and fun. Other children would tell my brothers and me that we were so lucky to have a pool and such a cool family.

My father was the youngest of three boys. He was a high school graduate but never made it to college. He had been an average student and athlete with a sarcastic sense of humor and enjoyed being with people. When I was growing up, he owned a bakery several towns away, as well as a few apartment complexes and some land. He worked seven days a week. He had all kinds of reasons for working so much, including his paranoia that employees would steal from him if he weren't there to watch over them. He kept an apartment above the bakery so that he could maintain a close eye on business, we were told.

My father would sometimes make up fun games for my brothers and me. He and I shared our own silly game where we'd race to the grocery bags when my mother arrived home from shopping and search for the peanut butter. Whichever one of us could stick his or her finger in first to get a taste would win. I know it sounds gross, but it was one of the few games my father and I shared, so I loved it.

My mother was the elder of two girls in her family. She did well in school and sports. She graduated high school and received her associate's degree in business. She met my father when she was in her twenties and enjoyed his sense of humor and outgoing personality. She got pregnant with my eldest brother while they were dating, so they decided to get married. I'm not quite sure if true love was involved in this scenario, but their decision to marry was firm.

My mother did a lot of things right as a mom. She was kind, and she taught me to be kind to everyone else. She took me to church. Although my mother was Protestant, she agreed to raise us Catholic, as that was my father's religion. He never attended church, but he still wished for us to be raised in this faith. My mother taught me that no matter how different someone is on the outside, we are all the same on the inside. Fun and spontaneous, she would sometimes take us on surprise rides with no particular destination, and she had this "magic box" hidden somewhere in the house (I still don't know where), from which she would, from time to time, pull out a new toy or game or something just as fun. My mother always prepared great food. She helped me join lots of activities, and she sent me to camp for five consecutive summers. She would sing songs with me, and we'd get silly together. I am so grateful to her for all of these special memories.

My Brothers, Ronnie and Paul

I was the only girl and the middle child. Ronnie was two and a half years older than me, and Paul was three and a half years younger.

Ronnie (the one who got the brains in the family, I always say) taught me to read when I was three. I remember Ronnie being an avid reader. As part of the book club he started for us, we would read as many Golden Books in one sitting as we could. Aside from our books, I wouldn't say that Ronnie and I were close, and I actually don't have many memories of our spending time together as children. Ronnie went off to Noble and Greenough School, a private school, following junior high and then to college at West Point in New York. When he graduated, he was stationed out in Monterey, California. After serving his time, he went to Georgetown University in Washington, D.C. for his MBA.

Paul, on the other hand, was the cutest kid I have ever seen. I clearly remember growing up alongside him, and we played together often. The night before Paul turned five, I was really upset because I didn't want him to get any older, thinking he wouldn't be cute anymore. Paul and I played "creative" games like Trip. Yup, it's just like it sounds. One person stood at one end of the hall, and the other sat down at the other end and extended one leg outward. As the other ran full speed ahead down the hall, the sitting person would raise his or her leg high, trying to trip the runner. A very high jump was required to avoid plummeting to the ground. *Ahhh, good times!*

I also played tricks on my little brother and would scare him with ghost stories and alien tales out in the woods of New Hampshire. I often had fun at his expense, but I meant it all in fondness. He was a funny, sensitive kid that everyone laughed with—not *at, with.* He was really, really funny.

He was an average student and tried a few semesters at college. He settled into some different jobs and made his way out to California to be near Ronnie while he was stationed there. Ronnie moved around, but Paul remained out west.

The Extended Family

We lived in a suburban neighborhood about thirty minutes southeast of Boston. My father's parents were Italian. As was traditional in the Italian culture, my father and his two brothers all married and had kids, and they all lived in the same neighborhood. My grandfather and father purchased land and built houses on it.

Growing up, I spent a lot of time with my cousins and my paternal grandparents: Nana and Grandpa. They were a funny couple. They would argue in Italian, but every once in a while, a "Dammit, Maude!" would come flying out.

Holidays were always about family . . . and food—specifically, pasta. At Christmas, we had pasta. At Thanksgiving, we had pasta. Easter? Pasta . . . and I didn't mind one bit. My grandparents made the best pasta and sauce I have ever tasted.

My mother's side of the family was much smaller. Her parents lived in New Hampshire, and they would sometimes visit us on holidays. Occasionally, we would head up to see them as well. My mother had one sister, with whom she was, and is, extremely close.

Grateful and Yet . . .

What I described above probably sounds to you like an ideal childhood. But that was our brittle veil and that was you looking in from the outside. Of course I am grateful for many aspects of my life growing up, but there was much more going on behind the scenes. Yes, my father paid the bills. Yes, we had enough food to eat. Yes, we lived in a comfortable home with a pool in the backyard. Yes, we went on field trips and took a two-week vacation each summer in New Hampshire at my grandparents' cottage. Yes, I appreciate all those things, and I am so grateful to have had the basic necessities to help me survive.

I understand that a father is supposed to be a provider for his family, but I believe a provider needs to do more than work hard to put "pasta" on the table. A true provider creates a safe and loving environment. He nurtures his family. He assures them through his words and actions that he will never consciously fail them. He cheers on their successes and provides a shoulder to cry on. No matter how busy a man may be providing for his family, his wife and children should feel him in their hearts.

By all appearances I had an ideal childhood. The trouble with appearances is that they can be quite deceiving, and few things in this life are black and white. The reality of my childhood was quite different from those appearances. My life was filled with utter chaos. Inside my pretty home also existed a world of fear, abuse, and oppression with my father at the core of it all.

My father was the scariest, angriest man I have ever known. He controlled each person in our family in various ways. He would react to random occurrences and conversations with a Hulk-like rage, which kept me on my toes at all times. My instincts told me that he was a cruel man and a bad person, but that was too harsh a reality for me to accept as a child. That's how I learned *not* to trust my gut. He was my father, right? Dads can't be bad, can they? I don't think young children can believe their parents are bad or wrong. I certainly couldn't. I internalized everything and believed I was the bad and wrong one. It would take me years as an adult to rewire this thinking.

As wonderful and as fun as my mother could be, she also stayed on the surface, never delving too deep into any topics or feelings. She was not one to enjoy conflict and could not address the "elephant in the living room." Whenever one of my father's blowups would occur, she wouldn't check in with us kids to see if we were okay. She was too busy just surviving my father's mental abuse, and I believe she existed in survival mode for much of my youth.

What should a mother be or do? A mother's role is easy to define on paper. She should nurture and provide a safe environment. She should shelter her children from harm just enough but not so much that they can't learn from life's lessons. She, too, should cheer on their victories and pick them up when they fall. However, in an abusive, broken household, those things are close to impossible for a mother to achieve. My mother resorted to keeping up appearances, so that we appeared to be a normal family. I got the sense she didn't want any of our teachers knowing what was going on at home. I don't know how much she told her friends or family. Today, my mother tells me that she was simply ill equipped to properly deal with my father's erratic, abusive behavior.

Dynamics Between Parents

When I picture my parents together back then, I only remember the tension between them. I certainly can't remember any fondness, affection, or even laughter. That's not to say they didn't share these things, but I don't recall witnessing any of them. My father put my mother down, made fun of her, and was just plain mean to her. She seemed intimidated by him and held back her words, thoughts, and feelings much of the time.

I learned a lot from this dynamic. My first impressions of a relationship consisted of control, manipulation, intimidation, humiliation, and secrecy. I watched very closely to learn how my mother avoided my father's wrath, and I tried to follow suit. She was better at it than I was, but I practiced very hard.

Clearly terrified of my father, my mother couldn't stand up to him or protect us from his anger. My father would often manipulate and guilt her in various ways with mind games like threatening divorce if she shared her displeasure about something he said or did. She'd always backpedal and do whatever it took to pacify the situation. He found ways to guilt and manipulate us all into getting his way. He blamed us for being unhappy rather than taking responsibility for his own actions and feelings. Many people are surprised when I tell them my father wasn't a drinker or a drug abuser. There was no outside influence on which to blame his horrific behavior.

My father cheated on my mother. Apparently he even cheated on her with an underage girl and went to jail for a brief period. How this fact eluded me until recently illustrates the finesse my family possessed in the fine art of secret keeping. When I learned this distasteful fact, it initially surprised me. However, as I weaved together the pieces of my childhood, the shock factor grew weaker. Nothing about my father's capacity to be a bad husband or father could surprise me. Many signs pointed to his unfaithfulness (which I didn't recognize as a child), such as when he would stay in his apartment above the bakery for longer and more frequent spans.

The hardest times occurred at the dinner table. We never knew what would set him off. We would be having a normal dinner, and all of a sudden, he would just snap. On rare occasions, he would make up a game to play with us at the dinner table, like guessing the manufacturing state of the ketchup. I lived for those rare moments, as they could convince me that everything would be okay—at least for an hour. But most nights were tense, and we just tried not to make him angry. One night my father smashed a clay pot Paul had made in school that day against the kitchen window and shouted at us, "See how crazy you people make me?" I just remember the crushed look on Paul's face. My mother sat there and said nothing. Unfortunately, each incident elicited the same response, or lack thereof, in my mother. She froze. And that's what we learned from her.

My father would smash things a lot. Sometimes, if the phone would ring while we were eating, he would hurl a dish or glass at it, then pick the receiver up and throw it, causing the receiver to bounce off the wall and come whipping back on its cord. Everyone would jump up to grab it so the person on the other end wouldn't hear the chaos and quickly hang it up. Normally my father was very aware of keeping the affairs of the family secret. But when he got angry, he didn't seem to care. My father's rage seemed to be a secret we all worked to conceal. We were the ones who didn't want anyone to know. We were the ones who kept his secret safe. I cannot recall a time when I was explicitly given the mandate to keep this secret. It was simply a given, an unspoken understanding in our house. No one could know that a tyrant ran our family.

Control and Withholding

My father never hit any of us as far as I am aware. He didn't need to. He controlled us without the use of physical violence. He outwardly withheld his love, and we tried not to make him angry. I became hypervigilant, trying to do everything right so I wouldn't set him off on a tirade. I took his cruel actions as punishment for something I must have done. I tried whatever I could to avoid his punishing behavior toward me, but my attempts never seemed to hold much weight. He withheld his love from me regardless of my actions. I tried to make him proud by concentrating on schoolwork and music, but all my efforts fell short.

My father also used money to control us, as the two went hand in hand. Once when I asked for some money to buy clothes with a cousin of mine in tow, he flatly refused. My cousin confided in me years later that she'd been appalled, as money was certainly not in short supply in our household and he never spent any of it on us. Not buying me clothes was just another way he maintained control over me. Kids at school teased me because I didn't have the "right clothes." Of course I'm not saying that not having the "right clothes" is an abusive trademark. If I had come from a loving home, being a fashion misfit would have been a manageable childhood reality. This was more about the withholding dynamic, which felt worse, because I got the feeling I did not matter enough for him to buy clothes for me.

My father used money to control my mother as well. One Christmas she opened a gift from him to reveal a box of cash. I am sure that sounds great to some people reading this, but this was an incredibly awkward moment. I could see she didn't know what to say. I could feel it. There was no tenderness between them at all. She just sort of said, "Ron!" And he kind of had a blank stare. She just uttered, "Uh . . . thank . . . thank you." I watched my father's expression. It is hard to describe the look on his face. The feeling I got from his expression was that he seemed somehow victorious when she opened that box, as if this gift held something over her. She certainly didn't seem thrilled to receive it. I wondered what that cash really meant.

My father's need for control grew worse as my brothers and I grew older. He would make me wait to take a shower in the morning before school, and then he'd go into the bathroom when I needed to get in there so that I couldn't use it. He would wear an expression on his face as if he had tricked me and won some sort of sick game. Aside from my out-of-style clothes, the kids also teased me about my greasy hair. Needless to say, I didn't have many friends in elementary school.

I know that I have repressed multiple other examples of how my father degraded me, and, quite frankly, I am grateful for the ability to repress things. Repression is sometimes a precious gift our minds offer us when faced with trauma. Various family members sometimes bring up uncomfortable incidents that I cannot recollect. For example, Ronnie tells me my father would often humiliate me in front of other people, and I truly have no recollection of the examples he gives. He also told me that my father would literally shove food in my mouth. I have zero recollection of this occurring. I tried for years to remember certain things, and now I have made peace with the fact that some things were just too painful to remember. It is also interesting to me, and I remind myself often, that just because I don't remember doesn't mean it didn't happen.

Winnie the Pooh

Once, when I was about five, I desperately wanted to watch a Winnie the Pooh special on TV. All day, my father reminded me about the show, getting me excited, saying he'd watch it with me. I even remember the blue polka-dot mug he let me fill with chocolate chip ice cream to eat during the show. He sat me in a chair in front of the television, and I was incredibly excited to watch the show and grateful that my father was in an unusually good mood. He turned on the TV and let me watch the commercials before the show. As soon as *Winnie the Pooh* came on, he snapped the television off and walked away. It was as if he had been planning it all day, building it up, reveling in the control he had over me. I was left sitting there alone with my ice cream in my little mug. Then he yelled for me to sweep the floor in the kitchen.

Now that I am a mother, it changes my perspective on the depths of my father's cruel nature. I cannot recall what thoughts went through my mind at that young age. I can only imagine that I thought I must have done something terribly wrong to deserve such a huge disappointment. I know my little five-year-old heart was broken.

At that age, a child cannot think her father is crazy, so she will internalize that feeling and think that there has to be something wrong with her, and that's exactly what I did. As an adult, I look back and realize that it was this type of strange control and oppression that molded me into the adolescent who would become the perfect target for sexual abuse.

Craving Attention

I can't look back on my childhood without a sense of longing for attention and craving to be seen. I sort of gave up looking for it from my parents. My mother was attentive in terms of caring for me and overseeing my schoolwork and activities, but I never felt that she was there for me with all that was going on with my father. I eventually resigned myself to the notion that I was never going to receive the kind of attention from my father that I desired. The times I did feel noticed by people were so seldom that they stand out in my mind.

An example of my craving for attention happened in first grade. We were on a field trip to a zoo with my teacher, Mrs. P. When I got home from the field trip, I told my mother I threw up on the bus, and Mrs. P had to clean it up. I have no idea why I made up this lie. On the surface it is just a funny thing that a six-year-old does. But I think there was something much more to it. I was craving someone to notice my pain and help me clean it up.

This lie was like I was telling my mother, "Look, I can't tell you this bad stuff, so I can tell Mrs. P, and she can clean it up and make me feel better." My mother wrote a note and had me bring it to school the next day. I didn't even look at the note, but apparently she wrote a note thanking my teacher for taking care of me on the bus. Mrs. P pulled me aside that day and asked me about it. I don't remember my reply, but I know I got in trouble for lying.

Mrs. P called my mom, and, when I got home, I went around to the back door and my mother was standing there waiting for me. I looked up. She asked me if I made it up and I said I didn't know. She kind of gave me an out saying, "Maybe you made up a story and then forgot to tell me it was just a story?" And I said, "Yes! That's what happened!" I find this whole story very strange, yet I believe it illustrates my inability to speak out at a very young age.

When I was in the second grade, my father saw me walking a toy dog named Digger around the neighborhood on a string. My mother said that my father came home and said he felt bad for me so he went out that night and brought home a Dachshund puppy. He pretty much told me that she was mine. He had this sense of guilt in giving me that dog, and I knew it. I couldn't pinpoint why, but it was evident. I named her Penny. I loved that dog more than anyone in that house did. She slept with me under the covers almost every night. She was a pretty high-strung dog. She would urinate when she got excited, even as an older dog. I think she was simply reacting to all the stress in the house.

One time my father gave Penny some wine to drink. I thought it was cruel and scary, but I went along with it, laughing, because I didn't know what he would do if I spoke out. She ended up running up and down the hallway for a long time and everyone was laughing. Then she got so sick, and I remember thinking that that was the cruelest thing anyone could do to a dog.

When Penny got older, my mother ran a small day care in our home. Penny was annoying to her because she kept urinating in the house, and my mother didn't want to have to deal with that anymore. So one day when I arrived home from school, I didn't see Penny anywhere. I was sitting at the kitchen table doing my homework, and my mother was at the sink. I was afraid to ask, but could no longer hold back, and I asked where Penny was. To this day, I can't remember her answer. I blocked it out. I found out later that she gave my dog away. She didn't tell me. I had no say in it. And I had no opportunity to say good-bye.

Penny always felt like the only thing my father gave to me and that maybe I mattered to him a little. The one thing my father gave me had been taken away from me, and I'm not sure if I ever really forgave my mother for that. She taught me a huge lesson right then that she would not be honest with me if she perceived that it would cause conflict. I also realized I could not trust her.

Over the years, I found my need and desire to be visible increase. For example, in the fifth grade, we had a talent show, and I immediately knew I wanted to be in it. All the other kids were either singing or doing some little dance routine, but I had the brilliant idea that I would dress up like Dolly Parton, complete with a big blonde wig and towel-stuffed bra, and lip sync the words to "Here You Come Again." My mother made me a pantsuit with sparkles and rhinestones. Not being popular and being teased for my newly budding breasts, I really have no idea how I had the courage to do this kind of a routine. But that night, waiting behind the curtain to walk on the stage, I felt so alive. I just had a confidence that I had never experienced before. I just knew it was going to be funny and people were going to love it. The music started, and I slowly walked on to the stage so the audience could see my exaggerated profile. The crowd literally roared with laughter, and, man, was I hooked on performing.

The lyrics hadn't even begun, and I knew I wanted a lifetime in front of people. I hammed it up for the whole song and loved every minute. Talk about feeling visible. When it was over, I got a standing ovation, and I had the biggest smile ever. I won first place in that show, and I clearly remember lying in bed smiling until late that night. Although my father did not attend the show, it was still one of the greatest moments of my childhood.

Don't Move

My father's disturbing behavior made me feel like I was crazy. On one occasion, I was seven and my father was sick in bed during the day. He was working evenings at this point and my mother had been out running errands. I brought cookies to him, thinking it might make him feel better. I thought he was asleep, but when I started to walk out, he asked in a threatening tone, "Where are you going?"

When I told him that I was just leaving, he said, "No you're not. You are going to stand here and you're not going to move."

Not wanting to upset him, I didn't question it and I stood there. I stood there for a really long time. The sun changed a bit outside, and I wondered what time it was. I tried to make up songs in my head to pass the time. At one point my legs started to get uncomfortable, so I shifted my weight a bit.

He heard me move and said, "You better not move. I have a belt over there, and I will use it."

So I became quite proud of how still I stood for what felt like an eternity. I heard the garage door open and realized my mother had come home. My father must have heard it as well because he suddenly looked at me and said, "What are you doing? Get out of here." Just like that.

All I had wanted to do was bring my sick daddy some cookies to make him happy, if just for a moment. I walked to my room and sat on my bed, wanting to cry. Instead, I felt an emptiness beyond tears, a feeling I wish on no one.

I distinctly remember feeling lost. That was a crazy-making experience. I thought that I must have done something wrong to deserve that punishment. I spent a lot of time that night burning into my brain ways to avoid any behaviors that might make him react that way in the future. There are times I wish I could go back to that little girl right now, put my arm around her, and tell her that my father was in fact the wrong one, and no one should ever have to go through something like that.

As an adult now, I have tried to construct some reasons or explanations for my father's behavior. What would possess him to make his little girl stand in place for hours and then pretend like nothing happened? I have never been overly successful in coming up with an answer that fits. He was controlling and cruel. I guess I don't really need an answer anymore for his motivations back then. It was what it was: sick and cruel. Perhaps it is a good thing that I don't understand the motives behind his behavior.

Every Man for Himself

One dinner, when I was about eleven, I had attempted to make a joke about something that my father took very personally, and he became furious. He tore the phone out of the wall, went downstairs (maybe to grab some of his things), left the house, and drove away. My mother and brothers shot daggers at me with their eyes. We didn't seem to get that it never mattered who or what set him off—he was going to go off at some point, and there was no stopping him. But this evening I was the lucky scapegoat. One by one, each family member got up from the table and went to their respective bedrooms—everyone but me. I sat at the table for a long time.

I desperately wished I could take back my words. I vowed to never speak during dinner again. I played and replayed countless scenarios in my head so that I could prepare for the next time. At least it wouldn't be my fault when my father's rage would explode upon us. Before leaving the table, I said a little prayer to God, despite feeling unworthy of prayer. I had just caused all this horrible chaos for everyone (from my young perspective), and God probably wasn't too pleased with me at the moment.

I just sort of half-whispered in my brain, *God, I am so sorry I made my dad so angry and everyone had to go through that. But if it's okay with you, could you just keep my dad away for a little while? I think it could help us. And please help me not say anything wrong ever again so that my dad won't get angry. Thank you for listening. I promise to try harder.*

Looking back on this, I am struck by a few things. Obviously, I am fully aware now that my father was responsible for his anger and how he handled it. He was so abusive, and I just can't believe how much I internalized as a kid. I spent most of my energy trying to prevent my father's anger from erupting. I was always editing my thoughts, words, and feelings before they left my mouth. I even made sure that I was in control of the emotions that showed on my face. And when I felt like I was nearing a danger zone, all I cared about was returning to any kind of normalcy.

I am also struck by how no one in my family ever addressed the reality of the situation. No one ever said, "Wow, Dad's crazy!" or "That was a rough night last night." My mother never pulled us aside to see how we were doing or to apologize to us that we had to live like that. I learned we weren't supposed to talk about the "elephant in the living room." Silence was the answer.

It amazes me how kids can learn messages like this without a word ever being spoken, and I often wonder how things might have been different for us if my mother had stood up for herself or for us kids. I imagine the landscape of my life would look quite different if she would have stopped, or attempted to stop, my father from saying terrible things to us. What if she had verbalized that what he was doing was wrong and hurtful? She may not have been able to stop him, but she would have sent a strong message to my brothers and me that this was not acceptable behavior. I probably wouldn't have felt so crazy or at least I might have felt some comfort if she had just asked me if I was okay, but it's really hard to guess.

I don't spend too much time wondering about "what ifs" anymore. It is what it is and was what it was. I know my mother looks back and wishes she could have protected us. She still doesn't seem to know how she could have acted any differently. I think she simply did not have the skills that were needed to stand up to my father. Everyone has his or her limitations, and that was hers. It has taken me years to understand and accept that she did the best she could at the time with the tools she had.

The other thing that lingers in my mind from that particular night is the fact that my father left the house, and we all just sat around the table in complete silence. No one knew if he was going to be gone for ten minutes or two months or forever for that matter. This type of behavior cultivated the feeling of "it's every man for himself" and "no one is going to validate your feelings or even notice that you have them." On this occasion and others too numerous to mention, I learned this erroneous rule: Do *not* trust your gut feelings because your gut must be wrong. If your gut is telling you your father is out of control, you are wrong. Believing such a thing felt overwhelmingly dangerous. Avoid danger, and ignore that gut feeling and convince yourself it is *you* who is crazy and cannot be trusted. This dynamic played a huge role in the rest of my story.

Squashed

One evening during dinner, my father was yelling about who knows what when he suddenly stopped shouting, looked at me, and said,

"Why aren't you eating your squash?" Terrified he was going to pick up my plate and throw it at me, I whispered, "I don't like it." And he screamed, "If you don't finish that squash in five minutes, I'm going to make you eat the whole pot of it!" So I tried a bite and gagged. I shot up from the table and ran to the bathroom, sure that I was going to vomit. My father let out a sort of maniacal laugh and yelled, "Aw, look at the little baby going to cry. . . . " In the bathroom, I sat on the floor, looking up at the ceiling. I prayed for God to take me away somehow. I wanted to be rescued.

I just couldn't wrap my head around my father laughing at me when I was so clearly upset, although this wasn't an uncommon response to a show of emotions. I think that may have been the first time I didn't think I was the crazy one. I didn't strategize how to avoid his rage as I had in all the other instances. I didn't sit there and say to myself, "Next time I will eat the squash before he can notice." I saw past his actual words and realized *he* was out of control. This realization scared me. If he became this out of control at dinner, what would he be like when something really bad happened? And one thing I knew: No one could stop him. My mother certainly couldn't. She didn't even try. She was as frightened as the rest of us. So who was going to protect us kids?

Living in Fear

Each family member reacted to my father's rage in different ways. Ronnie, my older brother, seemed to dig into his studies and activities. I became anxious, depressed, and withdrawn. Paul, my younger brother, would make up songs and sing them to my father in an effort to get him to be kinder to my mother. My mother spent her days overwhelmed and helpless. My father was oblivious and dismissive to all our reactions. These reactions to my father's behavior weren't limited to just the four of us. Three cousins recently told me they never felt comfortable around my father when we were kids. For example, my cousin Kristin recently told me that when she was about ten years old, she made some comment about my brother Paul to my father. My father started yelling at her in a belittling way, and she never spent time around him again. No one had ever treated her that way before, so she knew that this was not the right way to be treated. Instances like this give me the validation I craved as a child.

Validation at any point is incredibly empowering, but I believe that when you do not receive the validation during vital moments in childhood, it is much more difficult to integrate the information. If I had at least one comrade back then, I wouldn't have felt so alone, and perhaps I would have questioned my father a bit more and blamed myself a bit less. It would have felt so helpful to be able to think the way Kristin thought—*he is not treating me the way I deserve to be treated.* I simply didn't have that perspective because I was taught just the opposite by both of my parents' actions. This lesson had far-reaching consequences for years to come.

Another situation occurred, of which I never had a clue, until Ronnie disclosed it to me very recently. In the middle of my parents' arguments, my father would call Ronnie out of his room and make him agree with my father about whatever his point was in that moment. Ronnie witnessed some terrible arguments and brawls. Apparently one time, my father kicked my mother. Ronnie was very emotional when he disclosed this story to me, and he stated that when he witnessed this abuse of my mother, he "bawled his eyes out," which was rare for him to do back then.

The next day, Ronnie packed up his things and left the house to stay with his friend. I have no memory of Ronnie ever leaving the house. He apparently stayed up at my grandparents' house quite a bit, too. There was so much chaos and rage in our house that I never noticed that Ronnie wasn't even home. I can only imagine how envious I would have felt to stay anywhere else but home. To this day, I really enjoy staying at other people's homes. My home is just fine now, yet there is this feeling of escape deep inside me that never really left.

"You Are Fat"

My father was always overweight. He always talked about food and weight. He had been raised by two Italian parents, and food was a large part of their culture. I have always had body image problems since I can remember and will most likely always feel that I am the fat, ugly kid in the room. Many people ask me how I can think like this. I trace it back to my father.

He began commenting on the food I would eat and my weight when I was in the fifth grade. I started developing toward the end of fourth grade, which was earlier than many of the other girls in my school.

He once said to me, "No one is ever going to like you if you are fat. Put down the cookie."

That one sentence stung like a hornet. I can't explain why it was so devastating to me, other than it had such a feeling of shame associated with it. It was as if some rewiring took place in my brain, and I would never be the same. His opinion of me mattered so much, and somehow I had failed him. No matter what I did or what I weighed in the future, it was never good enough. I felt shame about my body, about certain parts of my body, and about my body as a whole.

What's interesting is that when I look at pictures from that time, I don't see a fat kid, but at the time I thought I took up so much space. I thought I didn't have as many rights as other people because of my weight. To be honest, this has been the toughest thing for me to shake all these years later. I will look at a picture and think, *Hmm, I look smaller than I thought I would.* But I look in the mirror and see something completely different. My brother Ronnie would make comments about my weight as well. I know that he was just emulating my father's behavior, but it still felt shaming, and I took it as a huge rejection. My mother would always seem supportive of me and help me try to lose weight. I was grateful for that support, but I always heard the message that my weight was a problem and I was not good enough the way I was.

One time, my elementary school principal was chatting with me in his office. I wasn't in trouble. I was just hanging out talking with him and he made a comment out of the blue about my weight. He said that I was probably going to be like his wife, and she always had a hard time controlling her weight. Looking back, I just scratch my head and wonder why on earth anyone would tell a sixth-grade girl something like that. He was a nice guy, and I don't believe he meant any harm or malice.

It amazes me that one or two criticisms from key people at key times in my life shaped my self-perception and body image. I have spent so much energy trying to rewire my "fat thoughts." To this day, I carry around the thought that I am a fat person who takes up a lot of room.

In high school my highest weight was about 140 pounds. Rarely have I weighed that much, except during pregnancy. It's funny to me now thinking about that number. 140 pounds at 5 foot 4 is not obese. Is it the healthiest weight I could have been? Probably not. But neither does it seem like an alarming weight to me—at least not reason enough to draw so much attention and self-criticism. At any rate, so much focus was placed on my weight throughout my childhood that it has taken me many years to challenge the thought that weight determines my worth.

I still struggle when I receive compliments, and I am much better now at just saying, "Thank you!" But inside my head, I am wondering why they think that positive thought about me. I sort of reject the idea that people find me attractive. There's also an issue of vulnerability for me. Being attractive can make me feel extremely vulnerable at times. I enjoy getting dressed up and going dancing with my friends. Yet, I am never truly comfortable—except on the dance floor when I am getting my groove on and couldn't care less about a thing!

Being plain and fitting in has always been my comfort and goal, and I find it difficult to understand why people find me attractive or smart. Will this ever change? I'm not sure. I have tried to make peace with who I am. Who cares what I look like? I'm a good person trying to make the world a better place. Unfortunately, my self-concept often conflicts with other people's perceptions of me.

Make Him Proud

As a child, I was fueled by the motivation to impress my father. Whether it was grades, sports, or general acts of kindness, I wanted so badly to make him proud of me and tell me something good about myself. This was a futile exercise. I *never* heard my father say, "Great job!" or "Wow, look what you've done!"

Children don't give up on their parents easily. I certainly didn't. I believed for a while that my father would one day come around and think that I was something special. The older I got, the less I believed this. My father just left me feeling invisible. I really didn't feel like I mattered very much in the world or in my family. I actually remember a time when I was riding my tricycle down our street and came upon a gatepost and stopped. I looked at the little post and wondered how long it would take for me to be taller than it. I then had the thought that it would be forever before I would "count." How old are you when you ride a tricycle—three or four years old? I was about four, and I was feeling invisible already. I also had the feeling that I would never make it out of elementary school. I just didn't think I was meant to survive. All I needed was a dad who was kind enough to make me feel like I had a place in the world. I just needed him to acknowledge me and to show me that he was glad I existed.

Is it really that hard to be a nice parent? Really, you don't have to be perfect by any stretch. Just don't be cruel, okay? All my father had to do was ask me how my day was, even once a week, and I would have been thrilled. I felt completely neglected by that man, and yet I believed I had something inherently wrong with me for him to reject me that way. So I spent most of my childhood trying to please a man who was incapable of being pleased.

The Car Accident

One day, when I was in the fifth grade, I was helping out at my father's bakery, and my aunt made a rare appearance. She spoke with my father on the other side of the room, and I knew something was wrong. They kept looking over at me, and I was convinced I had done something horrible and was in serious trouble. I don't believe this was a normal reaction for a child to have when witnessing such a scene. When they finished speaking, my aunt came over to me and said she was taking me home. I didn't question the reason. I got my coat and followed her to the car. I never felt as if I had the right to ask what was wrong, so I just sat quietly.

She explained to me that my mother and Ronnie were in a car accident. They were in the hospital, but I wouldn't be able to go see them. Apparently, my mother's car had hit a telephone pole, and my brother went through the windshield. He had hundreds of stitches on his head and face. My mother got hurt as well but not nearly as badly. My next recollection was later that night when I was lying in bed, and my father came in and sat on the edge to give me an update. I couldn't understand why he was having difficulty getting his words out, but then he broke down and cried. He hugged me and said that my brother would be all right. That was the first hug from my father that I can recall, yet the hug felt like it was for him, not for me. This felt like some bizarre movie where I had a different father. Again, all I said was, "Okay." I didn't feel safe asking questions, and I was actually surprised my father cared enough to cry about this.

The next day I went to school, all business as usual. I said hello to my teacher, sat down, and proceeded with my normal fifth-grade day. Around recess, my teacher pulled me aside to ask, "Andrea, why didn't you tell me that your mother and brother were in a car accident?" *Why would I tell him?* A car accident was miniscule compared to some of the other things that were going down in my house. My family did not speak of events or feelings or fears to anyone. A car accident was the most benign thing I could think of. So my response was, "I don't know." Then he sort of chastised me for not letting him know.

I walked away with the biggest lump in my throat and a deep sadness. I felt like I could not win. My life felt ridiculous. I decided being a secret-bearer was my lot in life, to carry unspeakable wrongs around in a backpack, and, if they ever escaped, I would be punished in ways I couldn't imagine. I'm not sure how that fear originated, but that's how I felt on a daily basis for years, and I am amazed by how powerful fear can be and how it kept me trapped.

My fear of my father's ability to "destroy me" dictated my every thought and action. He never had to lay a hand on me. His unpredictable rage and explosiveness instilled in me a knowledge that he could and would unleash the same fury on me, and I would die. Although, at times, death seemed like a welcomed option, the fighter in me refused to succumb. So I defended the secrets and played the role of happy girl. Therefore, disappointing someone like my teacher actually felt dangerous. What if he told my parents that I disappointed him? How would my father react if I were in trouble at school? I *never* wanted to find out.

Suicidal Thoughts

Many times I wished everything would just go away, that I could just disappear, or that someone would rescue me from my house. I began having suicidal thoughts in fifth grade. I had no real idea of how I would end my life—only a desire. But then, when I was in sixth grade, I learned about carbon monoxide poisoning. So one day, I went to the garage with the car keys, got into the driver's seat, and put the key in the ignition. There were two things that stopped me from turning that key.

One was the fear that I would screw it up. I was afraid I would do it wrong, and my parents would kill me. Ironic. But the other force that stopped me was much more powerful and longer lasting. I had a vision. I saw before me a vision of myself at about age thirty. I looked joyful and free with lots of happy people around me. I can't tell you for sure where that vision came from, but it felt like it was given to me by a guardian angel. This experience was far outside the realm of anything I had ever experienced, but I did not question it for a moment. That vision gave me clarity that my life would be different someday. I would be happy, and the pain would be gone.

I pulled the key out of the ignition, walked upstairs, put the keys back into my mom's purse, and went to my room. If I hadn't had that vision, I'm not sure if my fear of getting in trouble would have been enough to prevent me from attempting suicide. My gratitude for that vision is endless.

One night during junior high, I drank some of my parents' wine and called The Good Samaritans Hotline, a suicide prevention hotline.

Although the details of the call are fuzzy, I know that I was feeling desperate for some help or relief. I didn't know what I needed saving from—I guess from myself at that point. The next day my mother came into my room and asked me if everything was okay. I said everything was fine and asked her why. She told me that she found wine-soaked paper towels, an empty wine bottle, and the yellow pages open to the Good Samaritans. I panicked. I thought quickly and made up a story about how I knocked over the wine, it spilled, and I cleaned it up. As for the Good Samaritans, I told her a friend of mine was really upset, and I was trying to help her last night and gave her the number to call them.

I felt that it was critical for my mother to believe me. Why was I so afraid to reveal the depths of my depression? I had a fear (as well as a recurring dream) that I would get locked away in a mental hospital. I felt so out of control inside that if anyone knew, I truly believed the doctors would toss me in a cell and throw away the key.

A Glimpse Outside

As I grew older, I wondered more about how other families lived. Could we really be the only ones who had so much chaos inside our home? In sixth grade, I learned about a camp in New Hampshire that I thought would be an amazing experience as well as a way to meet other kids and find out that answer. I wanted in! I could not believe that kids could be away from home for two weeks or more. It sounded like paradise to me, and I begged my mother to let me go.

My father was not a fan of letting me go, and I never heard the reason(s) why. I think it was partially due to lack of control. He would have no say over who I met or what I would say to others. I just couldn't even imagine the freedom of being away for two whole weeks. But somehow, by some miracle, my mother was able to send me.

The first time I went to camp was the summer following sixth grade. My mother drove me up to New Hampshire, and when we arrived, I was ecstatic. I can't remember the three-hour car ride there, but I remember arriving at the top of the hill, looking down at the cabins and dirt road. It felt too good to be true. My mother barely got a good-bye from me before I was gone. I walked down that hill ready to meet anybody and everybody.

Those two weeks gave me a new perspective on life. I met girls from different cultures and backgrounds. I heard stories about other crazy families, and I was shocked that I wasn't the only one who came from a dysfunctional home. For the first time, I learned about divorced families, abusive parents, and kids who just weren't all that happy. I didn't say a whole lot about my own family, and, instead, I just absorbed my bunkmates' stories and filed them away. **I clearly recall the feeling, as if a window opened in my heart: I was not alone. This was a powerful realization.**

I was in heaven. I ate up the daily activities, and we sang at mealtimes and before bed each night. I bonded with my counselors. I laughed. I felt accepted. I didn't think about home for a minute. I absorbed every ounce of joy I could. When the last night rolled around, I sank into a deep sadness. I went back to my cabin after our final campfire, and I had an outpouring of tears I didn't really understand at the time. Losing this close, warm, safe feeling I had experienced for the very first time devastated me.

When I returned home, my father was downstairs standing on a chair replacing a lightbulb. My mother and I braced ourselves for his reaction. When I said, "Hi, I'm home," he ignored me, and I felt completely invisible. My mother stood by and watched. Keeping the mood light, she did the best she could to get my father to respond to me, but it wasn't enough. Feeling rejected, I walked away, and then quickly told myself, *Well, what do you expect? He didn't want you to go, and you went anyway. Of course he's angry. This is your fault, stupid.*

My father's reaction spawned a pattern inside me that I still have to practice a concerted effort to fight. The pattern looks something like this: Rejection hurts so deeply that I do everything I can to avoid it. I did this by becoming a people-pleaser. I became adept at reading people and situations and learned to quickly adapt to avoid conflict. While these skills served me well in my future careers, they were debilitating when trying to establish healthy relationships (there is more on this in later chapters).

To avoid conflict and therefore to avoid rejection, I would put myself down or take responsibility for others' actions. I would make fun of myself before anyone else could. This behavior served me well for a long time, but by the time I was an adult, I really believed the hurtful things I said about myself. I certainly don't recommend this coping technique to anyone.

Rescue Me

As a child, I felt helpless and hopeless. I had a sense that nothing was ever going to get better, nothing was going to change, and I couldn't picture myself growing up. I feared that my father could kill any of us at any moment—his anger frightened me that much. He was physically destructive in the house often enough that I believed it was just a matter of time before he was physically destructive with one of us. I would watch movies in which a girl would be rescued from some terrible person or situation, and I just prayed for that to happen to me.

Throughout my life, certain movies captured that old, trapped feeling from childhood. For instance, in my late twenties, while viewing the film *Forrest Gump*, I found myself triggered by different scenes. For example, when the character, Jenny, is a little girl, she and Forrest are running through a field away from her father. She kneels down and prays for God to turn her into a bird so she could fly far, far away. Whenever I watch that scene, I cry. It was as if the director had heard my silent childhood prayers and put them up on the screen.

I would try to get close to my teachers in school, hoping they would magically guess what was wrong with me. I befriended my teachers, hoping to be rescued because I didn't have the tools to rescue myself. I firmly believe that students should feel comfortable looking for support from their teachers as educators and mentors. In a perfect world, those teachers provide a safety zone, and they should be able to notice when something is "off" about a student and, in essence, rescue them from harm.

Separation

When I was in seventh grade, it finally dawned on my mother that she could, in fact, divorce my father. She says she remembers that exact day, and in her words: "It was like the heavens opened up."

Divorce was much less common back then, and my father had a short conversation with me about it, saying that "for whatever crazy reason," my mother wanted a divorce. I just listened. He was emotional, but I just sat still, afraid to have any reaction at all. I had no idea if this was a cruel joke or if he was serious. Then he made a statement I would never forget: "I'm a good person, you know!" I just looked at him blankly and said, "I know." He repeated himself a few times and then gave me examples of why he was a good person. I just nodded and kept wondering when the conversation would be over.

Afterward, I went to my room and thought, *Good people don't need to tell other people that they are good people!* I sat for a long time that night on my bed, wondering what had just happened. I could not allow myself to believe my father was actually going to be leaving our house. I braced myself for some strange twist that would surely follow. I went to school that week with terrible headaches and stomachaches. I held all my stress and concerns inside my body while I waited for the next shoe to drop.

About a week later, I came home from school, and my mother was waiting at the top of the stairs. She had a tentative look on her face, like she didn't know how I was going to react to what she was about to say. She said, "Dad moved out today."

Now, make no mistake. The moment those words came out of her mouth, I wanted to do the biggest friggin' happy dance you have ever seen. My prayers had been answered. *Was it really possible that dinnertime could be fight-free? That the fear and tension could be removed from my home? That no more screaming would be heard in that crazy house?* All of this went through my head in an instant, but I was concerned that my mother might get upset if I showed how happy and relieved I felt. So I just sort of said, "Okay."

I went to my room and pretended to do my homework, but I

couldn't focus. Processing this news took all my attention. I never thought there would be an end to his madness. I sat in my room that afternoon thinking that if I never saw my father again, I would be forever grateful. When my father left, my fears left with him.

My brothers and I went to visit my father about a month after he moved out of the house. He was living in the apartment above the bakery, and, when we went to visit, I was struck by how quickly he had settled in. Shortly after that visit, I met a lady he was dating. I was not very aware of grown-up relationship things, and I was a little confused about how he could be dating someone so quickly after leaving his family. She seemed nice, but none of this made any sense to me.

We had semi-regular visits with my father because my mother told me I had to see him. I never looked forward to the visits and couldn't wait to get home. A few years later, he moved into a beautiful house in Cape Cod. I had to spend some weekends there, and my stomach would be in knots the whole time. There was no tension and screaming like back at home, but I had all these leftover feelings about his behavior toward me, and I had nowhere to put them.

Interventions

My mother brought my brothers and me to family counseling for one session following my parents' separation. As we drove to the appointment, I felt like I was headed toward my doom. No one in my family ever spoke about the chaos we lived with, and I surely didn't understand why we were expected to start now. I couldn't imagine speaking about my feelings. I had no vocabulary when it came to things like this. There was this fear inside me that I couldn't pinpoint. It felt dangerous. I had learned there was actual danger in naming the truth, and I guess it was partly because so much effort had been placed on maintaining normal appearances.

Looking back, I want to shake myself and say, "Scream it out! Tell everyone what you're feeling! Who cares?!" But, God, back then, it was this unspoken expectation that we just kept our mouths shut. It seemed like my mother was attempting to gather up the pieces of her broken family. She wanted us to get the message that it was, in fact, okay, to speak the truth. It just took my father leaving to create a safe space for us to do so. I believe this is what my mother had hoped, but the damage had already been done.

When we started our session, the counselor asked us to take turns saying how we felt about the divorce. My older brother and I just sort of shrugged and said we felt fine. Paul was more vocal, and he continued counseling. The counselor later told my mother that we all seemed to be dealing with the situation just fine. As for my mother, she didn't have the tools to engage us in discussions about our feelings, and, even if she did, at that point I don't think we'd ever feel comfortable opening up to her. And so the stage was set for continued secrecy and silence within my family.

I did, however, begin counseling on my own soon afterward with the junior high school adjustment counselor. I had heard positive comments about how she had been helping some students, and I was desperate to find some relief from my pain. As silent as I had been in the past, I'm surprised as I reflect on the brave step I took to walk into her office. I sat in her office during my first visit and said nothing for about forty minutes. I wasn't trying to be difficult; I simply did not have the words to explain what I felt. I eventually warmed up to her, though. She was very sweet, and I finally developed the language I needed to discuss some issues concerning my father and his rage, and how I hated visiting him on the weekends. She asked me on more than one occasion if he was an alcoholic, explaining that this type of erratic, explosive, and unpredictable behavior was not uncommon in alcoholics. I sometimes wished he were an alcoholic, just so I could have some explanation of why he acted the way he did.

This experience of opening up to an adult who actually cared about my thoughts and feelings was crucial to my survival at that time.

Low Self-Esteem

As far back as I can recall, I have had low self-esteem. I didn't feel worthy of others liking me. It had been ingrained in me that no one would like me unless I was thin. I was never more than twenty pounds over-weight at any given time, but I thought I belonged in the obese cate-gory. I was convinced no guy would ever be interested in me. If I could fit in and look plain, I would be happy. I had no need to stand out. I just didn't want to repulse anyone. I also felt stupid. Although I took advanced classes, I knew I could never compare to my brother Ronnie's level of intelligence.

These are such harsh thoughts, and it makes me sad to write them. I realize now how much useless energy I exerted hating myself. I used to wonder how my life would have been different if someone took me aside in the fifth grade and told me I was smart, beautiful, and worthy. What if I received those messages prior to hearing the hurtful ones? Who would I be today? I don't really wonder about that anymore. I like who I am now. Part of who I am includes who I was and how I got here. And, unfortunately, feeling that low created an intense need to find someone or something to lift me up out of that darkness. I think I would have kept seeking relief until I found it, whatever the cost.

If you have never felt that bad about yourself, let me tell you that it is a very lonely, painful place to reside. I always felt like I was screaming inside for someone to notice my pain. I truly felt invisible. I just wanted someone to rescue me. The fact that few people seemed to notice my pain made my loneliness increase every day. I started to feel unworthy of being noticed. **This was a strange dichotomy for me: I put forth great effort hiding the secrets of my family, and yet I prayed for someone to break my code of silence.**

Childhood Friends

During childhood, I had very few friends. My perception was that I had no friends at all, but as an adult I now know that wasn't completely accurate. When I talk to some people who shared that time with me, they recall our being friends. However, I felt so isolated, alone, and invisible that I simply carried on friendly conversations and interactions without ever feeling like anyone knew me or what I was going through. I truly believed everyone thought I was weird and disliked me for it.

One girl in elementary school was particularly mean to me. I called her a few years ago while doing research for this book, and she told me she didn't recall ever having disliked me or bullying me. She said she remembered me as sweet and cute (which is odd since she was one of the main culprits who mocked me for my appearance). She did note, however, that I went through a plain, drained-looking stage in junior high. All those years I held on to the belief that she and others viewed me as an outcast. This conversation showed me just how confused I was.

Peers and friends mean everything to preteens and teenagers, and I despised this feeling of being friendless. I kept wondering what was wrong with me, and I tried to do all the right things to be liked, but my self-esteem continued to plummet when that didn't work. Everyone else seemed to have it so easy with tons of friends to talk to and hang out with. I felt embarrassed to have no one.

Childhood Activities

Staying busy distracted me from my pain. School was actually one of my favorite activities, and, as I recall, elementary school was one of my favorite parts of childhood. I liked my teachers, and I was motivated to achieve academically, partly to make my father proud. I didn't like weekends or long vacations from school because being out of the house was such a huge comfort. It wasn't until my own son lamented to me one day, "Why can't weekends last forever?" that I truly understood that most children don't mind being away from school. Even as an adult when I am inside a school, I feel comfortable, safe, and at ease.

As far back as I can remember, music also served as a great comfort and escape. I loved singing, playing instruments, and listening to whatever music was playing. I'm not sure where this deep passion came from, since no one in my family is musically inclined. The operas on *Mister Rogers' Neighborhood* were especially exciting, and I'd play along with my tambourine to Rita Moreno's punctuation song on *The Electric Company*, feeling pure joy; everything else just went away.

I started playing the violin in second grade. My playing was average, but I stayed with it. When I was in sixth grade, I had been practicing a particular piece of music quite a lot, and I wanted to play it for my parents. When the music concluded, my mother smiled, but my father simply looked at me and said, "When was the last time you cleaned your fingernails?"

Feeling defeated and deflated, I looked over at my mother, and she just said, "Ron . . . " This is just one more example of my attempts to earn my father's praise, which never came. I walked away, planning to do a better job of preparing next time. Nails would be clean, hair would be washed, clothes would be perfect—then he would love my music. I took some comfort in knowing that my mother recognized my defeat, but now I realize that had I been in her position, I would have said much more than *Ron*.

I became a cheerleader in junior high school. While I enjoyed the activity of cheering, I didn't know how to relate to the girls on the team. We would stand around at games and practices, and it was as if they were speaking a different language. Some of the girls made fun of me, while others ignored me. Looking back, I'm not quite sure what I got out of cheerleading. I was so depressed during that time that everything felt like a huge effort.

One day, my mother called me into the kitchen and asked, "Are you happy?"

I obediently replied, "Yes."

She said, "Well, your cheerleading coach just called and asked me if you are happy because you don't seem like you are happy at practices."

I really didn't know what to tell her. *Where to begin?* So I just assured her that I was happy.

Then she said, "Well then at the next practice you need to tell her that you're happy."

The next practice arrived, and the first thing I did was walk right up to my coach, and I simply said, "I'm happy."

And she replied, "Well good! Let's start seeing it then. Start smiling!"

I walked away and felt that same lump in my throat I'd had when my fifth-grade teacher scolded me for concealing the car-accident story. I had no idea how to proceed in life. I knew in my heart of hearts that if I let my guard down, the tears that fell would be endless. So the only choice in my mind was to act happy and together and to please others. **Wearing this kind of mask so early in life surely set the stage for later years when I would need to conceal my true feelings both from myself as well as from the outside world.**

I joined clubs and went through the motions of trying to belong, but practically everything I did felt empty. However, in sixth grade I performed in my first play and, similar to participating in the fifth-grade talent show, I loved being on stage where people had no choice but to notice me, and I could pretend to be someone else for a moment. I loved rehearsals, memorizing scripts, and bonding with the other actors and crew. I always fit in a bit more with these folks. We were all a little different, finding our own way through life, and I didn't feel judged in these circles. Feeling accepted, I found solace in theater and music. While I never became true friends with these people, I did find a place where I belonged for a short time.

I also played softball for many years, first for the town and then in high school. I was never a great player, but being good enough was fine with me. I never held expectations that I could be better than average.

In high school, I kept myself busy babysitting and working as a waitress at a local ice cream shop. I was in the Key Club and every singing group the school offered. I performed in plays, played softball, and maintained As and Bs. Most feedback I get from people regarding their perception of me during my high school years was that I was happy, smart, and successful. I'm not certain if I was trying to fool people into believing this or if I was just trying to find happiness in these activities. I do know that I had such a deep need to belong and feel accepted that I searched everywhere to fill my dark void with some light. I had no idea where that light would come from, so I kept looking.

Sexual Abuse

I believe my father molested me.

I know this is a bold statement to make. It took me months to decide to write it here. I have no idea how some of my family members will react when they read these words, but it needs to be said.

Do I have proof? No. But this is a question I have faced for many years. People have suspected and have gone as far as asking me if I had been molested. At a young age, I sobbed during movies and TV shows that addressed sexual abuse. I had just about every symptom of a sexual-abuse survivor: flashbacks, anxiety, eating disorders, shame, fear, dissociation, and so on. I had flashbacks of seeing my father's penis, and I would have extreme anxiety if I were in close proximity with him.

Many clinicians believe there are physical symptoms of sexual abuse called body memories. Sometimes the body remembers traumas that the mind forgets. I have had unnerving physical reactions to certain experiences. For example, during discussions of trauma and abuse in graduate school, the horrible details of a case would physically excite parts of my body that got triggered by body memories my mind could not access.

I do have a distinct memory of waking up in the middle of the night when I was very young to a strange, old man lying next to me in my bed. My parents had a party earlier that night with a bunch of friends, and one of them had made his way to my room. I froze, paralyzed with fear. I didn't have the sense that I could get out of bed and crawl into my parents' bed. What I remember is feeling that I had no choice but to lie there because I would get in trouble if I moved or told anyone this man was in my bed. I am not saying anything physical happened to me that night, but my reaction to some strange man in my bed bothers me. I had a vivid sense of not being able to move and not being able to tell anyone about it. Something about it felt familiar.

When I shared this memory with my mother years later, she claimed to know which guest it was and wrote off the incident as a confused, drunk partygoer dozing off in the wrong bed. But this raises a disturbing question: If she didn't know that a grown man had climbed into bed with her three-year-old, how could she have protected me if her husband had done the same thing?

Another memory involves my walking into my parents' room one night. My mother was sleeping on the couch in the living room. I remember staring at the doorknob, not wanting to turn it. Nothing in me wanted to walk into that room, but I knew I had to. I have this terrible feeling in my stomach when I recall the image of that door.

I remember the sound the door made as it opened, and I recall the darkness in the room. My memory halts there.

The next thing I remember is lying on the bed next to my father, staring at the ceiling. My cheeks felt wet, and I was wondering why I was crying. The next thing I knew, my father kicked me off the bed. My head rattled a bit once I sat up. I stood up and made my way out of the room in the dark. I don't recall the walk back to my own bedroom. I just remember feeling discarded the next day. I tried for years to recall the gaps in this memory. Yet now, I just accept the fact that the fragile parts of my mind must be protecting me from some pretty awful truths. Thank you, brain.

When I would stay at my father's house after their divorce, there were times at night when I would lie in bed. I would hear him walk by my room, and I would start to sweat. My anxiety would soar. And I would always shake my head and wonder what I was freaking out about. I knew he wasn't going to come in and do anything to me. But my body would react as if it had to be on guard for something. My body never failed me, but I didn't learn to listen to it for a very long time.

When I began my quest for healing, I desperately wanted to remember facts and details of my abuse. I thought I needed specific details to get treatment and to be able to tell the *right* story. I have worked through these limitations, and I now fully realize my story, the *right* story, is whatever my experience was. I am okay now living with doubt.

The reason this is such a vital part of my story is because these experiences, remembered or not, made me an easy target. Secretive boundary violations were familiar to me. When a man eighteen years older than me goes in for a kiss or when a trusted teacher tells me he can't imagine life without me and I don't run for the hills, this is a clear indication to me that this odd behavior was somehow familiar to me. I was just too easily able to adapt to this strange and inappropriate boundary shift.

Perceptions

I always felt like I was on the outside looking in on life—separated and detached from what was going on around me. As a child, I dissociated quite a bit, most likely due to a combination of having been the victim of molestation and the neglect and verbal abuse from my father. When someone dissociates, the brain performs an amazing skill of separating one part of the consciousness from another. For example, have you ever been driving for a while, and then you suddenly look around and realize that you don't remember driving for a chunk of time? Obviously you didn't leave the car, right? The brain can perform many operations without conscious thought. When a person encounters a dangerous situation, the brain can actually section off part of his or her consciousness to make the situation feel less painful. That's what my brain did for years.

Countless times at home or school, I would feel as if I were sort of floating above my body, watching everything happen. I had a very difficult time feeling like I was *in* my body. So when kids started making fun of me, I would pretend I was in a movie. This felt much better than feeling the sting of the insults.

Paying for College

The summer before college, I needed money to help pay for school. My mom was a single mother, getting next to nothing in child support from my father, and so she couldn't contribute. My father, on the other hand, had plenty of money. Everyone in the family knew he used money for leverage and control, and I swore he would never be able to do that to me. But when I realized I needed some help to pay for college, I felt stuck.

I was working many hours and saving whatever money I could save, but the college expenses were higher than I could manage on my own. I hated knowing my father would feel superior and dictate how he would "help" me financially. But in the end, I knew my education was my ticket out of that town as well as the key to finding a new life. So, I swallowed my pride. I called him and asked if we could meet to talk about something.

My father had me meet him at his "office"—the office by the garage at Nana's house. When I got there, he was sitting behind his desk. He had a smug look on his face. Hands behind his head, he said, "So, what's all this about?"

I took a deep breath and muttered the words, "I was . . . wondering if . . . maybe you could . . . help me pay a little bit for some of my classes."

He took a long, dramatic pause, and finally said, "I'd like to know one thing. What have you ever done to act like you're my daughter? How have you ever proven that you even care about me? You never visit me. You never call me. . . . "

I don't remember anything else that came out of his mouth at that point. And, as I tried to speak, I actually started to sob and hyperventilate. I couldn't speak or make any sense. I was distraught by my reaction. I had not prepared myself for this. I knew any number of reactions on his part were possible, but I believed I was prepared to walk away if he said anything negative. Instead, I just sobbed uncontrollably. I had never experienced such an outpouring of tears before or since that day. In retrospect, I believe a large part of the reason for my outburst was because I knew in that instant I was done with this man. This was a defining moment in my life.

This was no father. This was a man who had hurt me for the last time. For him to sit there behind a desk, watch me sob, and not move a muscle or show any concern, I could no longer associate with him. That sobbing was one giant grief reaction, and rarely did I look back. I would continue to mourn the loss of a childhood and the void that he left, but I never missed having him in my life. In a way, that day was his gift to me. I never felt any conflict for cutting him out of my life. He had brought that on himself.

FOR YOU, THE READER
CONSIDER THIS . . .

I realize I have painted a picture here that my childhood was filled with only turmoil and trauma. There were definitely times when I had fun and learned some positive lessons from those around me. However, this chapter serves to illustrate the child I was—what made me who I was and who I became as an adolescent. There are many other stories I could tell. In fact, I could write an entire book in this one chapter. But my purpose here is to set the stage for why and how I became such a perfect target. As you continue to read, keep in mind how my experiences as a child may have affected my needs, boundaries, and silence as a teenager.

For all readers:

- What are the key takeaways from this chapter?
- What dynamics were present in my home that shaped me into an invisible target? What words or actions formed my self-concept?

As a student . . .

- What messages have you received from your parents about communication, relationships, and boundaries?
- Do you have anyone to talk to if you are having problems at home?
- Is there an atmosphere of safety and open communication within your family?

As a parent . . .

- Are you turning a blind eye to warning signs in your child's behavior, hoping whatever is causing them will simply work itself out?
- What messages do your children receive from your actions and/or inactions?

As an educator . . .

- How do you identify a student who is having issues at home? What do you do once you suspect difficulties in a student's home?

- How much should you get involved with students' problems versus referring them to appropriate resources?

As an administrator . . .

- How do you handle a negative family situation brought to you by a student or teacher?

- What type of annual training do you have in place to identify and respond to concerns surrounding a student's home life?

- Are programs in place at your school to educate students about how to ask for help if needed?

As a survivor . . .

- Are there any secrets from your childhood that you still carry? How does that impact your life today?

- Do you see any patterns from your childhood that led you to become someone else's target?

- Are there any unhealthy patterns or boundaries learned from your upbringing in your relationships today?

Understand that what you experience as a child sets the stage for how you interact with the world as an adolescent and adult. Building a strong foundation of safety and open communication at this early stage can help provide the tools for healthy relationships and living in the future.

CHAPTER 2

The Man He Was

—◀○▶—

Just as it is important to understand the child I was to fully grasp my experiences, I believe it is equally important to understand the man Mr. Baker was. The background information in this chapter combines the details I recall with the perceptions and memories of people I interviewed who also knew Mr. Baker. While opinions of this man vary, one thing remains constant: Mr. Baker put forth much energy into gaining the trust of students, parents, and colleagues. How he abused that trust unfolds in the chapters that follow.

When it comes to Mr. Baker as a person, the information I have is limited, and much of it is based on my perceptions as a teenager who watched and listened to him in his role as my teacher and mentor. My knowledge and understanding of him was and is based upon what he chose to share with me and with others. I spoke with many former classmates while writing this book in an effort to learn as much as I could. I am aware that their feedback and memories were shared through the lens of adolescent impressions, and, as a result, it is quite challenging to paint a complete portrait of Mr. Baker.

However, the following are some basic facts that I can confidently share that will allow you a peek into the mind and world of this man.

Family

Robert Baker was born in Westwood, Massachusetts, and was the younger of two boys. He was a good student and athlete, he graduated from college, and he began teaching. He enjoyed sports, music, and friends. He loved animals and once had a pet squirrel named Funny Face. He wore a squirrel tie tack in remembrance of his pet. He also had a dog who meant the world to him, and he prided himself on how much that dog loved him. He would proudly tell a story about how the dog obeyed his command to come even when the dog was on its deathbed, and walking caused it excruciating pain. On several occasions, he said no human could care about him the way that dog cared about him.

Mr. Baker had an older brother named Jimmy. The two of them were pretty close and were interested in similar activities. They both enjoyed sports and as adults would play basketball together on occasion. They had a tradition where they would both predict the scores of each college basketball game during the season and then call each other to compare the scores. They went to concerts together and even liked to play music. Mr. Baker played the drums a little bit, and Jimmy played a little guitar. Jimmy also chose a career in education and was a high school math teacher in Dedham, a few towns over from Norwood.

Mr. Baker would visit with his aging parents, who still lived in Westwood. He described his father as a tough man and his mother as a bit of a hoarder. He would call his mother every New Year's Eve right at midnight to wish her a happy New Year in a silly, baby voice. They would all have lunch together occasionally on weekends, and the climate of these meals was pleasant and yet superficial. The family gave each other an abundance of gifts on Christmas.

Mr. Baker's family was very important to him, and although he wasn't overly affectionate or had an outpouring of kind words for them, it was clear that he loved them.

Marriage Dynamics

Mr. Baker married his high school sweetheart whom he had known since the first grade. Every day, he would bring in a lunch to school that she had made for him, and in those years that I ate lunch with him, it always looked delicious. She was a great cook, and he seemed to appreciate that.

He described the two of them as being quite different. She was content to stay at home and read, while he was more interested in being outside and active. Their differences made them drift apart over the years. He was fairly private when talking about his wife to the students, and he never seemed to include her when he would attend students' extracurricular activities or parties. He always wanted children, and, according to Mr. Baker, his wife was resistant to the idea. The two never ended up having children, and he seemed to resent his wife for this. Aside from that, the overall impression he gave about Mrs. Baker was fairly positive.

Reputation

My perception of Mr. Baker was that he had a reputation of being the junior high teacher who all the students wanted to hang out with after class. He would invite kids to eat lunch in his classroom, and sometimes during class, a former student of his would visit from college to say hi. Mr. Baker would halt the class lecture and catch up with whomever was visiting. The students would watch enviously as that former student got his undivided attention. He seemed to look at these visiting students with pride. While waiting for him to catch up with his alumni, many of the on-looking students (myself included) wondered if they would be so lucky as to be welcomed back by Mr. Baker in the years to come.

Mr. Baker also spent lots of time with students outside the classroom, getting friendly with their parents, attending their concerts, plays, sporting events, and parties. He bought a select group of lucky students Christmas and birthday gifts. It was just a known fact that this was how he interacted with lots of kids.

Mr. Baker was also known for being a tough teacher. He carried a great deal of pride in knowing that his exams were tougher than other teachers' exams. He felt strongly that he was preparing his students for the rigors of high school. The students who performed successfully on his exams earned his admiration and subsequent extra time and attention.

They would soon be accepted into his "circle," which consisted of the group of kids he would hang out with during lunch and after school.

Mr. Baker was also the coach for the junior high baseball team as well as the junior varsity baseball coach for Norwood High School for many years. He enjoyed coaching, and it seemed important to him that the kids view him as a cool coach. He had been an excellent baseball player as a student, and he enjoyed sharing his skills with the boys who followed in his footsteps.

Mr. Baker openly visited with students outside the classroom. One of his former students told me during our interview that Mr. Baker often had students at his house, and they would listen to music in his car for so long that the car battery would die. She admitted to feeling a twinge of jealousy back then, wondering why she hadn't been "chosen" to hang out in his car with him.

Mr. Baker did have a reputation for being one of the cool teachers. He listened to popular music and would speak the students' language. He also provided a shoulder to lean on if students were having difficulty at home or experiencing conflict with family, friends, or boyfriends/girlfriends. Students trusted him with their secrets and troubles, and he would listen intently and eagerly share advice. Word spread that Mr. Baker was the go-to grownup if you couldn't talk to anyone else.

Mr. Baker took himself very seriously. He was not someone who could poke fun at himself or laugh when someone pointed out a flaw of his. He had a temper that could flare fairly quickly and without warning. Many students noticed this and regarded him with some caution as a result. He commanded respect easily in the classroom. He sometimes would joke around with the kids, but he would also snap at a student for insignificant reasons.

Some of my former classmates shared similar perceptions about Mr. Baker. They felt like he was a trusted mentor who really cared about them. However, I also gathered some very different reactions from people that surprised me. There were those of the opinion that Mr. Baker was creepy. Some of the words and phrases used to describe him included: *yuck, ugly, creep factor, cruel, needed the validation of young women, quiet, homely.* Several of his former female students also told me he had been "flirty" with them. An interesting common theme emerged, though: Mr. Baker was not an attractive man. Everyone commented on his "ugly glasses and moustache," his "terrible attire," and his "bad comb-over." He was clearly not seen as the type of teacher girls would have typical crushes on.

Some men I spoke with sounded as if they resented Mr. Baker for spending so much time with the girls, as if he were competing with the boys for the girls' attention. Other men commented on how it was obvious that he played favorites with the "cool" kids and would neglect and ignore everyone else. Paul, a high school friend of mine, was on the J.V. baseball team when Mr. Baker was coaching. He confirmed the notion that Mr. Baker would pay lots of attention to the "cool" kids, and he would pretty much ignore the less popular ones. Paul told me he never liked Mr. Baker. He thought he had a bit of a cruel streak and didn't trust him.

I began to wonder if the folks who had bitter memories of him were the ones who felt he had creepy traits. It appeared to me as though the former classmates who considered Mr. Baker a great friend and mentor were the ones who were included in his circle. It's tough to like and respect a teacher who ignores you. Conversely, it's more difficult to view someone honestly when he offers you gifts and lifts your spirits.

On a whole, however, many former students spoke favorably about Mr. Baker. I know that Mr. Baker was well liked and respected by his colleagues and his students' parents. They all believed he was a great teacher who went the extra mile for his students. They knew he spent extra time making sure the students understood the lessons of the day. He was always cordial with his colleagues, but he tended to spend more time with the students. He certainly had no disciplinary actions against him. He just appeared to be an all-around nice guy who really cared about the kids.

Mr. Baker won teacher of the year at the junior high several times. He also was voted "Most Popular Teacher" year after year. So, I'd say Mr. Baker's overall reputation reflected a trustworthy, hardworking man who was well known for spending extra time and attention with kids.

FOR YOU, THE READER
CONSIDER THIS . . .

Mr. Baker was, by all appearances, a dedicated teacher and mentor for many years. His students, peers, administrators, and friends thought highly of him for his dedication and willingness to go above and beyond to be there for his students. No one would question his motives for doing so. He was the kind of teacher any student would love to have . . . or so it seemed.

As a student . . .

- Do you have a teacher who sounds similar to Mr. Baker?

- How would you feel if a popular teacher included you in his or her "inner circle"?

- What would you do if one of your teachers gave you a gift? What meaning would that have for you?

As a parent . . .

- Does your child spend time outside class with a certain teacher?

- Does your child have a teacher who is showing him or her extra attention?

- Whom would you approach with your concerns regarding a teacher's questionable attention?

As an educator . . .

- Do you have any colleagues who spend extra time with students? What possible repercussions and/or liabilities could arise as a result of this behavior?

- What are your boundaries with your students? In what ways might your actions be perceived by others?

As an administrator . . .

- What rules, if any, do you have in place for teacher-student interactions as well as teacher-parent interactions?

- What policies are in place at your school regarding gift-giving from teachers?

- What policies are in place at your school regarding teacher contact with students via social media?

As a survivor . . .

- How did your educator's reputation affect the way you interacted with him/her?

- Looking back, were there any warning signs, prior to the abuse, that this teacher was dangerous?

Not all attention from teachers is bad. There are a multitude of well-intentioned teachers who enhance our students' lives every day. However, there are also problematic teachers who use a cloak of popular, charismatic appearances to lure students into a world of abuse. It's important to remain aware of all interactions between teachers and students.

CHAPTER 3

The Grooming Process

◄○►

When Mr. Baker entered my world, I was clearly in a fragile state of mind. He had years of experience gaining the trust and admiration of students, parents, and colleagues. My obvious need to feel noticed and loved combined with his overeagerness to interact with students placed me directly in his crosshairs. It is essential to understand this dynamic between a child who feels invisible and a predator who recognizes the child's need to be seen in order to address such an issue long before sexual abuse occurs.

In all of my research about incidents of educator sexual abuse, several common themes emerge, and one of the most common tends to be that a grooming process is involved. The Vermont Department of Children and Families describes the grooming process as "a subtle, gradual, and escalating process of building trust with a child. It is deliberate and purposeful. Abusers may groom children for weeks, months, or even years—before any sexual abuse actually takes place. It usually begins with behaviors that may not even seem to be inappropriate." (http://dcf.vermont.gov/stepup/educate/how_it_happens/grooming)

It is critical that adults have an awareness of the warning signs of the grooming process so that they can intervene on a child's behalf. In the appendix, "Lessons from the Other Side," I go into greater detail about the warning signs. As I reflect on the period of time when I first met and got to know Mr. Baker, I recognize the series of events and encounters that allowed him to groom me into a girl he could easily lure into a world of sexual abuse.

Eighth-Grade Study Hall

I first encountered Mr. Baker in September 1980 in my eighth-grade study hall. I quickly noticed how the students gravitated toward him. He would play a type of Connect the Dots game with some students, who were mainly girls. Desperately lonely and craving attention, I wanted to play a "Connect the Dots" game, too! I wanted someone to ask me how I was doing and actually care about my honest response.

During study hall, I would go up to his desk to ask if I could play the Connect the Dots game with him. He would look up from his desk at me and just say, "No, go sit down." This rejection felt terrible, but being the needy kid that I was, I would try new and different ways to get his attention such as telling jokes or acting interested in things he would say. Yet every attempt was met with harsher rejection. Halfway through the year, I finally gave up and decided I did not like this guy one bit. He was mean and playing favorites, and that just wasn't fair. Why would I want to play some dumb old game with him anyway? I spent the remainder of the year pouting during study hall and getting my work done.

Ninth-Grade Science Class

When I got my schedule for ninth grade in the fall of 1981, my heart sank. I saw "Mr. Baker" written next to my science class. I did not want to deal with this guy every day for a whole school year. **It is funny how our instincts tell us everything we need to know.** I've often thought how different my life would have been if a different name were written in that space.

I walked toward his classroom on that first day, and he was standing by the doorway. He looked at me and said, "Oh God, I have you?!" And I replied, "Yeah, I'm not too thrilled about it either."

I walked into the classroom and took my seat. I hated that he didn't like me. I wanted him to like me, badly, but I pretended to hate him—I didn't want to show him my need for his attention and approval. Upon reflection of his initial rejection, I don't think it was necessarily a setup for the grooming process. He really could be a cruel person who ignored or teased those he considered unworthy of his attention.

For the first few weeks of class, Mr. Baker continued to ignore me. I focused on what he was teaching and tried to get the best grades possible. He was showing favoritism pretty early on in the classroom. He would tease some girls and make fun of some boys. He would throw crumpled up paper at kids if they looked like they were falling asleep. He could be funny at times, but I learned to keep my mouth shut and just be one of the students he didn't like.

I had this secret thought that maybe, just maybe, if my grades were good enough, Mr. Baker would notice me and believe that I was worthy of attention. **I wasn't aware of it at the time, of course, but I was simply replaying the attention-seeking dynamic I had with my father.**

Mr. Baker's perception of me seemed to shift when I got my first 100 percent on one of his exams. As I mentioned earlier, he prided himself on giving very challenging exams. When he returned my exam to me, he made it a point to express how surprised he was that I was capable of scoring 100 percent. I had the biggest smile, and he stopped and looked at me for a few seconds. I wasn't sure why he stopped like that, but I didn't care. He looked at me! He actually noticed me! I felt, in a very tiny way, that I mattered for a brief moment. Once he realized I actually had a brain cell or two, he seemed to pay attention to me more. My plan had finally worked.

Now that I was visible to Mr. Baker, he would call on me in class and started throwing paper at me. One time while he was showing a film in class, he threw something at my head during the film. It was actually a solid object, and it hurt. When I leaned over to pick it up, it was a film container. I looked at him, and, with a laugh, he told me to open it up. I opened it, and there was a note inside. Mr. Baker had just written me a note! No one had ever written a note to me, and now here was my teacher, throwing one at *me*! Something about it felt a little weird, but I didn't care. Here was the attention I had been craving my whole life. I suddenly felt visible.

The note read, "Wake up, will ya!"

I just smiled at him and nodded. (I hadn't been falling asleep, incidentally.) I saved that note for a long time. It felt special to be on a note-receiving basis with my teacher. I had won the jackpot. I would do anything to preserve the feeling that I mattered to someone who was so cool.

Lunch

I began eating lunch in Mr. Baker's classroom about a month or two into the school year, along with some other kids. I don't remember how it started—if he asked me to join the group or if I asked to join. Sometimes four or five other kids would be there, but sometimes it was just me. I remember feeling self-conscious about eating in front of him, but it didn't keep me away.

I had such a fascination for Mr. Baker. I was dying to learn whatever I could about his life outside the classroom. Do you remember seeing one of your teachers at a local store on a Saturday in jeans? You couldn't believe they had a life outside school, right? They actually wore normal clothes! There was something awesome about that. That's how I felt about him.

I loved to see what he would bring for lunch, as if it gave me a glimpse into his life outside school. As I mentioned earlier, his wife was an excellent cook, so he would always bring in delicious-looking leftovers. We would play games and discuss various topics when other kids were there. When it was just the two of us, we would talk about my family. I opened up to him about my father, feeling safe to reveal things I had never told anyone. He listened with rapt attention and complete attentiveness. Somehow, telling him my family's secrets was the easiest thing to do. He would give me advice and put my father down—just a little bit. It felt amazing to have someone validate the hell I had gone through.

Mr. Baker also made me feel smart by talking to me on a level that felt so mature. I believed he really saw *me*, and I no longer felt invisible or insignificant. He would compliment me on my maturity level and point out the ways I was beyond my years compared with my classmates. He would tell me he couldn't talk with the other kids or even some adults the way he could talk with me. Hearing him say such things shocked and thrilled me. I was beside myself with pride to know that I was making such an impression on him. Now, as I write these words, I roll my eyes; this was all so clearly contrived and purposeful, but to the impressionable, needy kid I was, it felt significant and spontaneous. I believed it all.

A Free Pass

Mr. Baker would occasionally write me passes to get me out of my least favorite class, Ancient Civilizations, with Mr. S. If I didn't have a pass, I would tell Mr. Sweeney that I needed to go to my locker, and I would end up in Mr. Baker's class, sitting on top of a desk, swinging my legs and chatting away. Once, Mr. S actually threw open Mr. Baker's classroom door and yelled at me to get back in his class. I just laughed and followed him back to class, while Mr. Baker smiled and showed no sign of concern. At that point, I felt untouchable. If Mr. Baker had no problem with me blowing off the class, why should I worry about it? Basically, I would have done anything to spend time with Mr. Baker. As an adult, I've often wondered why Mr. S did not express concern about my being with Mr. Baker during class.

Babysitting with Denise

My friend Denise had Mr. Baker for science during ninth grade, but she was in a different class. She told me that she sometimes called Mr. Baker at home in the evenings. I thought it was so cool that she was actually having conversations with him outside of school. She even talked to his wife sometimes. The jealousy drove me crazy. So, sometimes when Denise and I were babysitting together, we would call him. We would get all giggly and silly, and he would just chat away with us. Connecting with him outside of school felt almost intoxicating, and I began to call him on my own from home.

He had such a mystique about him that I felt drawn in like a magnet. He remained very private about some things, but when he would give me glimpses of his life outside school, I just wanted to hear more. During our phone chats, I would ask him questions about off-school topics, like what he and his wife did for fun and what type of friends he had. Sometimes it would seem like my questions would catch him off guard, and he would delve into the conversation, revealing more and more personal information. I would breathe in his every word. I truly was in awe of this man. However, this was not in a sexual, crush sort of way. In my eyes, Mr. Baker had celebrity status, and I felt myself getting pulled in further by his charm and charisma.

"One of you is smart and one of you is pretty."

Years later, Denise told me that Mr. Baker had once said to us, "One of you is smart, and one of you is pretty." I don't remember him saying that, but Denise admitted his words had stayed with her for years because she had tried so hard to figure out which one she was. Such a statement is terribly manipulative and an underhanded way to stir things up between friends. I believe this was part of his grooming process to see which of us would react more. This speaks of what a troubled man he really was. No adult in his or her right mind would toy with kids like that, even if he or she were not a child predator.

The Gift

On the last day of ninth grade, I went to Mr. Baker's classroom where we chatted for a while. Then, he told me he had something for me. He said, "I realized I've become attached to you and I'm really going to miss you this summer." Then he handed me a wrapped gift. I opened it to reveal a windmill-shaped music box that played the theme song from *Romeo and Juliet*.

I remember feeling a couple of things. I felt terrible I hadn't gotten him anything. It actually hadn't even occurred to me. The other thing I felt was . . . funny—funny in my gut—but I had no idea why I felt this way. I now know that this was a red-flag feeling, which I hadn't learned to recognize as a child. I never could have recognized that the music box was a conditional gift at the time, but thinking back now, that's the feeling I got—a creepy one. The awkwardness I felt probably showed.

For the first time all year, I wanted to leave his classroom as quickly as possible, but I didn't want to hurt his feelings. Here I had prayed for someone to pay attention to me like this, and it would have made sense for me to feel ecstatic that my cool teacher would miss me so much that he bought me a gift. Instead, it felt creepy.

Counseling

I had been meeting with the school adjustment counselor for much of the ninth grade to help me work out my feelings surrounding my parents' divorce and my relationship with my father, but I never mentioned my friendship with Mr. Baker. I eagerly headed down to the counselor's office on the last day to say good-bye. I showed her the gift from Mr. Baker and told her that I felt kind of funny and bad about it. When she asked why, I replied it was because I hadn't gotten him anything. I also told her what he had said when he gave it to me.

To this day I cannot explain her response, which was "Well, maybe he has feelings for you."

To that I replied, "What?! Ugh no! He's married! He's a grown-up!"

She actually said, "Well, people have affairs, you know."

I have run that statement through my head hundreds of times. Why would a school counselor say something like that? I have come up with two possible reasons: 1) She was fishing for more information, or 2) She was completely clueless.

Even if my answer had suggested to her that there was no cause for concern, her handling of this matter was a major failure. In fact, her mention of affairs freaked me out even more. Her words somehow made me feel as if what Mr. Baker had said and done were acceptable behaviors and that there were even acceptable reasons behind them.

I am not saying that anyone should panic if a teacher gives one of his or her students a gift, but I do know that gift-giving is a hallmark of the grooming process. In my case, gift-giving was a prevalent theme. I will revisit this topic later. For now, it is just food for thought.

Camp Visit

During July and August 1982, following ninth grade, I worked as a counselor in training (CIT) at the camp I had been attending in New Hampshire. I used a pay phone to speak with Mr. Baker. I would also chat with his wife when she answered. She would always ask about camp and treated me kindly.

During one conversation, Mr. Baker told me he missed me and that he wanted to drive up to see me. It felt so unreal. I wondered why he would possibly want to drive over three hours just to see little old me. Naturally, I said it would be more than okay for him to do that. Then I counted down the days until his arrival.

The night before he visited, I went out to a bar with some of the other counselors with a borrowed ID that said I was twenty-two. I had several strawberry daiquiris, which I had never had before, and I unfortunately loved them. I got very drunk. I woke up the next morning with my first hangover.

As soon as Mr. Baker arrived, he asked if I was sick. I proudly told him about the evening at the bar, expecting him to think of me as more mature and cool. But he got very angry. I had never experienced such anger from him directed at me. His anger reminded me of my father. However, he wasn't angry because I had put myself at risk or because I drank alcohol. Instead, he had asked, "How could you be so inconsiderate? I drive all this way, and you can't even feel good for my visit? You are so selfish."

His words crushed and confused me. I truly believed he would approve of my drinking and even think of me as older than fourteen in spirit.

We went for a bite, and I told him about camp. I tried to keep the mood fun, but there was tension present, which was unfamiliar. When he dropped me off, I felt like I had hurt him deeply with my selfishness and thoughtlessness. I swore I would never let anything interfere with my time with Mr. Baker again. I was replaying the distorted father-daughter dynamic I had grown accustomed to, always vowing to get it right the next time to avoid making him angry. I took full responsibility for his behavior.

Visits from High School

I began high school in September 1982. I didn't get to see Mr. Baker around the corner every day, and I missed his caring expressions and his funny words. It wasn't too long before I began making trips to see him after school by taking one of the school buses that stopped near the junior high. I would go to his classroom to hang out, and we would talk as long as we could. I remember feeling so proud that I had made it into this elite group of alumni, so to speak. I had always looked up to the high-schoolers and college students who visited him as if they were some sort of heroes, and now I had become one of them. The younger kids would look up to me because Mr. Baker was happy to see *me*.

We would sit in his classroom and talk about lots of things—music, sports, school, my family, my life, and so on. The details of the conversations and the feelings surrounding them are hard to recall. Back then, it was so vivid and exciting, but now it is a distant memory that is difficult to access. I do, however, remember a strong feeling that I *needed* to see him and have him in my life. He had essentially become my best friend, and I told him everything a tenth-grade girl would tell her best friend. *Everything.*

I had no expectation that *he* would tell *me* everything in turn. He gave me tiny pieces of safe information, and I cherished those pieces. The fact that he shared anything with me—that he trusted me with any confidential information about his life—made me feel very special. Things progressed quickly in the early part of tenth grade. I would feel incredulous when he would tell me that he looked forward to my visits. From my perspective, no one gave a shit about me—I was virtually invisible—but here was my idol excited to see me. I mattered! His attention became addicting, and I, of course, wanted more and more and more.

Mr. Baker validated me. **His attention made me feel like I had worth. This hooked me completely, and I cannot think of a single thing that would have convinced me to stop visiting him or communicating with him.** With him, everything felt okay. I had been severely depressed and suicidal when I first met him, and it felt like the depression was actually lifting. I felt such sweet relief that I would do anything to preserve this feeling of well-being. All the answers I needed were within him, and he shared them so eagerly. The more he helped me, the easier going he seemed, and he gradually opened up to me more and more.

We danced a strange dance, and the boundaries were so blurry.

Was he still my teacher? **No.**

Did he feel like a mentor? **Sort of.**

Did I call him Mr. Baker? **Yes.**

Did I tell him things a person would tell a friend? **Absolutely.**

Did we share mutually? **Not really.**

Did I feel excited and giddy around him? **Yes.**

Did he look at me for long periods of time? **Yep.**

Was he a boyfriend? **Absolutely not.**

Did I have a crush on him? **Nope.**

Could I picture my life without him? **Absolutely not.**

See? Blurry . . .

On the days I visited him at the junior high, he would drive me home, and he would share new music with me. I loved those rides, and I wanted them to last for hours. When we arrived at my house, we would sometimes sit in his car for a while. Our time in the car never felt long enough to me.

Years later, my mother told me that my sitting out in the driveway with him made her crazy. Yes, she was grateful I had someone to confide in because I clearly couldn't confide in her. She was glad I had a father figure to lean on, and she thought Mr. Baker's mentorship would make a huge difference in my life. However, she also had the feeling that it was a little strange for a grown man to be parked outside her house with her fifteen-year-old daughter.

I don't know what prevented my mother from walking outside and asking me to come inside. She probably found this type of conflict too tough to handle. Had she done so, I would have been horrified. My anger and embarrassment at her interfering with my "important time" with this "important man" would have been explosive. That wouldn't stop me as a mom today. I would march outside and say, "Thanks for giving her a ride! Bye!" Then I would have a number of questions to ask my child. But things were different back then. My mother knew I was lost and looking to find my way through this difficult time. She didn't know how to handle this weird situation. She did her best.

Conversations

The conversations Mr. Baker and I shared were the highlights of my days. I believed we were kindred spirits—like he really got me. We would talk about music, the meaning of song lyrics, sporting events, and so on. As time went on, he began telling me more and more about his relationship with his wife. He never painted her out to be a bad person. He just said they were growing apart. He wanted to have children but she didn't, and he told me he felt betrayed by that. He also complained that they didn't have things in common anymore. He made it seem like she was the reason their marriage wasn't working and why he was becoming "drawn" to me.

I met Mrs. Baker several times, after having spoken with her on the phone multiple times. My mother invited them over for dinner once during my tenth-grade year. She probably wanted to "keep her enemies close," but I would like to think this was her way of getting involved in my life. This was likely the first time I met Mrs. Baker. I thought she was beautiful, classy, and elegant. From my point of view, it seemed like she loved Mr. Baker. When I recall that night, Mr. Baker seemed uncomfortable, not the usual self he presented to me during our alone times. At one point during dinner, Mrs. Baker winked at me, which made me feel special. She just seemed so kind. The experience was really weird, yet cool, getting a glimpse into Mr. Baker's private world like that.

Body Image

During this grooming period, I remember feeling extremely self-conscious around Mr. Baker when it came to my weight. I would have died if I knew he thought of me as overweight. *Is he looking at me?* I would wonder, never considering he might see me in a sexual light.

As mentioned earlier, I had always walked around feeling like a misfit. I saw myself as the fat, ugly kid and had it ingrained in me that no boy would ever like me. I owned this label so that other people's disapproval wouldn't hurt me so much. So when Mr. Baker tolerated being around me and even liked to be with me, it somehow felt healing. This incredibly cool guy was really *seeing* me, and he wasn't running the other way. Let me clarify again: in my mind, his interest in me was not of a sexual nature—not one bit. **This was more a case of being seen, of being *visible* to someone I admired and respected. Somehow my value increased as a person. I still felt fat, but with Mr. Baker in my life, it mattered a little bit less.**

The Diary of Anne Frank

Over the summer, our friendship strengthened through phone calls and visits, which continued into the start of the eleventh grade. I auditioned for the play *The Diary of Anne Frank,* which was being produced by a local community theater group. I had always been deeply touched by Anne Frank's story and wanted to be a part of it. When I told Mr. Baker I planned to audition, he was not as positive as I had expected him to be. He did not like my passion for being on stage. He would often refer to it as a crutch, which I never understood. The larger reason was likely that he didn't like me socializing with others outside his influence.

I auditioned anyway, and I got the part of Margot, Anne Frank's older sister. I loved everything about being in that play—every rehearsal, person, and prop! The cast and crew were mostly adults, who I felt could teach me so much. I enjoyed talking with them and feeling that special bond among us. I think we all got just how very special this project was.

Mr. Baker and his wife came to one of the performances, which made me both excited and nervous. I wanted him to see me on stage and to be impressed by my acting, hoping this would somehow put me on his level in his eyes. Afterward, he told me that he liked the show so much that he wanted to see it a second time. His wife didn't join him for the second performance because "it was too emotional for her to sit through again." Whether that was the truth, I will never know.

I was flattered that Mr. Baker took the time to watch the play again. He later commented that he was intrigued by my performance, which was absolutely thrilling for me to hear. To receive this attention and approval from someone I respected so greatly filled a deep void that I had carried for years.

Back Off

A month following the close of *The Diary of Anne Frank,* my mother went to the junior high to meet with Mr. Baker. She asked him to stop spending so much time with me. She told him that while she truly appreciated all he had done for me, she was afraid I was going to get hurt. Mr. Baker had acted shocked by my mother's concerns. He had reassured her that he would never willingly hurt me, but if that were her concern, he would, of course, back off. Years later, she told me that the thought of Mr. Baker doing something inappropriate had never even crossed her mind. She was simply worried I would develop a crush on my teacher and naturally get hurt as a result. Knowing my mother's difficulty with conflict, I imagine this was difficult for her.

Later that day I stopped by to see Mr. Baker, who appeared anxious and upset. He had two pieces of yellow paper with handwritten notes on both sides in his hand. I immediately thought I was in big trouble for something. The idea that he was angry or disappointed with me felt unbearable. As he read me the notes, I slowly got the picture of my mother's visit to him. She had never expressed any concern to me about the time I spent with him, and I had no idea she had even really noticed, so I was completely taken by surprise.

I panicked. How could anyone think about taking away the one thing that brought me relief and joy? Mr. Baker was *the* most important thing in my life. I felt semi-happy for the first time ever, and now my mother was trying to say this was a bad thing? I didn't think there was anything inappropriate about our relationship. He had never touched me or said anything of a sexual nature to me. I certainly didn't feel like I had a crush on him. He wasn't even cute. In fact, I actually found him unattractive. Balding, ugly mustache, and glasses—just an old dude in my mind. But the beauty of his friendship outshone all of that in my mind. An unfamiliar anger bubbled up inside me. It felt like a grave injustice.

I watched him put the papers aside, and then he made the following statement, which will forever be burned in my memory: "She's asked me to back away from you, and I guess I should abide by her wishes. But I've grown so attached to you, and I just don't think I can do that. I can't handle being away from you."

After typing his words above, I paused for a good ten minutes, completely struck by the contrast in my reactions to his statement as a fifteen-year-old kid versus a forty-five-year-old woman. My fifteen-year-old self felt shocked, excited, flattered, frightened, happy, confused, lucky, worried, guilty, and hopeful. Today, as a forty-five-year-old woman, I am still shocked, but now I also feel sick, angry, repulsed, determined, nauseated, saddened, and worried.

I was beside myself. *Mr. Baker had grown attached to me? It wasn't just one-sided?* This was difficult for me to grasp, but I believed him wholeheartedly. I wanted to jump up and down and shout woo-hoo! **I mattered in the world . . . in this important man's world. This was the pivotal moment that completely hooked me to him. Nothing could ever make me walk away now.**

There was another feeling beneath this excitement—a strange feeling in the pit of my stomach (a gut feeling)—that was hard for me to identify. Just like many other times in my life, my body told me something about this was awry, but I had been taught to ignore such feelings. Today, I call this warning from my body a "red-flag" feeling. **These flags were always flying in my face, and I dismissed this one as well.** I focused, instead, on all the positive feelings buzzing around my head and body.

I was so caught off guard by his words that I was speechless. So, he and I made an unspoken pact that we would forge ahead against my mother's wishes. Unfortunately, the request she made of Mr. Baker pushed us even closer together. Many teenagers rebel, of course, but up until this time, I had been doing exactly what I thought was expected of me. I didn't have any rebellious urges prior to this, and I don't think this was a case of "acting out." This was honestly an act of desperation. I *needed* that man in my life to keep my depression and suicidal feelings at bay. I made the decision to do whatever was necessary to preserve his place in my life.

I went home and shouted at my mother, "How could you take away my only friend?!"

I stormed out of the house and walked several miles to a friend's house. Meanwhile, my mother called Mr. Baker and said, "Well, now you've done it. She has run away. Are you happy?" Apparently, she had also asked him not to tell me she had made the request. Mr. Baker responded with concern that I had run away but acted innocent about our conversation.

I ended up at my friend Karen's house, but then her mother drove me back to my place. It turned out that my mother was throwing me a surprise birthday party that night. So when I got home, one of my brother's West Point buddies took me to a movie to get me out of the house, as my mother had arranged.

When we returned from the movies, I walked into a little gathering of family. I needed to act surprised and happy, but inside I felt like I was dying. I was so confused. With my years of practice wearing a mask during times like these, I came across as happy, surprised, and grateful, but inside, I was losing my mind. *How had Mr. Baker become so important to me? Why was it wrong to be close to him? Why couldn't he be at my party?*

Secret Meetings

After the confrontation, Mr. Baker and I started meeting secretly. I would tell my mother I was going to hang out with a friend, and then I would walk to the elementary school, where he would meet me in his car. We would just drive around or go to an ice cream place a few towns away. Sometimes we went to an arcade in Framingham.

Whenever Mr. Baker would drive me home from school, he would drop me off at the elementary school, and I would walk home from there. If my mom asked me where I had been or who dropped me off, I would make up something. I felt a level of familiarity, aliveness, and excitement in the secrecy. Secrets weren't new to me, and my mom hadn't really fostered honesty and trust between us. From early on, I got the message that secrets and shame and unacceptable behaviors were kind of the norm. It never dawned on me that hanging out with Mr. Baker in secret was something I should tell anyone about.

FOR YOU, THE READER
CONSIDER THIS . . .

Extra attention, gifts, compliments, a caring ear, a common bond . . . all of these things made me feel incredibly special. Mr. Baker had found a way to fill my dark and lonely place. In my mind, he was my hero. I looked up to him with admiration and awe. I had spent so many days as a child praying to be rescued, and I believed he had done just that. This filled me with gratitude, and I felt I needed to repay him.

It is no surprise to me that it was so easy for someone to gain my trust and admiration. I was begging for my father to love me and pay attention to me. Anyone's focus on me was such a welcome change in my life. If it hadn't been Mr. Baker, I am convinced someone else would have taken advantage of my neediness. I may have ended up with an abusive boyfriend, or I might have turned to drugs or stealing—anything to distract me from my pain. It just so happened that my void aligned perfectly with Mr. Baker's target practice.

As a student . . .

- Is there a trusted adult in your life you can talk to about your problems?
- What does an appropriate boundary with an adult look like to you?
- What is the difference between a caring adult and an adult who is manipulating you for his or her own gain?
- How can you trust your instincts when your gut tells you something is not right?
- Who can you turn to if a teacher is making you feel uncomfortable?

As a parent . . .

- Can your child talk with you about anything?
- Does your child have a teacher who spends time alone with him or her?

- What would you do if your child tells you that her teacher is her friend?
- Who would you go to with concerns about a teacher's inappropriate boundaries?
- What would you do if you have concerns that something inappropriate is going on with your child's teacher, but your child insists there is nothing to be concerned about?

As an educator . . .

- What are appropriate topics for you to discuss with students?
- Do you think it is okay for a teacher to give a student a ride home under certain circumstances? To give a student a gift?
- Is there ever a valid reason for a teacher to spend time alone with a student outside of class?
- Could any of your interactions with students be viewed as inappropriate or questionable regardless of your intent?
- How would you react to a colleague spending a lot of extra time with a student?

As an administrator . . .

- What protocols are in place to determine appropriate interactions between teachers and students?
- How do you address parents' concerns of suspected inappropriate teacher behaviors?

As a survivor . . .

- Looking back, was there a grooming period prior to the abuse?
- Was there a void that your abuser filled in your life? How is that void filled now?
- Are you able to meet your own needs now, or do you wish for another person to do so?

Concerning the school counselor's response . . .

- What do you think her response should have been?

- Do you think she should have reacted differently?

- What would you do or say in this situation?

- How do you get the most information out of a child without scaring them? And what do you do once you have the information?

- Do you go to that teacher and confront him? Do you go to the principal? Do you talk with the parents?

This interaction between the counselor and me was reason enough for me to write this book. The lesson here is to stop and think. There is a fine line between a teacher who is highly dedicated to his or her students and a teacher who has inappropriate boundaries. The safest practice for both students and teachers is to have an awareness of appropriate boundaries and guidelines for interactions.

CHAPTER 4

Crossing the Line

———◄○►———

Mr. Baker crossed the line with me when I was in ninth grade. This fact is indisputable. Giving me a gift on the last day of school and telling me how attached he had become to me clearly went beyond acceptable social boundaries between teacher and student. However, the focus in this chapter is on when I recognized, as I was in the midst of the experiences, that Mr. Baker had crossed the line with me. Depending on when and where you see them, blurred and crossed lines can take on different appearances.

Gifts

Following my mother's confrontation, Mr. Baker continued making it a point to spend time with me on the phone and in person. As we became more and more familiar with each other, our "friendship" grew and deepened. He told me he saw me as more of a peer than a kid, and, quite often, that's how it felt to me. His tone became softer and kinder, and he would often share with me that I held a special place in his life. I began to notice that he was looking at me very differently, too. While I couldn't identify how those looks differed. I knew they *felt* different. But the more Mr. Baker affirmed I was special to him, the more infatuated and attached I became.

While I had become somewhat accustomed to the occasional gift from Mr. Baker throughout tenth grade, in eleventh grade his gifts graduated to jewelry and crystals, and they began to take on a different meaning to me. (My gifts to him consisted of records and cards and anything that a teenager could afford.)

I felt overwhelmed and uncomfortable when, at Christmas, he pulled out a trash bag full of gifts for me. I would have been so much happier if he had handed me one wrapped gift, but the enormous amount of presents he put before me made me feel unworthy, inferior, and, most important, scared.

I kept getting the feeling that I owed him something; that those gifts were a conditional expectation to receive something in return. It was obvious that I could not give to him equally, so it was this emotional expectation I didn't quite understand. I now look back and realize that there was also a sexual expectation as well, but I did not realize that at the time. **I just felt pressure to be on an adult emotional level with him. Although I felt kind of mature, I had no tools for that level as an adolescent, making it a very confusing dynamic.**

Mr. Baker and I shared a love of music and song lyrics, and he would introduce me to musicians and bands I had never heard of before by making me music tapes. He even made me cassette tapes with love songs that would make me swoon. I would make him tapes as well, trying to capture lyrics that seemed to pertain to how I was feeling at the time. One song that stands out in my memory is Lionel Richie's "Stuck on You." The line I loved back then was, "Got this feeling down deep in my soul that I just can't lose." I cringe as I type those words now, but, back then, I tried to find any song that could express how I was feeling so that Mr. Baker could fully understand me.

First Kiss

Mr. Baker invited me over to his house one afternoon in December of my junior year while his wife was still at work, claiming he really wanted me to see his Christmas decorations. I went over, and we sat on the couch, watching the blinking tree lights and talking about his different ornaments. My torso was turned toward the tree, and he sat just behind me. Then, seemingly out of nowhere, he put his arms around my waist.

He had never touched me like that before, and I felt very unsettled by the contact. Yet, I was also excited, as this was completely uncharted territory. I felt so close and safe with him, but I certainly did not feel sexually attracted to him, and I had no idea he felt physically drawn to me. So this overture came as a big surprise. Still, I didn't question him or address it. I just sat there, my breathing labored, feeling as if I couldn't say a thing.

Then he said something that totally blew me away: "I need to tell you something, and I don't expect you to say anything back, but I *need* to say it. . . . Somehow I have fallen in love with you, and I never expected this to happen. You don't have to say anything, but I can't go on without you knowing how I feel."

Time just sort of stopped for a moment. I felt conflicted between feeling incredibly flattered that this amazing man could feel love for me and knowing somewhere deep down inside me that this was very wrong. This stuff was not supposed to happen. But then again, considering the messages I'd received as a child and what went on in my family, how could I judge any "supposed to's"?

I didn't reply. The conversation continued, but I can't remember any more of our exchange. When the time arrived for him to drive me home, he stopped me at the front door. He placed his hands on my shoulders, leaned down, and kissed me gently. The kiss lasted about five seconds. I experienced another swirl of emotions—disbelief, pride, excitement . . . and fear. **I was scared. I felt like I had just done something illegal. I didn't think about it in terms of him doing something illegal**—it was *me*. Then we turned and left.

We didn't talk much on the drive toward my house. He did let me know that it was important that no one could know about that kiss. He explained that nobody would understand how special our "relationship" was. My brain was a cloudy mess. I just kept looking in the side mirror for police cars. I knew inside that something very wrong had just occurred.

That night, I sat in my bedroom with my head spinning. I had so many confusing thoughts and feelings, and no one to share them with. Mr. Baker had become my sole confidante, and I couldn't share these feelings with him. I would never have dreamed of letting him know I felt frightened or confused. With very little awareness, I had no tools to speak the truth.

This profession of love and this kiss were the fairly concrete line-crossers for me. I sat on my bed and shook my head. *Was this really happening?* I felt like I was in a movie. I suppose I had become accustomed to believing I led a surreal life, and that this was just another phase in it.

Mr. Baker made me feel special. Maybe this is what happens when a man finds you special—you just oblige. **I felt like I had no right to determine if this is what I wanted. Mr. Baker was the adult, the teacher, the role model, the authority figure, the father figure, the hero. . . . I had been taught to respect authority and to not question what was being asked of me. So, regardless of any negative feelings I had around this experience, this was apparently the way it was to proceed. My job was simply to figure out a way to make sense of it all, comply, and enjoy it.**

I didn't really pause much after that night. It was clear to me that this would be my new life. I had a giant secret to protect. This man, eighteen years older than me, was in love with me. I knew he was going to be sexual with me, and I needed to be okay with it.

I Love Him, I Love Him Not

When Mr. Baker first crossed that line with me, I felt so many emotions —excitement, confusion, shame, and guilt. Mainly, I felt the need to eliminate any negative emotions as quickly as possible. The pain I had felt over my father's lack of love and affection for me was now being greatly overshadowed by these big, grown-up thoughts, feelings, and actions. I actually welcomed the replacement, and I rationalized my concern. If Mr. Baker said this was okay, that's all that mattered to me.

Shortly following that afternoon at his house, I went on a ski trip with my friend Karen. I didn't tell her what had happened between Mr. Baker and me. I wouldn't have even known where to begin. Besides, he had told me not to say anything to anyone—ever.

I vividly recall waiting for the chairlift with Karen at the bottom of the hill. We got on the lift, and the following progression of thoughts went through my mind:

What the hell happened with him?

He's in love with me?

I can't believe I didn't say anything back.

He must be so sad.

I just don't think I'm in love with him.

He's not even cute!

He's old and he's married . . . but he means so much to me.

He is my best friend.

I don't know what I would do if he wasn't in my life. I need him so much.

That kiss was scary, but it was kind of exciting, too. Maybe that's what it's supposed to feel like.

This man is so amazing and I look up to him so much, and he actually has those kinds of feelings for me?

Who else would ever feel like that about me?

I finally matter to someone.

Maybe this is what love is. Maybe being in love means you can't live without that person.

I've never had a crush on a boy—I am just messed up, so that's why I am not physically attracted to him. I've never been attracted to anybody.

Well, that's it. I must be in love with him.

Yup, I love him, too!

I had convinced myself from the bottom of the chairlift to the top that I felt for Mr. Baker what he felt for me. I had talked myself into it. By the time I reached the top of the hill, I felt less angst about the situation, but it all felt so surreal. This was a declaration of sorts—I was to be with Mr. Baker. He had chosen me, and my life would take this new course. I felt hopeful he would make me happy and take away the sting of my father's lack of love or presence for the rest of my life. Yes, this would be a pleasant, exciting distraction from everything else. Most important, though, I thought, **"It must be okay if Mr. Baker says it's okay."**

I wholeheartedly believed what Mr. Baker had said: Other people wouldn't understand how special our relationship was, how important I was to him, or how much he needed me. Clearly, I meant a lot to him, or he wouldn't put himself at risk like this.

I never stopped to think about Mrs. Baker in all of this. She didn't even enter into my consciousness. I was so good at compartmentalizing things that I easily filed away the fact that he even had a wife.

When I look back now, I feel terrible remorse. How could I not even consider her or her feelings in any of this? Then I recall my young age and level of need back then. I had been a lost soul, desperately looking for love and belonging. I had spent my entire life ignoring my gut instincts and just doing what I was told, while wearing a mask that reflected someone else entirely.

Feelings

Mr. Baker began proclaiming his love and need for me more often, and I soaked it up. No man had ever told me he loved me before this, and now that I got to hear it on a consistent basis, it felt great, and I didn't want to let it go. I also considered myself fortunate to have won his affection over all the others at school who would have loved to be close to him. I wondered what it was about me in particular that warranted these extreme feelings and risky behavior, but I didn't question him. **I now understand that he had been grooming many girls over the course of his teaching career, waiting for just the right target to grab the bait. At the time, I saw it as some magical equation that had fallen into place for both of us.**

As time went on, Mr. Baker seemed to have an increased need to see me, talk to me, and know what I was doing, thinking, and feeling. I took that as a sign of how important I was to him, never realizing that it was actually his need to exert his control over me that was increasing. Whether it was right or wrong, I would have done anything to make sure nothing interfered with my "rescuer's" loving feelings for me. He cared about me in a way I never dreamed anyone could. How could I let that escape?

FOR YOU, THE READER
CONSIDER THIS . . .

Mr. Baker had gone from teacher to mentor to friend to boyfriend in a matter of two years. This was how I saw the progression of events. He had slowly and carefully constructed a path to build my need, trust, and affection for him. The intense emotions and physical interactions were overwhelming and confusing. However, any discomfort, fear, or concern I had was greatly overshadowed by my trust in this man. I believed I knew in my heart that he could only have my best interests in mind. Hadn't he always wanted only the best for me? He always wanted to help me feel better about my life and myself. Surely he wouldn't do something to me or put me through something that could harm me.

As a student . . .

- At what point do you think Mr. Baker crossed the line with me?

- Was there a point when someone could have intervened?

- If you were either the target or simply a bystander, would you feel comfortable reporting any possible concerns at this point?

- If so, who would you tell and what would you say?

- What fears would you have if you reported?

- What does love feel like? What is the difference between infatuation and love?

As a parent . . .

- How do you approach your child if you suspect he or she is being abused?

- How do you explain what love is to your child?

- Who can you go to in the school to express your concerns?

As an educator or administrator . . .

- What are appropriate topics of conversations and interactions between teachers and students?

As a survivor . . .

- When your abuser crossed the line with you, what was your first instinct? Did you act on it? Why or why not?

- If you were to go back to the day your abuser first crossed the line with you, would you react differently?

There is an undeniable power differential between a school employee and a student. Crossing the line, regardless if a student is willing, is an abuse of power and is never acceptable. Period.

CHAPTER 5

A Secret Life

————◀○▶————

Some friends have asked me how I feel about sharing my story for everyone to read. I have worked through much of the pain and grief caused by the years of abuse. I now view it simply: I carry no shame about this. This is no longer my secret—it's Mr. Baker's. I didn't do anything wrong. The wrongdoing happened to me. Why should I hide anything? If these words, thoughts, and feelings are put on paper, and someone reading them can gain some personal insight or relief from them, then isn't that worth enough to put myself out there? Maybe part of the reason this happened to me is because I am someone who can speak out. Maybe my story can stop this from happening to someone else.

High School. I believe high school is supposed to be about learning, maturing, friendships, first relationships, peer pressure, exploration, individuation, and so much more. Some people go on their first dates in high school. They date, they hold hands, and they call each other incessantly. First love is supposed to be all encompassing, and you want the whole world to know about it. You have your arm around that person, showing him or her off to anyone in your path, and all your best friends know who you are dating.

Typically, that first relationship is with someone who is experiencing those same "firsts" with you. You are supposed to go to class, study hard, maybe have a part-time job, participate in some activities, fight with your parents a bit . . . you get the idea. This is the ideal. My high school experience was a far cry from all this, and no one knew.

Hiding It from My Mother

Once my mother had approached Mr. Baker and asked him to stop spending so much time with me, I felt I could not be honest with her about the time I spent with him. I had an overwhelming need to protect my relationship with him because his attention provided me with my only sense of joy, peace, and meaning. I led a secret life and became adept at lying and sneaking around. Some of this was less difficult than I'd anticipated, since my mother worked until way after school was dismissed. As I mentioned in an earlier chapter, I would simply tell her I was with friends.

When I saw Mr. Baker on the weekends, he would pick me up at the elementary school and we would drive several towns away. We would spend as much time together as we could pack in at the arcade, movie theater, or ice cream shop, and then he would drop me off at the school and I'd walk home.

When we talked on the phone, I would whisper in my room or pretend I was talking to someone else. We had code words for certain things. For example, if I remember correctly, I would say "twenty-four" if my mom was within hearing distance. There was no instant messaging, no cell phones or texts, or Internet back then, so I had to talk with him on the phone to arrange plans and secret meetings.

My father was absent from my everyday life, so there was really no need to hide my relationship with Mr. Baker from him. I still saw my father occasionally on weekends, but I just didn't have enough of a relationship with him to tell him anything of a personal nature. I recall on my seventeenth birthday, my father took me out for dinner, and I mentioned to him that Mr. Baker was taking me out as well. My father told one of my brothers that he didn't like Mr. Baker involved with me like that, but I got the feeling that he just felt jealous because he didn't spend much time with me. It certainly couldn't have been that he was concerned about my safety.

The Shift

As Mr. Baker and I carried on with this secret life, some dynamics between us started to shift, but only subtly at first. He slowly began showing more interest in my whereabouts and which kids were in my classes, and his questions had less to do with *how* I was doing and more about *who* I was interacting with. Also, the strangest details would make him angry. For example, if I mentioned a boy from my class, his temper would flare because I hadn't mentioned that boy's name previously. He would also ask many questions I just didn't know how to answer, and he would become angry by my inability to respond. These reactions confused me, and I did not understand why our relationship was changing in this manner.

The level of physical contact between us shifted as well. After Mr. Baker violated my boundaries with that first kiss by the door at his house, he assured me that we would take things slowly, at my pace. At the time, I believed he was making the kindest of gestures, and I was grateful he did not expect me to perform some of the sex acts I had only just begun to learn existed. **Little did I know, this was all part of a typical pattern employed by pedophiles as part of the grooming process: gradual sexual encounters and interaction to gain trust.**

I was extremely nervous about being physically intimate with Mr. Baker. Nothing about being with him in that manner felt natural to me, and nothing about it was for me. Everything I did, I did to keep him happy. My need and desire to please him far outweighed my fear or anxiety about having sex. Another shift occurred in that he began to be less complimentary of me after we became sexually involved, and, of course, I would try harder to earn his compliments.

Sexual Firsts

When close friends asked me who I had lost my virginity to, it made me so sad to realize that I had lost it to a perpetrator. Outside of a few random kisses with boys, all of my sexual firsts were with Mr. Baker—

and all before I was eighteen. Most of them were performed with great reluctance.

I cannot remember much about the first time we had intercourse. I believe we were on the living room floor in his house on a blanket. I feared his wife would come home, so I just prayed it would be quick.

I felt surprised and betrayed when the "slow pacing" Mr. Baker initially insisted upon got lost by the wayside. The level of intimacy and acts expected of me rapidly increased in intensity. When he would try giving me oral sex, his moustache would rub against my skin, and I would go into utter panic. My reaction to this made me think I was crazy. I had never even heard about oral sex the first time he tried it. Frankly, I just didn't understand why he was doing that weird thing to me, and I felt sick and scared by it. I didn't pull away or ask him to stop because I just didn't know how to voice my disgust.

I would perform oral sex on him because he acted like he would die without it. While I did it, I would sort of float away to the ceiling—a coping mechanism that I now know is called *dissociating*. Whenever we were physical together, I would pretend I was in a movie or something, so it would feel less painful and traumatic.

Mr. Baker never seemed to notice any of the intense negative reactions I was having. He would get very physically active with me, and his intensity would frighten me. Nothing in me wanted to interact with this man in this manner, and I was not in any way ready for this level of sexual activity with anyone.

Why couldn't we just hang out at the arcade?

In the middle of a particular sex act, he would just continue going, almost as if I wasn't even there. He would get this strange and ugly look in his eyes whenever he was being sexual with me.

Sex soon became the priority for him whenever we hung out. He would find different places for us to have sex. Sometimes we did it at his house. Other times, we used his brother's apartment. Usually at night, he would park somewhere remote, and we would do it there.

I do not remember one time when I actually felt safe having sex with Mr. Baker. However, I put forth a great deal of energy into acting like I was excited to be with him sexually. I was so accustomed to pleasing people and wearing that dreaded mask of happiness that it seemed natural to keep doing it, as horribly uncomfortable as it was.

Above all, I wanted to be sure *he* was happy. I very much wanted to enjoy sex with him, but the truth is, there were times when I prayed to God during the physical acts that he would just let me die right there so I *never* had to do that again. It was that bad at times. I couldn't understand how a man who had initially been so kind and loving could turn into this sex animal, seeming to be completely clueless of how it was affecting me. It was apparent even back then that he was uninterested in my feelings.

Sometimes he would give me alcohol to make me relax. His specialty was melon ball cocktails because they were sweet, and I guess he figured I would drink more of them than other types of liquor. Once I became so dizzy that I couldn't stand up straight. He pinned me to the ground and ravaged me. I was so grateful that time for being numb and out of it. He never used any protection. He would pull out of me—that was it.

On my eighteenth birthday, midway through senior year, he ejaculated inside me and said, "There's your birthday present. Don't go and do something stupid like get pregnant."

Statements like that confused me to no end. Was I supposed to be grateful? I remember feeling scared when he said that. *Pregnant? Could I really get pregnant by this man? Would it be my fault?* I believed *everything* Mr. Baker told me. What on earth would I do if I ever got pregnant?! I pushed that thought quickly out of mind and decided to feel grateful that someone felt comfortable being that close to me. I trusted Mr. Baker enough to believe that nothing bad would happen to me.

Faking It

I don't recall *ever* enjoying being kissed or touched by Mr. Baker, and I never had an orgasm with him. I would pretend to have one during sex just so he would hopefully stop sooner. I had no idea what an orgasm felt like, but I had watched enough movies to copy what I saw.

Again, I never, ever felt safe with him sexually, which was a far cry from how he used to make me feel when we were just "friends." If I could dissociate enough during the experience, I could sort of numb out and tolerate whatever he was doing to me. That was about as pleasurable as it would get for me.

Still, I did my best to pretend with him that I was into it. In later years, I couldn't pretend as well. I just cried a lot during sex, hid it from him, and headed to the nearest bathroom as soon as he was done so I could dry off my tears and recover my composure as quickly as possible.

Expectations Versus Reality

When I really thought about what was going on in my life, I was always taken aback by the contrasts between my behavior and what other kids my age were doing. A main example was riding the school bus during my junior year. Here I was, sixteen years old, having a teacher touch me in ways I had never experienced before, yet I was still riding a school bus to and from school. This thought would occur to me *every time* I stepped on that bus, and it left me feeling terribly lonely and like an outcast among my peers.

My life did not make sense to me at all when I would take a close look at it. Yes, when I was with Mr. Baker, it would make sense, but only in the moment. It was difficult to step in and out of the contrasting roles of my life. Sometimes I felt so misunderstood and mistreated by my teachers because I thought they should treat me like an adult. If I could "handle" this situation with Mr. Baker, I shouldn't have to deal with homework and exams and adolescent things like SATs and PE class. Of course I got along with my teachers because I was compliant by nature. I just internalized the confusion and became anxious and depressed—those things I thought Mr. Baker's attention had chased away.

The Necklace

Among all the gifts Mr. Baker gave me over the years while I was still in high school, there was one that held particular significance for me: a necklace. I thought it was the most beautiful thing I had ever seen. It was made of an interesting stone with a tiny painting on it—a dark sky with a mountain and moon. It hung from a lovely silver chain. It meant so much to me, and I found this one of the most challenging ones to hide. I wanted to share with others how much Mr. Baker meant to me and how much this gift meant to me, but I had to hide it from everyone as usual, including my mother. I always found a good excuse to explain away Mr. Baker's gifts, saying it is just what he did with all the students he liked. However, hiding the gifts and the fact that they spoke of how "special" I was to Mr. Baker was always such a painful conflict for me. So, I wore that necklace in my senior picture. It was my statement that I was with him, without having to tell anybody the truth about the situation. Now, when I look at that picture and I see that necklace, I cringe. **It's like a stamp of abuse on my chest, yet at the time, I thought it was a statement of love.**

Fun and Games

Fun and Games was an arcade in Framingham, Massachusetts. Framingham was about thirty minutes or so away from Norwood. We would drive to Fun and Games and spend hours playing pinball and video games. We felt safe there because we didn't think anyone would recognize us. I remember trying to act like he was just my friend. I didn't want people to suspect that he was my "boyfriend." As always, I was led to believe that it was my responsibility to protect this secret.

One time, I was getting quarters from one of the adult staff members. He had seen us there many times. He looked at me with a strange smirk and said, "So how old is that boyfriend of yours anyway?"

I looked right at him like he was insane and said, "He is sooo not my boyfriend, hello?! He's old—he's just a friend of the family."

He just smiled and said, "Oh yeah, okay, whatever."

I walked away, blushing in a panic. I told Mr. Baker about the conversation. He looked pissed off and annoyed with *me*. It was as if it were my job to not look so young or not raise any suspicion. I just remember feeling like I was not doing a good enough job of hiding my reactions and feelings. I assured Mr. Baker that I had convinced the guy that he was, in fact, just a friend of the family.

The rest of our time there that day, I just wanted to run. I found myself wondering how long we would need to keep up these appearances. I had the skills to present a relatively convincing façade for the benefit of others, but I just didn't know how long I wanted to keep that up.

SAT

Near the end of my junior year of high school, I was about to take the SAT. Mr. Baker was going to be taking me to Fun and Games right after it was over. He told me that he would wait in his car outside the school. I asked him what would happen if the other kids at school saw me get into the car with him. He told me that I had better finish the exam early so that no one would see. I told him that leaving early was not an option in these exams. (Wasn't he a teacher? Shouldn't he have known this?) His response to this was, "Well then, you better not linger afterward talking to boys or anything."

Again, he placed the responsibility on me for protecting the secret. How well do you think I could focus during that exam? I was a complete basket case.

I broke out into a sweat at one point during the test—not because of the content of the exam, but because I kept envisioning everyone seeing me get into his car and talking about it. *What if they told a teacher? What if talk got around and people found out the horrible things I was doing?* All these "what if's" replaced remembering the algebraic equations and vocabulary words I had studied. When time was up, I rushed out of that classroom and made my way out of the school, as fast as I could. There he was, waiting, looking angry that other kids were around. I could not win, no matter what. He set up the situation to control me—to make me feel that I was wrong and inept. In retrospect, he did that quite often. Of course, I couldn't recognize that at the time and, yes, my SAT score was terrible—well below what I probably should have been able to score. Did that low score really impact my life terribly? No. Did the experience of taking the test under duress impact my life terribly? Absolutely.

Dining Out

Occasionally Mr. Baker would take me out to dinner. We sometimes went to a restaurant near Fun and Games called Houlihan's. Going out to dinner with him was always awkward. I felt so conflicted. On one hand, I wanted to seem all grown up, like him. I think he brought me to restaurants so that it felt like we had a mature, adult relationship. I loved going because that was what adults did on dates, but on the other hand, we would get strange looks from the staff and other patrons. I could tell people were trying to figure out just what type of "relationship" was sitting at table number twelve. It clearly wasn't father/daughter—you could see it on our faces. I was too young and he was too old for us to be dating. Was it uncle/niece?

I would try so hard to not look at their expressions, but I kept getting drawn back in. I would be so confused about how to act. He would get angry with me if I wasn't showing him enough affection, yet I could not hold his hand or look into his eyes for an extended period of time. There was a danger that I always felt just under the surface. It was my job to protect this secret. Maybe he set up these situations to test me. He couldn't have been overly concerned about getting caught if he kept putting us in scenarios in the public where people could react.

One phrase I have learned from my research always rings in my head when I think about all this: *above suspicion*. Dr. Robert Shoop is a professor with a focus on sexual harassment, abuse prevention, and risk management. I have heard Dr. Shoop speak about the issue of educator sexual abuse, and he uses the phrase "above suspicion" often, and it seems to sum up so many dynamics. I truly believe Mr. Baker felt like he was above suspicion. He was an adored teacher who always went the extra mile to make kids feel special. Nobody would ever suspect any wrongdoing on his part, and I think he knew that. So he would toy with me in these scenarios, reminding me of the control he had over me. He was testing me to make sure I could protect the secret.

Integrating Friends

We integrated some of our friends and family members into our "relationship," while keeping up the pretense that we were just friends and everything was normal. I enjoyed sharing our time with other people, usually because we got along better when there were buffers. I felt like the chance of my saying something to anger him decreased when others were around. I had an easy time pulling off this "friend" act. Acting was all I knew.

On one occasion, when my friend Kirsten was joining us to see a movie, Mr. Baker picked us up at her house. As we were heading to the door, her mom asked her, "Is this guy . . . okay?"

Kirsten and I reassured her that he was just a really cool guy who liked to take students out. End of story, and out we went. This would not be the only time an adult would question Mr. Baker's intentions and be brushed aside by this type of answer. Kirsten believed what she was telling her mom, and I was proud to be so convincing.

Most people knew I was close to Mr. Baker. However, I rarely felt safe enough to tell anyone the truth about what was going on. Mr. Baker had drilled it into my head that no one was to know the true nature of our "relationship." I was well aware of how loosely people held on to the promise of not sharing secrets. Because of this, I not only held on to my own secrets, I also put forth much energy into ensuring people believed Mr. Baker and I were just good friends.

New Year's Eve

During my senior year, I went to a New Year's Eve party at my friend Christine's house, and I had been drinking quite a bit. I looked around at everyone and noticed how happy and at ease they all seemed. I felt like a complete imposter. I was having fun, but I felt guilty for doing so. I had the thought that I was not allowed to like any of the boys at the party because that would mean I was betraying Mr. Baker.

I had a moment of clarity, in my drunken haze, when I felt entitled to tell someone my truth. *Screw him,* I thought. *He's home with his wife. Why can't I at least talk about whatever I want to talk about?*

These impulses didn't occur often, so I quickly reacted. I pulled Christine aside and said I needed to talk to her. We went to the corner of the room, and I spilled my guts. I didn't know what reaction to expect from her. She didn't seem very surprised by the news. I guess most people wondered about it all.

She reassured me that, above all, she would not tell a soul. I made her double and triple swear that she would keep it to herself. She also warned me that I would probably regret talking to her about it the next morning. She told me to never regret it. She said she was there for me and would take my secret to her grave. I was so grateful for her friendship in that moment. Somehow the weight I had been carrying felt a little lighter.

Many years later, I had a conversation with Christine about Mr. Baker. She told me that she always regretted not telling someone about what was going on. I apologized for making her promise to keep the secret, and she apologized for keeping it. It was a strange but wonderful conversation. I find this very important to write about now. The most important thing in the world to me in high school was to keep the secret to myself or at least with one friend—to protect Mr. Baker at all costs. I would have done just about anything to follow his directions and hide the truth. If anyone asked or confronted me, I would have denied it all in a very believable manner. I would have hated anyone who betrayed my trust and broke my silence for me.

How ironic is it that Mr. Baker was the one betraying my trust? Back then, I could not see this truth at all. I needed someone to disregard my armor of deceit and silence and expose the abuse for what it was. It didn't matter that I would have hated it; it needed to be done.

I want people reading this to know that the number-one priority must be to stop the abuse from happening regardless of what the victim says, does, feels, or acts. Sometimes kids need adults to take charge of a situation, regardless of whether or not they understand the reasoning behind it. Sometimes kids need to take matters into their own hands if they know their friend is being abused or engaging in something that might hurt them.

Brigham's

Throughout most of high school, I worked at an ice cream shop called Brigham's. They had the best-tasting vanilla ice cream, hands down. I really enjoyed working there. I loved the girls I worked with, and I enjoyed the customers who became regulars. Mr. Baker would come in and visit once in a while. When the girls would ask me about him, I would just act casual, explaining he was once my teacher but now he's a really cool friend. I would emphasize that he was friendly like this with *lots* of his former students.

Sometimes Mr. Baker would call the store and ask for me. I would be happy to talk with him, but I worried what the others thought. Once after I ended a call with Mr. Baker, my boss said, "That boyfriend who calls you is a man! He sounds *very* old." I couldn't even begin to deny that I had a boyfriend or go into the long explanation I had all worked out, so I simply said, "Nope." My boss just shook his head.

I often think of the adults in my life during that time in my life. My friends' parents, other teachers, my boss . . . How they must have wondered about my relationship with Mr. Baker. What happened to those thoughts? Why didn't they follow up on them?

One time, after Mr. Baker and I had argued earlier in the day, he came into the shop wearing a very serious look. He waited in a line of customers, and, when it was his turn, he simply handed me a plastic bag in front of the other girls, who of course were wondering what the heck was in the bag, and then left.

I went over to the side of the counter and looked inside, being careful not to allow anyone to see its contents. It was a songbook from the soundtrack to the movie *Top Gun,* which we had seen together. I am not sure what message he was trying to convey, but it was the most awkward moment.

This is just one example of the conflicting messages he would give me. *Hide this secret, but don't deny me when I am present with you. I* never felt like I could make sense of that conflict.

Wife's Discovery

During my senior year of high school, I was at Mr. Baker's house after school one day. We were upstairs in his bedroom—in his bed. Downstairs, I had left my shoes and jacket. We were fooling around, and I heard the front door open. We both froze and just listened. There was a long pause, and then the door slammed. His wife had come home early. I thought I was going to die in that instant.

Mr. Baker panicked and scrambled to get his clothes on. He kept saying, "Dammit, I didn't want her to find out this way!"

I just kept pleading, "Tell her I'm so sorry, tell her I'm so sorry!"

Up until that point, I had distanced myself from the fact that he was married. I just put it out of my mind and compartmentalized it, as I explained earlier. When that door opened and my heart stopped, the fact that he was married had just become very real to me. The remorse I felt was greater than anything I had ever experienced.

He drove me back to Brigham's. I don't think I was scheduled to work that day. He just dropped me off there, saying he had to go find her. I begged him to call me when he could to let me know everything was okay. He assured me that no matter what happened, he wasn't going to "leave me out in the cold."

I believed him, too. Looking back, I doubt he was worried about leaving me anywhere but at Brigham's. As he drove away that night, I believed in him, trusting that he would work things out, as if that afternoon had never happened.

I can't recall how much time went by, but when I finally saw him again, we went for a long drive to get ice cream and talk. I wanted to know everything—every word and reaction she had about him and toward him.

He told me she cried a lot and said, "That was Andrea, wasn't it?" And he had acknowledged that it was. He then said, "She isn't too pleased with you right now, Andrea."

Apparently the blame was on me. I just looked at him sheepishly, believing it was entirely my fault. I felt like I owed the world an apology for my existence. That feeling continued for many years. I willingly accepted the responsibility, continuing this self-destructive mind-set. I didn't feel like I could walk away from this situation. It was all his choice, his call. He informed me that he told her he would not "leave me out in the cold" and that she chose to stay with him, fully aware that he would still be seeing me.

I find it extremely difficult to believe any of that now. I don't even know if she guessed it was me. If she did suspect that an underage student was up in that bed with her husband, why wouldn't she have reported it? Was she under his control as much as I was? Perhaps she was just caught up in the realization that her husband was cheating on her. I will never know the answers to these questions. What I do know is that this was one of the most horrible memories I have—more horrible than all the abuse he put me through. I hate that she had to experience that.

Over the years I have considered contacting Mrs. Baker, but the fear of upsetting her and opening old wounds has prevented me from doing so.

TONY Award

Norwood had a tradition of giving out the TONY (Ten Outstanding Norwood Youth) Awards. During my senior year, I won this award, and there was a ceremony for all of the nominees, which was taking place the week after I had been "caught" by Mr. Baker's wife.

I wished Mr. Baker could be there, but considering what had just happened, that would be impossible. However, I had asked my father to attend, and I was really excited for him to see me get nominated. I thought maybe I could finally win his approval or respect somehow. When the evening arrived, my mother and I got all dressed up and drove to the event. There was no sign of my father.

I waited as long as I could prior to the event and eventually went to a pay phone to call him. I asked him why he wasn't there, and at first he acted surprised it was that night, and then he said I had never gotten back to him with ticket information, so it was my fault he couldn't make it. Clearly he had forgotten all about it. I hung up the phone and walked back to my table.

I think my mother could see what had just occurred by the expression on my face. I felt so dejected and rejected and invisible, all at once. The feeling was all too familiar and heartbreaking. The award ceremony proceeded, and I was announced as one of the winners.

I can't remember much about that evening except having the overwhelming feeling that I was a complete fraud. Here I was voted one of ten outstanding Norwood youth, and I was involved with a married teacher. Even my own father knew I was not worthy enough to win that award or surely he would have shown up, right?

A reporter interviewed me, and then told me that an article would appear in the paper the next morning. There was a big group picture and a lovely article featuring me! Instead of feeling excited and proud, I woke up the next morning in a complete panic. The article was on the front page of the paper, and all I could think about was Mr. Baker's poor wife seeing it and reading about me. I was beyond horrified and remorseful.

The moment I arrived at school, I ran to the pay phone and waited for Mr. Baker's call. (We spoke every morning at the same time on that pay phone.) When he called, I warned him about the article and told him to get rid of that paper before his wife saw it. I was sure the article would be too much for her to bear. He just listened to my fumbling, rushed words, and agreed to remove the paper before she could see it. When we hung up, I felt relieved yet responsible for so much. I felt like I had the weight of the world on my shoulders.

Filled with dread and wanting to cry, I was unable to focus in any of my classes. I felt hopeless and clearly saw that this was not how my life was supposed to be at such a young age, but I had absolutely no clue how to change it. I still needed Mr. Baker in my life, and yet it wasn't feeling as magical or breezy as it had a few years earlier. The old, familiar angst and pain had returned.

Jimmy

Mr. Baker was very close to his brother, Jimmy, who taught math at Dedham High School. We would often do fun things with him, such as go to the beach and concerts and play tennis. Once, when Jimmy was out, Mr. Baker and I went to his apartment. Jimmy came home early while we were having sex in his bed. I froze, once again, not knowing if this was going to become some huge ordeal or not.

Mr. Baker jumped up and whispered to me, "Stay here and be quiet."

I didn't know if I was supposed to hide or what. He went out to meet Jimmy. I overheard him saying that I was there and was not feeling well. So I quickly adjusted my demeanor and pretended to be sick by curling up in a fetal position. Then a moment later, Jimmy walked into the room with Mr. Baker behind him.

Jimmy said, "You're not feeling well, huh?"

And I just kind of moaned, saying my stomach was a mess. I didn't think that he believed it, but I will never know. They both walked out of the room, letting me rest.

I just lay there wondering if I was going straight to hell. I hated myself so much. Why was my life this way? I wondered what Jimmy must have thought, having a teenager lying in his bed, sick or not sick. Everything felt like it was starting to spin out of control.

I felt the peace and calm that Mr. Baker used to bring to my life slipping away from me. Very seldom did I feel that all was better because of him. Things became more and more complicated. There was also this eerie familiarity of conflict avoidance with Mr. Baker. The same dynamics seemed to be popping up with him as they had with my father. I would consistently act and speak in ways that I hoped would avoid angering Mr. Baker or cause any possible conflict. I wasn't quite sure how I had landed in this situation.

Anxiety

I had a lot of physical complaints back in high school that I believe all stemmed from keeping this big secret trapped inside me. For someone who initially brought me so much "joy," I sure didn't feel great. The adrenaline rush I got from secretly talking and meeting with him took its toll on my body. I had constant stomachaches, headaches, heart palpitations, chest pains, nightmares, and severe insomnia. I felt like I had this giant anvil placed on my shoulders anytime I wasn't with Mr. Baker. It was a weird catch 22—being under his control created this unhappiness, yet when I was with him, the misery lifted for only a short time. I had an intense fear of anyone discovering this secret, and yet part of me wished the whole world could know so my pain could lift. I wanted people to see my pain because I felt so lonely in it.

My senior year of high school continued to be plagued with decisions and anxiety. Upon graduating from high school, Mr. Baker insisted on trying to spend as much time as possible together that summer, since I would be embarking on a new life chapter soon (I will discuss the details of how and where I decided to attend college later in the book). I juggled working several jobs and secret meetings with him throughout that summer. I found myself wondering how I would be able to attend college and maintain this stressful balancing act in just a few short months.

The Basement

We didn't go back to Mr. Baker's house for about a year following his wife's discovery. As horrible as that day was, after some time, we were able to go back to our old routines, and I was able to move past the trauma associated with being caught in his home.

During my freshman year of college, I was home for the weekend as usual. He picked me up at Brigham's. I was supposed to be home by a certain time because I was going to share a ride with Eddie, a guy in my neighborhood, who was also heading back to the school that night. Mr. Baker drove me to his house, where we had sex. Just as we were about to leave, Mr. Baker looked out the window and saw that his wife was pulling into the driveway. Panicked, he hurried me down into his basement.

The basement was dark and completely packed with stuff. With barely any room to stand, I was stuck right at the bottom of the staircase. I cannot describe the terror I felt. I couldn't bear the thought of his wife seeing me there again.

I heard her come in and casually say hello to him. He was trying his best to sound calm and normal. They chatted for a while. She asked if he wanted a drink, and he declined. It was odd to hear him interact with her. She sounded happy to see him and not as estranged as the picture he painted. At one point, she opened the basement door and started down the stairs. I squeezed my eyes shut and held my breath. I prayed so hard she would not see me.

She grabbed something near the top of the stairs and shut the door. She told him she was going upstairs to take a shower. As I heard her climb the stairs, there was a long pause. I wasn't sure which one of them was going upstairs. Then, a few moments later, the basement door opened, and I heard footsteps coming down. I could not tell if they were hers or his.

I opened my eyes to see him smiling at me.

Smiling?

He sort of laughed at my expression. He gave me a twenty-dollar bill and told me to go out the bulkhead, run behind a few houses, cross a street, and get to the nearest pay phone to call a taxi. I was absolutely terrified. I asked him all these questions.

What if she saw me?

What if a neighbor saw me?

How was I going to get back to school on time?

He just hurried me out of there, chuckling and saying it would all be fine. The journey from his basement to my car was horrible. I was crying and panicking and wondering how I would get back to my car in time. Here I was, eighteen years old, still feeling like a child, crying in the streets and looking for a pay phone. *How is this my life?* I wondered.

I never did get back to my car in time. I got back to my house, and my mother told me Eddie had to leave. I had no explanation for her other than I lost track of time. I felt so sick to my stomach. My life felt completely out of control. I drove back to school very late and slipped into college mode as best as I could. I didn't tell anyone what happened. I felt so lost and alone. I wanted it all to just go away, and I wanted someone to make it go away for me.

The next day, Mr. Baker called me on the dorm pay phone. He was talking as if nothing was wrong. I meekly brought up the events of the previous day.

He just said, "Oh, that was no big deal—everything is fine."

I was shocked. My world was in a tailspin, and he minimized it. And I had absolutely no voice, no words to speak to him. I did not have the tools to confront him about the situation or tell him how it made me feel. I wanted it all to be over, but I had no idea I had the right to even want that. I continued to feel that he was in charge and would tell me how things were to be.

I simply told him that I missed him and couldn't wait to see him next weekend.

That was a lie.

I still thought I loved him, but I didn't want to deal with a married man any longer, and I also did not enjoy how he made me feel most of the time. What a switch from ninth grade, I realized. Unfortunately, I just knew that Mr. Baker was in charge of everything, and I had no say in this. So, I continued seeing him.

Fun Times

The times we had together weren't all horrible. We enjoyed several activities together. He got me to play tennis regularly, although he would get pretty intense when we played. We would also go hiking in the mountains of New Hampshire and do other fun things. But somehow, more often than not, they would develop into tense situations.

He even taught me how to golf and bought me a set of golf clubs. I want to say that we had a great time golfing, but I just remember tension. One time, as he was about to tee off, I was talking more loudly than was desirable. He got so angry with me. He blamed his bad shot on me and would not talk to me for the rest of the game. He would also get really frustrated when I couldn't apply the pointers he gave me to my game. Hell, I couldn't even get the damn ball up in the air, and I really didn't care. I just wanted to have fun, but he was just too competitive. Soon, we stopped playing golf because it wasn't worth the aggravation.

I found myself in this pattern with Mr. Baker that would resemble the same pattern I experienced growing up with my father. I would cling to any good time I had with him and think that everything was repaired, and the good times were here to stay. One particular time that stands out in my mind is a trip we took to stay at a condo in Waterville Valley in New Hampshire one summer during college. We had a great time. We had no stress or arguments. I felt like we were couple.

We played tennis, went hiking, went floating down the river on rafts. We got along really well for those few days. I remember feeling very conflicted that weekend. I was always so upset about our relationship, wondering how I could develop a plan to leave him . . . yet there we were, having this great weekend away, and I felt guilty for having such negative thoughts. I thought that everything had changed, and he was going to be nicer. The calm didn't last very long, of course.

When we returned home, so, too, had the tension and control. I felt more confused than before the trip. How could I have such a great time with him, yet be so stressed out and unhappy at other times? Why couldn't he just be that nice and relaxed all of the time?

Much later, of course, I learned that this is another part of the cycle in abusive relationships. It is sometimes referred to as the "honeymoon period." After a conflict, the storm passes and the abuser tries to lure the victim back into a trusting state. He will act sweet, bring flowers, or generally try to restore a peaceful setting so that the victim has this false sense that the relationship can be saved.

I can relate very strongly to all parts in the cycle of abuse. This particular phase was a very difficult one for me to both recognize as well as resist. The moment we had some laughs, I wanted them to last forever.

We went back to Waterville Valley another time during the winter to ski. I arrived later than he did because I had a late afternoon class. When I arrived, I was looking for the correct condo. I clearly remember this moment: I heard voices and laughter and looked up. A group of college kids were partying in one of the condos. When I saw them, the worst feeling of longing came over me. I felt like that was where I belonged, not with this much older guy. I wanted to learn how to party. I wanted to feel like a normal college student. I guess I had just convinced myself that that wasn't the life I was to lead. With emptiness in my heart, I found the right condo. I remember taking a deep breath and telling myself to suck it up and have fun.

Transition to a "Couple"

There was a point when the secrecy and status of our "relationship" shifted to one we did not have to hide from everyone. Sometime during college, Mr. Baker felt comfortable enough to allow people to see us as a couple. He explained to people that we "hooked up" when I was an adult in college. He instructed me to give the same explanation. I didn't want to hurt him in any way, so I agreed to share the same story of how and when we "hooked up."

Mike, a math teacher at Norwood High School, was one of Bob's closest friends. Bob started bringing me to Mike's house to hang out. We had some of the best times at Mike's house. We would grill steaks or make nachos and drink strawberry daiquiris. We would play pool and listen to music. We went to concerts together. This felt like a safe environment for us. Mike knew we were together and was fully accepting of us. It had this glimpse of a normal relationship where we didn't have to hide our feelings or actions. It was one of the few safe places most of the time.

From Mr. Baker to Bob

In the beginning, I called him Mr. Baker. I called him that for a long time, both to him and to others when talking about him. After a while, I stopped calling him Mr. Baker because it reminded me of how strange this relationship was, but I couldn't for the life of me call him Bob in his presence. That did not feel right either. He was not Bob; he was Mr. Baker. Midway through college, I started referring to him as Bob when talking to others, especially to my friends. The problem was, I never felt that teacher-student dynamic go away. There was a power differential that existed throughout every facet of our "relationship." This is a major problem with teacher-student abuse. The foundation is not set on equal ground, so the student always takes a deferential stance.

Softball Games

Bob joined a softball league once I graduated from college. I really enjoyed going to his games. I met the wives and girlfriends of the players, and they just accepted us as a couple. I had my spiel that I gave anytime someone would ask about us: that he was my teacher years ago, and he became a friend of the family, and then throughout college, we got closer and now we were together. No one seemed to question it.

I enjoyed being able to call us a couple. It all seemed easy at these softball games. It was what I had desired for years. He was busy playing, and I could just socialize. He couldn't get aggravated with me that way. As great as that was, it wasn't all perfect. I had to make sure that I would watch Bob every time he was at bat or a play was coming his way. He would get upset with me if I missed seeing a play. It was as though he needed constant reassurance that he had my undivided attention, which resulted in high levels of anxiety for me.

At one point, Bob and I joined a co-ed league for one season, and I had a lot of fun playing on the same team as him. One play in particular comes to mind when I was playing catcher and Bob was in the outfield. The batter hit the ball way out to him, and he caught it. Another runner was trying to slide on home. He threw the ball to me, I actually caught it, and I tagged the player out! Ah, that was a great moment! Bob high fived me, and I felt so proud. Despite the good feelings, I clearly remember praying I would catch that ball so Bob wouldn't get pissed off that I'd missed it.

Those were the kinds of experiences that kept me with him for so long. **Like in gambling, intermittent gratification seems to make it all worth it. The gambler may not hit a winning number for ages, but when he does, he forgets about all the previous losses for a while.**

This is how it felt with Bob. When we had a good moment or laugh, I would forget about all the stress and concern over our relationship. Then, I would bend over backward trying to keep these great moments coming. This unhealthy cycle was identical to the cycle I had with my father. I was simply repeating what I knew.

Grad School

I graduated from college with a bachelor's degree in communications with a specialization in communication disorders and a minor in psychology. Although I really loved learning about communication disorders—audiology and speech pathology, for instance—I just didn't feel in my gut that following that path was my calling. I knew I wanted to go to graduate school, mainly because I loved being a student. I just didn't know what to specialize in. So, I worked for a year as a teacher's aide in an elementary school special-education classroom. I enjoyed it and learned a lot, which led to lots of discoveries about myself and which path I should take. I realized the most rewarding part of the job for me was listening to what the kids had to say and helping them with their lives (more so than with their math problems).

Life issues were something I had mastered. I was accustomed to having problems, thinking about problems, analyzing problems, and relating to problems, so I decided to go into a program and field where I could focus on solving problems. I considered becoming a psychologist, and I researched the field and found that the most versatile degree seemed to be a masters in clinical social work. With that in mind, I investigated the graduate schools in the area and narrowed down my search to three. I applied to all three, got accepted to all three, and chose to attend Boston University.

I lived at home while attending BU. The first year we had three days of classwork and two days of an internship. I really enjoyed those classes, and my internship was at an amazing place called the Baird Center—a residential and day school program for kids with emotional difficulties. I got a few kids as individual clients with supervision to help me process the experience to make sure I was on the right track.

Looking back, it is difficult to comprehend that I was supposed to be helping kids sort through their lives, when mine was such a mess. I couldn't think or see clearly. I had terrible boundaries. I could not be firm or strict. I had zero faith in my abilities as well as zero faith in myself, yet I was supposed to be a role model and a therapist for these kids.

Gary was a counselor who worked at the Baird Center full time. He was a tall, handsome guy who was great at his job. I was drawn to him for a number of reasons. Back then, I had a very weird way of sectioning off the reality that was my life. When I stepped onto the Baird campus, it was like Bob didn't exist. I felt like I could be myself more than usual.

I also developed a justification in my head that I should be able to date other people. I had felt so conflicted about Bob for years, and I knew that he was bad for me and that I should just leave him. However, the self-defeating thoughts and blurred boundaries he had fostered in me during my formative years made me feel trapped in our "relationship." But here on campus, I could leave those thoughts behind and bravely open myself up to trying to have some kind of normal dating experience (when I could sneak it in)—although I really had no way of knowing what "normal" looked like.

Gary and I began talking a lot and flirting a little. One day while we were in one of the offices, I coyly asked if he wanted to get a drink sometime. It surprised me that I'd had the courage to ask him. Something inside me just busted out in that moment! He brightened and said sure. So we went out for drinks and soon thereafter we started "dating."

I have a hard time remembering much about my experiences with Gary because it was overshadowed by my experiences with Bob. I do remember that I told him about Bob and my dilemma over not knowing how to break free. Along with many others, Gary could not understand why I couldn't just tell Bob it was over, and I couldn't explain why I was so stuck. No one seemed to get the dynamics, perhaps because I downplayed the fact that I never had a voice of my own to start with—that Bob had grabbed a hold of me when I was a kid and never let go.

When Bob sunk his hooks into me, I wasn't yet an adult with a mind of my own. He didn't give me a chance to grow into adulthood, so my life at this point was just one big continuation of adolescence.

Shortly after we began hanging out, Gary ended the relationship with me because he wasn't interested in sticking around with Bob in the picture. I was sort of relieved, though, because I was not ready to leave Bob. I had been hoping that Gary, or any guy, would magically understand my dilemma and just deal with the fact that I had this man in my life, and then still be willing to see me when I was available. This was a clear case of not understanding appropriate boundaries, and when I look back now, I think, *Crazy!*

FOR YOU, THE READER
CONSIDER THIS . . .

There was not a single segment of my life that was unaffected by my situation with Bob. Eventually, the difficulties and pain outweighed the initial reasons I felt drawn to him. I never understood the reasons the dynamics of our relationship had changed so dramatically. As time progressed, so did his need to control me. My mixed-up feelings grew, and I started to gain some clarity. Bob was not quite the savior I first thought him to be.

For all readers . . .

- Why did leading a secret life feel familiar to me?

- What parts of my childhood set the foundation for me to be able to compartmentalize this secret?

As a student . . .

- Can a relationship be healthy if it has to be kept secret?

- What would you do if a friend swore you to secrecy about her involvement with a teacher?

- Who could you talk to if you know a student and teacher are having a relationship?

- If you are in an abusive relationship, did this chapter of my book shed new light on your situation?

- Who does a secret generally protect?

- Would you recognize if you were being groomed by a teacher?

As a parent . . .

- Do you keep secrets in your home?

- How can you open the lines of communication with your child?

- Are you always aware of your child's whereabouts?

- If you suspected your child was lying about something, what steps would you take to learn the truth?

As an educator . . .

- Have you ever seen a coworker with a current or former student outside of school?

- Do any of your coworkers claim to be friends with a student?

- How would you express your concerns to your coworker or supervisor if you suspected educator sexual abuse?

As an administrator . . .

- What protocols are in place to address concerns about inappropriate teacher-student interactions?

As a survivor . . .

- Did your abuser keep you silent? How?

- Have you told anyone your story?

- If you could go back and change one thing about the silence or the secret, what would you change?

- Are you still protecting this secret? Is it really your secret, or does it belong to your abuser?

- Is your abuser still working with students?

- Is your silence placing other students at risk?

Secret. That word is so charged. Always think about who a secret protects. If you are being asked to keep a secret, especially from family and/or friends, there is the potential for someone to get hurt.

My senior class picture, wearing the necklace that Mr. Baker gave to me.

CHAPTER 6

Control

—◄○►—

The more intense and involved my "relationship" with Bob became, the more control he exerted over me. The comfort I had received from him in ninth and tenth grade diminished by my junior year when he began sexually abusing me and continued to decrease steadily thereafter. Although I was young, impressionable, and clueless about the matters and dynamics of healthy relationships, some of Bob's controlling maneuvers were still obvious to me. Other controlling behaviors would only become obvious to me later in life as I reflected on my experiences. This chapter provides some examples of the various types of control Bob displayed with me over the years so that you can become more familiar with these troubling behaviors.

I think Bob needed to keep me close to him mentally, emotionally, and physically so that as I grew up, I wouldn't leave him. Also, I think he needed me to depend on him for making decisions so that I would not think for myself. He was deeply afraid of the repercussions for his indiscretions with me when I was underage, and if I were to become a more independent thinker, he would risk my telling the wrong person the truth about us.

I also got a sense that Bob was a very insecure man. Controlling a child gave him a sense of power he did not have in other areas of his life. I was confused and upset by the control he held over me. What was even more difficult for me to process was how familiar the control felt and how unprepared I was to handle or fight it.

Controlling me wasn't difficult. I was primed to be controlled—I had years of experience under my father's control. On top of that, I think Bob thrived on controlling me. He appeared to love watching my face and seeing me squirm when I did not know how to react to things he would say or do.

Anger and Fear

Bob revealed his anger to me more and more as time progressed. Much like my father, Bob had a temper that would erupt at unpredictable times and for bizarre reasons. How do I explain my fear of his anger? It felt like a childlike fear, as if I were going to be in BIG trouble when my dad got home. I made every effort I could to prevent Bob's anger from occurring, just as I had with my father.

Nothing about this fear was rational. I had been under my father's controlling influence and transitioned right into Bob's. This fear of sparking their anger caused me to act or *not* act in ways that contributed to feeling I had no voice and that I was invisible. My father's anger had produced in me a deep fear of conflict. If I sensed that someone was about to become angry, I would panic and find any way to prevent it. I can now see that Bob used his anger, and my fear of it, as a means of controlling me—just like my father did with our family.

Isolation

Bob often put down my family and friends. He would tell me that he didn't like them because they really didn't care about me the way he cared about me. It was all part of trying to isolate me so that I would depend on him more, giving him control over my actions. He also didn't want others to have any influence over my way of thinking about him or how I dealt with him.

This is all part of the cycle of abuse. **An abuser isolates his victim so that the victim avoids anyone who might pull her away from the abuser.**

I would usually feel guilty if I chose to spend time with family or friends rather than with Bob. He would often suggest that I cared more for them than I did for him if chose to spend time away from him when the time he could give me was so precious and fleeting. He would tell me that he had to work very hard to make time for me, considering he was married.

I never wanted him to feel that I cared more for others than I did for him, and I definitely didn't want him to be angry or upset with me. So, I often made excuses to friends and family about why I could not be with them at some event or other. Sometimes isolating myself from other people would make me feel lonely, but I was confused. I misinterpreted Bob's control and manipulation as love and concern. I didn't have a father who wanted to spend more time with me, and he never showed me what fatherly love and concern was even supposed to feel like. And here I was getting the attention I had desired for so many years from a father figure, and I thought perhaps the isolation from others was a normal trade-off.

Concert

One evening, I was performing in a choral concert at another high school, and Bob was able to attend. The dress code was formal, so I borrowed a prom dress from my friend Karen. I was so excited for him to see me perform. However, I had a horrible case of strep throat, and I had to take my ACT exam the next morning. So I had a lot going on— to say the least. I probably should have stayed home in bed, but I never would have missed a concert.

After the concert, the plan was for Bob to drive me home. All I wanted to do was lay my head down and sleep for a week. He knew how sick I was and that I had the ACT in the morning. We drove away from the school, and then he pulled over somewhere. I have no recollection of where specifically he parked. It was pitch black out, and there were no lights. I asked him what was wrong. He didn't say anything. He immediately shoved his hand down the front of my dress, grabbing my breasts. I was caught off guard, and, frankly, I was frightened. He seemed out of control. He started kissing me hard and was pawing and groping me under my dress.

I wanted to cry and scream, but I had no voice. I was too afraid to tell him to stop. I must have had a fever because I got really dizzy and lightheaded. I just remember praying he would finish whatever he needed to do quickly so I could get home and into bed.

I can't remember anything after that or whether he dropped me off at my house or down the street. I do remember walking into my bedroom and wanting to cry, but my tears literally felt stuck. Something sort of felt dead inside me.

As I write these words, I can't believe what a sick person he was. In a million years, I would not tolerate anything remotely like that now, but back then, all I could think about was that there was something wrong with me. I loved him, so why wasn't I able to enjoy being with him like that? I felt bad that I had "rejected" him because I was sure he could tell I wasn't into it. As was my pattern, I took on responsibility for his actions and behaviors. It took me years to recover from that dynamic—and I'm still working on some of it today.

Inability to Say No

Following the experience after my choral concert I felt I could not reject Bob sexually. It was the unspoken rule that I needed to comply. He used controlling and manipulative behaviors to regulate and control my actions and reactions. He would use the silent treatment or he would yell. He would give me a look that could stop me in my tracks. He also praised me for things that were just twisted. He would thank me for being sexual when he knew I didn't want to be. I would feel so sorry for him when he would explain to me how he and his wife were no longer intimate and she didn't provide release for him.

There would be times when he would kiss me or grab my breasts, and I would try not to gag or cry and just pray that he didn't see my reactions. Saying "No" was not an option. I had learned that from a very early age, so this was just a continuation of the lesson. He was exerting control over me sexually as well as in other areas of my life. To say this confused me is an understatement. He could be still be fun and silly with me, and we would still talk about music and do fun activities, and, just like with my father, I would hang on to those times and try not to let go. The intermittent control and anger that arose felt all too familiar. I responded the only way I was raised to respond. I would try to please him and avoid any and all conflict within my power. I said yes to whatever he wanted.

Senior Prom

By my senior year, my secret life weighed heavily on my shoulders. I had convinced myself I was deeply in love with Bob, but it was getting increasingly more difficult to carry on with these compartments in my head and in my life. This is probably why I broke my silence to my friend, Christine, at the New Year's Eve party, as I mentioned earlier. It was a step in the right direction, but a very small one indeed.

I felt frustrated by the feeling that I was missing out on normal high school activities, such as attending parties and dating. Honestly, I did not have a romantic interest in anyone in high school. I was more interested in staying sane through this crazy experience. However, I simply wanted to know what the experience felt like to date the way normal people did. I didn't actually believe any boys would want to date me, but I was curious about how other people my age lived.

I made a firm decision to go to my senior prom. I knew that this was a rite of passage I would someday regret missing. There was a boy from my class named Paul who was participating in the senior class play with me. He was a nice, quiet guy. Apparently, Paul had a little crush on me (which he disclosed during my research for this book), but at the time, I could not imagine *anyone* liking me that way.

During a rehearsal break, Paul asked if he could talk to me in the hallway. I went outside with him, feeling very jittery. He sweetly stumbled his way through asking me to the prom. I remember this moment but not much else because I started to dissociate. I felt dizzy and my thoughts sort of just floated away. I couldn't feel myself inside my body at all. I should have been excited by this invitation, but all I felt was danger. I felt like Bob would kill me for my betrayal if he found out. I felt so torn. After all the kindness Bob showed me, a boy was talking to me and moving in on his territory. That's how Bob would have seen it anyway.

Yet, that tiny part inside me . . . that teeny, healthy, wise, old soul who knew what I needed . . . that part of me was screaming inside of my head, yelling, "SAY YES, STUPID!" It turns out that that voice was stronger and more influential at that moment than the disassociated, guilty part of me. I accepted his invitation to the prom.

Now I had to figure out a way to tell Bob, which made me a complete wreck. *Why did I listen to that voice?!* So many times I faced that same struggle—follow my old-soul instinct or do the safe thing and keep Bob happy. I had no plan in place to tell him about this. I thought maybe I could get away with not telling him. Maybe prom night would arrive, and I would just tell him I was sick or had to do something with my family. He would never find out that I even went.

But wait—what if he talked with some of the other kids, and they told him that I was there? No, that wouldn't work. I felt stuck.

One afternoon, Bob gave me and another girl, Laurie, a ride home from our play rehearsal. We were talking about many different topics. Then, suddenly, Laurie started talking about the prom. I felt lightning shoot through my body—the type of danger signal I would always feel when I thought Bob would get mad at me. This physical reaction was identical to my experience with my father's rage.

I tried to change the subject, but Laurie didn't take the hint. Why would she? I had assured her and everyone else that Bob was a cool friend I shared everything with. Then she said, "So you're going with Paul, right, Andrea?"

I felt sweat bead up on my forehead, my heartbeat quickened, and my breathing became labored. "No!" I said, acting as if I couldn't believe she would ever dream up such a wild idea.

"But everyone is saying that you guys are going to prom together," she insisted.

"I don't know where they came up with that one," I said convincingly. "But no, I'm not going with him."

Time stopped. I glanced over at Bob, his knuckles white from gripping the steering wheel so tightly. He kept his eyes straight ahead. He inhaled loudly through his nose, as if to hold himself back from exploding.

I recall exactly where we were when this all went down—a hill right near my house, the same hill my mom and I would drive down when I was a child and I would pray I wouldn't see my father's car in the driveway. I was thankful to be so close to home, which felt safe in that moment.

As Mr. Baker pulled up to my house, I said good-bye to Laurie. I looked at him to say good-bye, but he wouldn't look at me. I gave him a slight hug, which was met with a cold shoulder. I went into my house, and the relief I felt to be home quickly turned to panic—a panic attack, actually.

I felt like my bedroom walls were caving in, and I could not catch my breath. A sense of impending doom I had never experienced before filled me. I found myself furious with Laurie and with myself. *Why did she have to bring that up? Of all the things we could have talked about, why did she have to pick prom? And why did I ever accept Paul's invitation? I knew better than that. Look how much I just hurt Bob. How could I be so selfish? He had helped me through so many things. He listened to me; he bought me so many gifts. He befriended me when no one else would. He rescued me from the pain and loneliness of my childhood. And this was the thanks I gave him?*

I desperately wanted to see him right then and there and run into his arms and apologize for hurting and betraying him. I wanted to make things right so badly. I hated the not-knowing part. Not knowing when I would have the chance to talk to him again made me feel crazy and out of control. This was just one example of the crazy dance that continued for years.

When I finally did see him again, I was really afraid. It triggered the same kind of fear I had around my father. My father didn't have to do very much for me to think he could kill me—literally kill me. It was the same with Bob. I always ended up feeling that there was something I could have done to prevent him from getting so angry.

When I got the chance to speak with him, I explained to him that I never said I was going to the prom with Paul. I said that there were weird rumors about everyone going with different people. Believe it or not, I did tell him that I was thinking about going to the prom, though. I wove it into the conversation. I told him that it had nothing to do with loving him any less or liking a boy or anything like that. I simply wanted to experience the prom like everyone else. I was afraid I would regret not going when I was older. Somehow, he understood that enough to not fight me on it, and, truthfully, I was shocked by that. That inner wisdom told me I had to fight for certain things, and I had actually been prepared for a fight.

The prom was quickly approaching, but I had not canceled with Paul. My mother was so pleased I had a date for the prom, and I talked with the girls in school about the prom as if it were the most normal thing to do. I felt like a phony. If they only knew I was cheating on my boyfriend. As bizarre as it was, that's exactly how I felt: like I was cheating on Mr. Baker. I felt so guilty to be lying to him. I also felt bad that Paul had no clue what was going on with me. I wasn't even sure if I was using him or not. I had no intention of dating him after the prom.

When the prom was just a few weeks away, I decided I *had* to tell Bob that I was going with Paul. So I drummed up a scheme. We were talking one day, and I announced that the prom was coming in a few weeks. I told him that I learned that they would not sell single tickets—you had to buy them in pairs. I decided (gulp) to ask for his advice. I appealed to his know-it-all side. I said, "I don't know what to do! I really need to go to this thing to get it out of my system and be able to say to my kids one day—I went to my prom. That's really important to me. But I can't go alone. What do you think I should do? Should I see if someone asks me, or should I just ask that Paul kid, the one Laurie mentioned? He's so shy that he would never ask anyone. What do you think would be best?"

Now, I have no clue why he did not freak out about this. Perhaps when I mentioned telling my future kids about prom, he realized how important it was to let me do this without a fight—likely to protect himself. But I will never know. Somehow, I was sly enough to get him to advise me to ask Paul to the prom. I checked and double-checked with him on this, and he acted okay with it.

Interestingly enough, I remember little about prom night, so while researching this book, I contacted two people. The first was my former high school PE teacher, Mrs. K. She and I used to talk in the mornings before the start of the school day when I was in high school. She reminded me that I would sometimes share details and concerns about my "friendship" with Mr. Baker. Mrs. K reminded me that I'd told her Mr. Baker had strongly discouraged me from having pictures taken with Paul prior to prom. I have no recollection of this request or demand. Mrs. K told me that although she thought it was odd for Bob to have an issue with that, she had just shrugged it off. **She believed Bob was a great teacher and knew he had been a key player in helping me battle some tough, lonely times.** Later, Mrs. K had been devastated to learn the true nature of Mr. Baker's interactions with me, and she shared her deep regret for not acting on her initial instinct.

The second person I contacted was Paul. He filled me in on more than a few blank spots from that evening. We did have pictures taken, both at my grandmother's house and at his house. He said we danced a bit at the prom and mentioned I seemed nervous, so he just assumed I didn't have feelings for him.

I do remember this: When Paul dropped me off at my house that evening, I feared Bob would be waiting down the street. I knew Paul probably expected a kiss good-bye. I was terrified that Bob would see, and I didn't want to devastate him like that. In my mind, Bob was nice enough to allow me to go to my prom, and I couldn't betray him any more than that. So Paul and I never kissed.

During our conversation, Paul admitted he had a crush on me and had always believed I agreed to go with him to the prom because I felt sorry for him. He seemed relieved to discover the real reason I seemed disinterested in him, although he was devastated to learn that I had been enduring such abuse while he knew me. I reassured him that I was very good at hiding most signs of the situation, so there was no way he could have known.

In the end, I *am* glad I went to my prom. I feel sad that I cannot recall basic memories such as having pictures taken or what the party room looked like. I don't think my life would have been crushed had I missed the prom, but I am pleased that I pushed myself to accept the request of a sweet boy. I wonder how my life would have been different if I had been able to open myself up to Paul's kindness and interest back then. I just don't think I would have known how.

Route 27

One evening, just before dark, while driving home from Fun and Games on Route 27 (a roadway that still brings up an intense, visceral reaction for me), Bob pulled over and parked the car, right on the side of the road. I had no clue what he was doing, but I remember being too afraid to ask. He opened my car door, took me by the hand, and led me up over a hill. There were trees and dirt and leaves. He laid me down on the ground and sexually assaulted me. I was terrified. I had no idea where we were, if there was some crazy maniac in the woods, or if someone would see the car pulled over and wonder what was wrong and come up the hill to look for us . . . so many thoughts went through my head.

As afraid as I was of all those other things, I was most afraid of Bob seeing me cry. I just knew he would be angry with me if I got upset. I remember him being inside me, and my head kept hitting a rock as he penetrated me more deeply each time. I started to panic, worrying that I would need stitches. *How would I explain that to my mother?* So I floated away in my mind and pretended to be somewhere else. I also pretended to like it, too, because Bob needed that reinforcement. If I didn't seem like I was into it, he would get very disappointed in me. I didn't want him to be upset with me. It was a convoluted mess.

When he finished, he helped me up and we walked down to the car. I tried my best to wear a natural smile. We didn't talk very much the rest of the way home. I looked out the window and told myself that something must be wrong with me. I knew plenty of girls my age who enjoyed sex. *Why was sex such a scary thing for me? Why did I always end up crying?*

Then I chastised myself for crying so easily. I started drumming up funny things to think about during sex so I wouldn't get upset anymore. This thought process helped me endure the rest of that ride home. I was able to calm down and breathe more freely. I felt proud of myself for thinking of a way to conquer whatever was wrong with me.

As I write these words, I feel such a need to put my arm around that girl and tell her that none of this was right, none of this was her fault; she was a victim. A note on healing: The more I heal from these wounds, the more compassion and acceptance I have for myself. No one should have to endure what happened up over that hill. But I survived. No matter what mind games I had to create to survive, I survived. Nothing can take that away from me.

War and Rape

Bob and I went to the movies a lot. He enjoyed seeing war movies, such as *Missing in Action,* but I despised them. He had a "thing" about making me watch these movies, especially knowing how much I would squirm while watching them. He would mock me if I looked away from a violent or troubling scene, and I would feel bad that I couldn't "take it." One film had a particularly disturbing scene that I couldn't shake in which a soldier was raping a little girl.

I couldn't watch it. I refused to watch it. I got up and went to the restroom, panicking inside. I sat on a toilet and wept. I had no real understanding why I had such a visceral reaction, but a panic attack ensued. Part of my panic included worrying what Bob would say to me when I returned. I don't know how long I stayed in the restroom. When I finally returned to my seat, I looked straight ahead at the screen, and not at Bob.

He leaned toward me and whispered, "You bailed, didn't you?"

And I denied it. I told him I had to use the restroom because my stomach was upset.

He just said, "Yeah, right" with total disgust in his tone.

I felt like I had failed him. He needed me to be strong and handle anything I saw. I could never figure out why he wanted me to watch stuff like that, but I was determined to do a better job of it next time.

He barely spoke to me on the way home that night.

On My Shoulders

Every now and then, Bob would tell me it was my responsibility to protect his job. He would reiterate that no one would understand how special our relationship was and that he would be fired—and did I really want that responsibility on my shoulders? This logic began in high school and continued well into college and beyond.

About six years after we met, I told him we were having an anniversary. He looked at me with disbelief, and I thought he was surprised the time had gone by so fast. He swiftly corrected me: "Andrea, you cannot mark our anniversary that way! No one can ever know when this started—I thought I made that clear to you. Do I need to explain it another way?"

I just hung my head a bit and said, "No."

He said, "I told you . . . no one will understand this except you and me. You have to get this out of your head, or my job is at stake. Do you want to see me lose my job?"

I reassured him that I would never tell anyone how young I was when our relationship started. I just let him know it was special to me that he had been a part of my life for so long—ever since I was a teenager. This didn't help the situation very much.

"Andrea . . . it started when you were in college. We were always friends, but once you went off to college and came back, we just got closer. That's all. Got it?"

I agreed, and I never spoke of it again. I never questioned the responsibility of upholding his secret. It was clearly my secret, according to him. I don't think I need to spell out how good it feels to write this book and expose *his* secret.

Book of Questions

One time, while driving to Fun and Games, I took out the *Book of Questions*. It was filled with hypothetical questions, and we would take turns answering them. I got to the following question: "If you could be one person for a day, who would you choose and why?"

I gave an answer that I would be some actress (I think it was Kristy McNichol or some other popular actress back in the eighties).

Bob got really quiet. His silent treatments always scared me. Finally, after about ten long minutes, I asked him what was wrong. He looked at me with such anger that all I wanted to do was to make it go away.

He finally said, "I cannot believe you. I can't believe you would choose to have someone else's life. You wouldn't even know me. I guess that's how much you love me, huh?"

I had no idea how to respond to that, except with my usual knee-jerk response: "No, No! I didn't mean that! Of course I want to be me. I love having you in my life. It was just a dumb question, I didn't mean it!"

I always became desperate to make things right as soon as possible. It was like there was such a danger when he was not happy with something. **Looking back, I can't say what that danger was at all, other than a conditioned response. But at the time, it was my whole world; it was an unspoken given that he would destroy me if he wanted to. It was the exact same feeling I had had about my father.**

I had an inherent knowledge that this man could actually kill me if he got too angry. Yet, I felt that his love for me would win out over his anger or control.

Head Flicking

Bob would do various things to me and around me that would remind me he was in control of me. One particularly annoying behavior was that he would flick me in the head—hard. Lord, did that drive me crazy. And most of the time I would let out this nervous giggle and "pretend" to yell at him. He would just laugh at me. He would try to flick me when I wasn't looking. I wanted to kick him in the groin every time he did it, but I would have this stupid giggle reaction, so, of course, I could not be taken seriously.

After a few years, the giggles stopped. I would look at him and ask him to stop doing it. He would continue to laugh, and once I even replied, "I'm not laughing. Please stop."

This didn't seem to faze him, and he would continue to do it.

This was actually the dawn of seeing him in a different light. He was like a little boy pulling my ponytail. Only now I saw it as worse than that. He was inflicting pain on me, despite my requests for him to stop. One time I actually yelled at him. It was the only time I had ever yelled at him.

He just laughed harder and said, "Andrea, I'm only doing this so you can see that it's no big deal."

I said, "If it's no big deal, then stop flicking me!"

He argued his case and never stopped doing it.

I find it difficult to describe how frustrating this was for me. I felt helpless. I also wondered what else he could do to me. I remember wondering one night, after we had argued about this, how he could really care about me if he was purposely doing something he knew hurt me or drove me crazy. Sometimes physical abuse is easier to read than emotional abuse. I believe this was physical abuse. No, it didn't leave any marks, bruises, or scars, but he was hurting me for his own pleasure. That is abusive, in my book.

He actually slapped me in the face once. We were discussing something simple—there was no major argument. I joked about something he disagreed with, and he lightly slapped me across the face. It was as if he were testing the waters.

The head flicking had been going on for quite some time. Then we had a face slap. Lovely. I looked at him with fire in my eyes, stood up, and said very slowly and quietly, "Don't you ever do that to me again. Do you understand me?"

And he apologized. I could hardly believe it.

I have often wondered why it was so easy for me to literally stand up to him when he slapped me. I think it had something to do with the fact that I had never been slapped before. I had never seen anyone get slapped. It was not in my "vocabulary," so to speak. This reinforces my suspicion of having been sexually abused by my father. When this adult role model became sexual with me, it didn't feel foreign to me.

Something about the boundary lines being crossed in that area and not being able to say no to sexual gestures seemed familiar. However, this slap was clearly wrong in my mind, so it was easy for me to know that he had no right to do that to me.

"I can bury you."

Bob was adept at using words to control me, as well. There was much power in what he would or would not say to me. His silent treatment could bring me to a halt in seconds. He would make subtle comments that didn't faze me at the time. Now, looking back, I realize how damaging and controlling they actually were. He would insult me and call me an idiot. He once described a woman his friend Mike was dating as classy and elegant. He said to me, "I told Mike that you could never really be classy or elegant, but you sure look good around the house." And I believed this hurtful statement. I believed everything Bob told me for many, many years.

Other times he would say things such as, "You know, I could bury you."

I never knew if he meant he could literally bury me, if he could destroy me mentally, or if he could just bring me to tears. The specific meaning didn't matter to me. I believed him. He said this from time to time as a casual reminder of his control over me. His threats took a toll on me after a while. There was a long time when I thought, *What's the point in trying to fight him? He will always win. He could bury me if he wanted to. The sooner I accept my life with him as my fate, the happier I will be.*

Mountain Dew

Bob kept plastic two-liter bottles of Mountain Dew on the floor next to his refrigerator in the kitchen. I never thought anything of it. One day I was trying to be silly, and I opened the nearest bottle, put it to my lips, and took a swig right out of the bottle—something I never normally did. As the liquid touched my mouth and throat, I experienced a horrific gag reflex and began to cough. My throat burned as if I swallowed a torch. I looked at Bob through tears and coughs, and he just looked at me like I was a complete idiot.

"What the hell are you doing?! I put antifreeze in there!" he shouted.

He had put antifreeze in a clear Mountain Dew bottle and left it right next to the other bottles—that all looked the same. Why would someone do this?

I couldn't even respond because I was coughing, and I ran to the bathroom. Bob just sat on the couch and didn't come to see if I was okay. I stayed in the bathroom for a long time, drinking water from the sink faucet. I remember dropping to the floor and crying, trying hard to not let him hear me. I felt like an idiot drinking out of the bottle that way. *Why did I do that? I have never done that before.*

What were the chances that the one time I took a swig from a bottle, he had filled it with antifreeze? I did not stop to question his motives. I felt too sick to analyze anything. I was just angry with myself that I had done such a stupid thing.

As I write these words now, I question Bob's reasoning for doing this. It is difficult for me to believe that he had no thoughts of malice in this dangerous move. Do I believe he tried to cause serious physical harm? I don't really think so, but I do believe this was some sick maneuver on his part to remind me that he could "bury me."

"You will never pass."

Bob was not too keen on the idea of my attending college. It was difficult for me to understand why a teacher could be anything less than supportive of my furthering my education. I realize now that he was afraid of losing control over me. He played up the level of difficulty in college courses. I graduated high school with A's and B's (not a single C). Yet he would tell me that college math would be too tough for me, and he didn't want to see me go through that frustration.

He would say, "Why don't you stay home? Soon I will be leaving my wife, and I can support you."

Something deep inside me knew that I wanted so much more for myself than that.

I believe there has always been a healthy part of me, no matter how deeply it was buried, that knew what I needed to do. And somehow, by the grace of God, I found the strength to exert myself just enough to get what I needed. So I told Bob I would get whatever tutoring was necessary to pass those classes.

I only applied to two colleges—Bridgewater State College and Providence College. These were the closest schools to Norwood and Walpole. They were close enough where I could live in a dorm and still come home on the weekends. It was very important to me that I lived in a dorm. Bob wanted me to stay home and commute. He emphasized all the bad influence others would have on me. He also tried to guilt me into staying home, saying that he wouldn't get to see me or call me as much if I were away. I stressed to him that it would be easier for me to focus on classes if I lived there.

I reassured Bob that I would come home every weekend to see him if he was available. I agreed to keep my job at Brigham's in Norwood and work there on the weekends all throughout college. It was a compromise I felt was fair. I could have applied to so many other schools in any state really. Part of me really wanted to travel to California or something —get a fresh start, meet new people, and so on. But I knew Bob would not approve of that. I felt completely controlled by even just the expression on his face. Somehow I pushed through that control enough to move into the dorm at Bridgewater State.

Incidentally, I graduated 24 out of over 1,200 in my class at Bridgewater State. I thought it was a fluke, because I believed what he told me—that I was full of lack. I lacked intelligence and the resources to succeed without him.

Disney College Program

During my senior year of college, I was living in a great apartment on campus with five other women. This apartment living was the best. We felt sort of grown-up, I think. I loved my roommates. They were all strong, intelligent, funny women. I had filled most of them in on the Bob situation, but I hadn't really filled them in on the whole truth. They could see how unhappy I was, and they really struggled to understand why I didn't just blow him off and tell him to go to hell (their words, not mine). They tried different conversations and interventions with me to help me break free, but to no avail.

I was walking to one of my classes when a flyer posted to a bulletin board caught my eye. A recruiter from Walt Disney World was coming to the campus that week to recruit students for their college program. I walked away thinking, *Wow, that would be such a great opportunity for someone to just get away and have a ball.* I didn't give it much of a second thought because obviously I would never be able to get away like that. Bob didn't like me spending a weekend at school to get work done. I could not imagine him saying, "Sure! I think it would be really good for you to live 1,200 miles away with a bunch of college kids! Have a great time! Don't worry about me—I'll be right here when you get back!"

Nope, that great opportunity was meant for someone else—not for me.

I returned to the apartment, and one of my roommates was talking about the Disney recruiter. She was excited, saying she was going to make an appointment to meet with her. I instantly felt a pang in my heart that surprised me. I was very sad I couldn't live my life that way—just decide to do something and do it without checking in with anybody.

My thoughts must have been transparent because she said, "Andrea, you should do this!"

I laughed at her and said, "Yeah, right. Can you imagine Bob's reaction?"

She let out a few expletives with his name in the middle of them, and said, "Just go meet with the recruiter to get some information. You don't have to decide right now. Just go find out!"

I tried to explain to her that I didn't want more information because it would be that much more difficult turning it down. She walked away saying, "Just go meet her, will ya?"

I couldn't sleep that night. I tossed and turned. *Damn her for planting this terrible seed in my brain! She clearly does not understand Bob or his anger. He needs me. He needs me to be around. I am not one of those people who can do things like this.*

I wasn't sure why I was struggling so much with the idea of heading to Florida. Something kept tugging at me, like a child tugging on my sweater, wanting me to go in the direction of the toy section of a store, when I knew I had to go to the housewares section. It was much like being asked to go to prom. I knew Bob would be furious, but it was that same familiar tug that knew I should follow a different path.

I woke up the next morning exhausted but clear. I was going to meet with the recruiter to find out what was involved. There was no harm in that. I also knew that under no circumstance would I tell Bob about this meeting. My roommates were shocked and thrilled. I reminded them that I was just going to gather information, but they knew that I would not be able to resist.

I met with the recruiter the next day. She was a lovely woman who clearly loved her job. We chatted about lots of things, including my love for theater and music and acting. We shared stories about our favorite plays and musicals, and she explained how the internship worked. It would consist of approximately three months of a combination of working at one of the Disney theme parks in Lake Buena Vista, Florida, as well as weekly business classes. College credit would be granted upon the completion of the program. Interns would be paid as well, and the housing fee would be deducted from the paychecks.

She described the various jobs and the housing arrangements. She told me she would be in touch very soon with a decision of who would be accepted into the program. We shook hands, and I walked back to my dorm.

That walk was torture for me. Who would not want to do an internship at Disney World? I could have three months away from Bob. I would be free from studying, working, and responsibilities. I started to picture Bob's reaction to the news, but then I started rationalizing that three months really wasn't a long time. Surely he could understand this was a chance of a lifetime. I got back to the apartment and talked about the meeting with my roommates.

They were my cheerleading squad. "Go Andrea! You can do it!"

I gradually worked my way to accepting the idea that I may actually get to have a shot at this.

Later that evening, the phone rang, and my roommate, Kim answered the phone. She said, "Andrea come quick, it's the recruiter on the phone for you!"

I was surprised because the recruiter wasn't supposed to get back to any of us for a few weeks. She told me that she really enjoyed meeting me, and she had a different opportunity that she wanted to run by me. I listened as she described the opening of a brand-new theme park—the Disney MGM studios (now called Hollywood Studios). They were having a grand opening in May, and they needed some interns to open the park. There were attractions called the Great Movie Ride and the Back Stage Tours. They needed college kids who had an inclination toward theater, and she thought I would be perfect for it. The catch was, this was an extended internship. This would go on for about eight months! My heart sank. Just when I had made up my mind that three months was a manageable amount of time to justify, she put a monkey wrench in it all.

I thanked her very much and asked if I could have some time to think about it. She said that because this internship started earlier than the others, I would have to let her know within twenty-four hours. Twenty-four hours?! That wasn't enough time to tell Bob and get his permission! I had a feeling that he may just notice I was missing if I were gone for eight months. I agreed to call her one way or the other by the next evening.

I hung up the phone, and three of my roommates—Heather, Nilde, and Kim—were sitting on the floor watching me. I started to get all choked up and anxious. They wanted to know every word that was said, so I explained the scenario. They shouted with delight for my opportunity. They also, I'm sure, were thrilled that I had a chance to get away from Bob for such a long time. I was so conflicted.

They helped me so much that night. They allowed me to voice all my fears and concerns. They met each one head on with logic I could not argue against. They just kept emphasizing that this chance may never come again. This argument is what won out over all my fears. I knew I had to do this. How, I had no clue. I would work the details out later. I called the recruiter back and accepted the internship.

Telling Bob

I delayed telling Bob about the Disney program for as long as I could. Then there came a time when I realized that the more time went by, the angrier he would get at me for waiting so long to tell him. We were out one night at a restaurant having dinner, and I decided to spring it on him then.

I had rehearsed my words very carefully. "So, I wanted to tell you about something that you probably aren't going to like. I want you to just listen first, and try to understand where I am coming from with this, okay?"

He just glared at me. I started sweating a little, and my throat got very dry, but I continued.

"I found an internship for next semester—it's a great opportunity that I will probably never run across again. I want to make sure I get everything out of my college experience before I'm done. It's even a paying internship, which is even better than the typical ones. I really want to give this a try."

He simply asked, "Where is it?"

I smiled nervously and said, "Well . . . it's actually at Disney World. . . . "

The world stopped for a few minutes. He looked down and didn't look up for a while. I didn't speak. I had no idea if he would get up and leave or throw something at me or start yelling.

He finally looked up and asked, "So you mean to tell me that you would actually *choose* to be that far away from me? Even when you know how tough things are for me at home and how much I need you?"

I didn't know how to answer that question. I tried to think of a response that would be acceptable to him. I came up empty-handed. He continued with questions and comments, guilting me to no end for even considering it. I just sat there listening to him.

I felt many emotions in that restaurant. I felt bad that I hurt him. I also felt frustrated that he couldn't understand why this would be good for me. I didn't know if I had the right to feel angry with him. He finally asked me if I was going to say anything at all. I looked at him and tried to plead my case. I emphasized how it would be an opportunity for me to be on my own, but in a controlled environment. He said that was a pathetic excuse.

I listed a few other reasons, and he just shot them down one by one. I gave up trying to convince him this was a good idea. I also realized I wasn't going to receive his permission. We finished our dinner in silence. Something was different this time, however. I knew I was going on that college program. He would hate it and kick and scream, but nothing was about to make me back out. I was frightened, but I was going.

We never discussed the time-line details of the internship. I happily avoided them at all costs. As the days marched closer to my departure, I became more conflicted about leaving. Bob would flip-flop between emotions of anger and self-pity. Then we went skiing for a day up in New Hampshire. He was still acting bitter toward me, but he was able to suspend his bitter tone just a tad that day—until we were riding on a chairlift and he asked the big questions.

"So when do you leave for this *internship*?" (He kept calling it bull-shit because . . . how tough could working at Disney World be?) I told him that I was leaving in the middle of January. He nodded his head quietly, calculating the time that remained.

"When does it end?"

I pretended this question was no big deal, but inside I was dying. *Here goes nothing,* I thought. "*Umm,* I think it ends August twentieth."

He lost it. "What the hell are you talking about?! AUGUST?" Showing the count on his fingers, he shouted, "That's eight months! I thought you said this was a *semester* internship?! How many semesters last eight months?!"

I fumbled to find my words. "Well, this is sort of a special project that they chose me for. . . . " And I continued to explain about how the MGM studios were opening, and they needed interns to spend extra time there.

His expression froze, and he seemed to fade off into the distance. As nervous as I was, I had a hard time containing my excitement when I talked about it. We barely spoke for the rest of the day and the drive home. I cried quietly during most of the ride, wishing he would just have a change of heart and grant me his blessing. He never did.

Continued Calls

One way Bob exerted his control over me was via payphones and scheduled calls. Bob would call me at designated times, either at home or on a pay phone. I would go to great lengths to be prompt. If I missed one of his calls, I would either miss him terribly or not know when we could talk again. Or I would panic because I knew he would be fuming.

Pay phones were popular back then. The pay phones had numbers on them, so you could call a pay phone. He would make this a useful tool because no outgoing/incoming numbers would show up on his phone bill. He would have me meet him at a specific phone booth at specific times. In high school, there was the pay phone in the hall. Then, during college, there was the pay phone at a nearby sub shop. Also there was the pay phone in my dorm freshman year of college. It was no easy feat trying to make sure nobody else was using the phone at the designated time.

I felt so much pressure to be available for his calls, but he could not always call me when he planned to. I gave him all sorts of concessions because I didn't want to interfere with his marriage. But if, God forbid, I was not at the phone when he demanded, he would become furious and jealous. So, I just did about everything in my power to be prompt—then all would feel right with the world. He was happy; I was happy.

I also had to be sure to have enough quarters on hand to call him. A typical call would cost $1.50 or so. Then every few minutes I had to deposit more quarters. On one particular occasion, we were on the pay phone in my dorm, and he was very angry with me for something. I ran out of quarters, and it was also time to go to dinner. I had missed dinner many times due to our calls, and if I asked him to cut it short because of dinner, he would say that I obviously didn't care about him if I could blow him off that easily. So it felt easier just to skip dinner and talk with him for as long as he could stay on the phone.

But this *one* time, I ran out of quarters, and he was fuming about something. I ran off campus to a local store and got some quarters, then found a pay phone and called him back. I could hear him smiling as he talked. He was so pleased he had this much control over me—even an hour away.

During my Disney internship, these arranged times to talk allowed him to keep me in his grasp. I would give him my schedule for the week, and he would choose the times he would call me. Once I told him that a few girls were planning to go to the beach, and I was excited to be joining them. He became quiet, so I asked what was wrong.

"Well," he said, "I was planning to call you this afternoon, but I guess your new friends and the beach are more important than me. I knew this would happen. I told you this would happen. Guess it didn't take very long for it to kick in, did it?"

I reacted to that statement the same way I always reacted—in a panic. Just like I always rushed to make sure things were right again with my father, I quickly reassured him that I had not lost any love for him.

"No!" I hastily replied, "No, it's not like that at all! I don't have to go to the beach at all. I just thought I would go with them, but I would rather talk to you. I don't want you to feel that way. If I am all the way down here, you need to be reminded of my feelings for you. Don't worry—I will be home at two o'clock."

Looking back, I'm sure I heard victory in his voice, and somehow he convinced me that I had won, too. When he was not angry, I was not stressed. Staying home from the beach was a small price to pay to keep the peace with him.

This peace-making dance was all too familiar for me. The steps were instilled in me throughout my childhood. I watched my mother do the same dance moves, year after year. And I practiced the same routine with this man, well into college and beyond. It was the only dance I knew. Incidentally, he never did call me that afternoon.

Andrew

While working at the Great Movie Ride, I met a guy named Andrew. He was by far the most attractive man I had ever met. I had a terrible habit of not making eye contact with people I found attractive, somehow afraid I would offend them if they knew I was attracted to them, and Andrew was no exception. Andrew and I got to know each other well, as we worked together and hung out at parties. Soon I learned, to my surprise, that he had taken a particular liking to me. Surely this gorgeous man could not find *me* attractive. I was not even in the same league as he was! But we started flirting, and, before long, we were an item.

This was the first experience I had with an open relationship, and I was filled with excitement, joy, and true appreciation for the experience. It was the first time I kissed someone I was truly attracted to. He was a loud, fun, outgoing, adventurous young man who wanted me by his side. And he didn't seem like he was just tolerating me—he wanted me! He liked everything about me: my hair, my body, my laugh, and even my dark side.

As safe and accepted as I felt with Andrew, I was not at a place in my life where I was able to have sex with him. I had a genuine fear of sex, and it worried me that I would never be able to enjoy a healthy sexual relationship. Fortunately, Andrew was patient and understanding. His acceptance of my difficulties made me care about him even more.

I opened up to him about my family and the whole situation with Bob, minus when the "relationship" started. Andrew had a hard time comprehending why Bob would be involved with me or why I wouldn't just walk away from him. He would also question my feelings—if I really cared about him, how could I even consider going back to Bob once the internship was finished? I tried to explain to him that it was not that simple. I tried to explain my fears, but I could never seem to convey the answers in a way that made sense. I didn't blame Andrew for being confused; most people would have had a difficult time understanding the level of control Bob had over me and just how paralyzed I had become.

Bob's Visit

My internship was in full swing when Bob came down to visit. I had mixed feelings about seeing him. It wasn't like I missed him. The only thoughts I had about him were relief—relief that I could be myself without being questioned or criticized.

I had been dating Andrew for a few months at this point. I tried to explain to Andrew why I needed to visit with Bob. I forced myself to be okay with the fact that he was not pleased with my decision to have Bob visit. I needed Bob to see me in this new light: independent, self-sufficient, and happy.

Bob informed his wife that he was coming down to see me—at least that's the story he gave me. During this trip, his wife moved out. I couldn't imagine how bad she must have felt about Bob's visit. My guilt felt all encompassing. Also, I had taken some comfort knowing Bob was not always available, which gave me a little freedom. But now, with her gone, I had no excuse for not being able to handle this relationship.

I suspended my concerns as best as I could and prepared for his visit. I arranged for a few days off. We stayed at a little motel, and it actually felt nice to see him. He wasn't nearly as angry or bitter as I had anticipated. It was a strange but refreshing experience to see him in a new environment. I was more in control of our time together than he was, and this felt fantastic. I drove him around to see the places I had visited. He was mostly quiet, taking everything in, but it wasn't a punishing sort of quiet; he was just processing everything.

We went into the Disney theme parks and had a wonderful time, enjoying the rides, the food, and the atmosphere. I also arranged for him to go on the Great Movie Ride, the attraction I had been working on for the past few months. Although it was my day off, I was able to go to wardrobe, get my "costume," and rotate in to be the "tour guide" for his ride. I told my new friends—and Andrew—about taking him on the ride.

I snuck Bob into line and hopped on a vehicle. Andrew hadn't seen us, so I was relieved that I avoided that conflict. I felt proud that Bob was watching me run this ride like a champ. He had a little smile on his face the whole time. There was the possibility that he would make fun of me later, but I didn't care. I was obviously happy and in my element. As the ride pulled up to the platform, I was wrapping up my spiel for the guests.

Suddenly, Andrew appeared from around the corner and greeted everyone in the vehicle. I panicked. I could *not* have Bob know anything about my relationship with Andrew. So I kept talking with the guests, ignoring Andrew completely.

Andrew said in a loud voice, "How about Andrea, ladies and gentlemen, isn't she awesome? Let's hear it for her!"

He started clapping, so the whole crowd clapped as well. I blushed, smiled, and just shook my head. I glanced over at Bob, and he was staring down Andrew. He slowly shifted his gaze to me.

I just shook my head and whispered, "Ugh, he's such a dork."

That seemed to address the issue enough for the moment.

I told Bob I would meet him outside the ride in a few minutes. Andrew asked where Bob was because he didn't think Bob had been on the ride. I explained to Andrew that Bob had been sitting right next to me. Andrew found that hard to believe. He hadn't noticed anyone because no one on the ride looked like they could be with me.

"You know," I explained, "the bald guy with the moustache and glasses?"

Andrew's eyes widened. We were twenty-two years old at the time. He could not imagine an "old guy" like that being with me. Andrew seemed hurt and confused by this, but I knew I had time to deal with him once Bob left.

When I took Bob back to the airport the next day, he said something that blew me away. "You were right, Andrea. You are on your own. I didn't know what to expect, but it's good to see you navigating your way around this town."

With that, I threw my arms around him in the biggest hug I could muster. It felt like I had just won my dad's approval.

In retrospect, I think Bob wanted to leave me with a positive comment so I would want to return to him. It worked. That one kind sentence made it a bit tougher to say good-bye to him. I sent him on his way and promised I would be back in a few months.

As the end of the internship approached, my feelings toward Andrew grew more serious. The carefree feelings I had when the internship began started to take a backseat to an impending feeling of anxiety and darkness. I had to return up north and leave behind Andrew's kindness, returning to Bob's control. I just didn't feel as if I had any say in the matter.

Andrew and I had shared a few sad moments those last couple of weeks in Florida. I tried to reassure him that I would work on leaving Bob at some point, but, in my mind, I knew this was a lie. I wanted to believe my words, but Bob was simply too powerful a force for me to contend with.

I drove away from Andrew with the heaviest of hearts. I had had the eight-month experience of a lifetime, and I believed that I would probably never feel that sense of freedom again.

Leni's House

Following my college graduation, I decided to pursue a master's degree at Boston University. This two-year program was intense, and I found myself constantly juggling my studies, part-time work, and this conflicted situation with Bob. Trying to integrate Bob into this new life increased the tension and frustrations between us.

After grad school, I worked at Bay State Community Services as a clinical therapist. (I'll share more details about this in later chapters.) I met some fantastic people, including Leni, a coworker in whom I confided quite a bit. I even brought Bob to one of her get-togethers. Of course, I was overwhelmed with anxiety because I had told her and some of my other coworkers about my concerns regarding our "relationship." But here I was, bringing Bob to meet them and wanting them to be nice and act like everything was fine. **I had become quite adept at compartmentalizing things in my life, especially things relating to Bob, so I expected everyone else to be able to do the same.**

I was incredibly tense during that get-together. I found myself mentally pleading with everyone, praying they could read my desperate expression. I just needed them to be nice to him so he would never suspect I had complained about him. I was scared. This gathering was another bridge between the secret world and "coming out," so to speak, as a couple. I was mixed up emotionally, and I didn't know what I wanted. In the end, none of my coworkers mentioned any of the troubles I had expressed, and Bob was unaware of any concerns that may have existed.

By this time, I knew without a doubt that Bob was bad for me. I knew he was no longer a positive influence in my life. I also knew I needed to get away from him, but I had no idea how to do it. I truly did not believe I would ever live a life free of his control. At times, I would even doubt my desire to leave. So I tried to make the best of the situation and enjoy the moments I could enjoy, wanting to ensure that, while I was with him, things went as smoothly as possible.

First Apartment

After working at Bay State for a year, I received a pay raise. I had been living at home with my mother, and I needed a place of my own. I spent a great deal of time mentally gearing up to present my case to Bob. I knew he would not be a fan of my increasing independence. It is likely he believed I would go straight from home to him—no in-between. I had an opportunity to rent an apartment from my friend Colleen's father for $500 a month. At this price, I could easily afford my own place.

I drove to Bob's house to give him the news, playing a song from a cassette over and over and over the whole way there. It was "Passionate Kisses" by Mary Chapin Carpenter. That song spoke to me. One line of the song commands the listener to "give me what I deserve, 'cuz it's my right." I kept repeating the speech I had prepared in my head, and sang that song at the top of my lungs all the way to his house.

When I arrived, Bob and I chatted idly for a while as I worked up my courage. Then I presented my case to him, keeping the focus on what would be in it for him: more privacy, less sneaking, easier phone calls, the ability to have him over whenever we (or rather, he) wanted, and so on. My heart raced as I spoke.

He watched me present my case with a weird look on his face, almost as if he were trying to determine if I were being honest or if I were trying to get away with something. In the end, he halfheartedly agreed to the idea, and that was all I needed. I thanked him for giving the "okay." He knew I was asking for permission for what I was going to do, not telling him I was going to do it. He loved it; I could see it all over his face.

FOR YOU, THE READER
CONSIDER THIS . . .

The secret life I led as a child and into my young adulthood brought me into a world of verbal, emotional, and sexual abuse. While I was aware that things weren't right with Bob the older I got, I hadn't yet realized that his abuse of me had already been taking place prior to that first kiss.

Bob was initially subtler in his delivery. I saw him as a kind, valiant knight who had rescued me from my childhood pain. In reality, he was a strategic and abusive perpetrator who gained my trust, built me up, and then began to tear me down and control me in every way he possibly could. I was left confused and desperate to get back that feeling I was special and everything was going to be okay—a feeling I would never experience with Bob again after that initial joy began to disintegrate. I was torn between efforts to make things go back to the way they were and finding a way to be free.

As a student . . .

- What are some similarities between my relationship with my father and the dynamics with Bob?

- How did growing up with fear and abuse impact the way I interacted with Bob as I got older?

- Why do you think I didn't just leave him once I graduated from high school?

- What are different ways a person can be controlled? How does denial play a part in the control?

- Do you know someone who is in a controlling relationship? How could you help her recognize the signs of control and abuse?

As a parent . . .

- How do you teach your child the difference between a healthy relationship and a controlling relationship?

- Does your child see you as a positive role model regarding healthy relationships?
- Is your college-age child still in contact with a former high school teacher? Do you know the details of how their relationship developed?

As an educator . . .

- Would you question a colleague's adult romantic relationship? Do you feel you have a right to?

As an administrator . . .

- Do you think it is within your authority to question if a teacher in your school is dating a former student?

As a survivor . . .

- What acts of control, if any, did your abuser employ?
- How did the control make you feel? How did the control affect your actions or inactions?
- Do any of your current relationships have controlling facets?
- Have you developed a need to control people or your environment as a result of the abuse?
- As a result of/response to the abuse you endured, do you see any qualities of your abuser in yourself now?

Control plays a huge role in abuse. Sometimes it can be difficult to recognize when you are in a controlling situation or relationship. It's generally much easier to spot a controlling situation when one is not the target of the control. Gentle support and encouragement along with honest acknowledgment of the controlling and abusive nature of the relationship can be extremely beneficial for someone in this difficult situation.

CHAPTER 7

Breaking Away

—◄○►—

As Bob's control and abuse increased, I became more anxious, depressed, and confused. My need to break free from him grew stronger. I had no voice with this man, and I did not know how to speak my feelings or think for myself. I felt as if I were still a child asking for permission for everything. It would take breaking my silence and proclaiming the truth to finally guide me toward the path to freedom, and I needed skilled professionals and caring souls to show me the way.

By the time I was twenty-four, I knew with 100 percent certainty that I needed to leave Bob. Anyone in my life who knew about our relationship was painfully aware that nothing good could ever come of his presence in my life, and they were very verbal about it. I felt so weighed down by anxiety when dealing with Bob that I could not think clearly half the time. My judgment was cloudy, and my coping skills—as unhealthy as they were—were dwindling rapidly.

Suicidal Thoughts

Many times during college and graduate school I felt really low, trapped, and helpless. I had resigned myself to living an oppressed life, but I kept waiting for someone to rescue me. My hopeless feelings sometimes led to depressive and even suicidal thoughts. I didn't want to actively kill myself the way I had thought about as a kid when I took the keys to my mom's car. This was more of a passive feeling, like hoping a terrible accident would end things for me. For example, I would hope someone would push me off the train platform while waiting for a train, or another driver would swerve into me while driving. I never shared these thoughts with anyone. I felt ashamed by them.

As I slowly allowed people to know the truth about my relationship with Bob (while still keeping silent on when and how it started), they would become so frustrated by my reluctance to leave him. No one could ever understand why I didn't just walk away. I could never explain to them why I felt so paralyzed. What was the main reason for my inability to leave him? It would take me a few more years to truly understand the reasons behind it all.

Attempted Breakups

I did try to leave Bob several times. I would always gear myself up and tell myself I could do it, but, inside, I knew I didn't have the strength to fight him for my freedom. Sometimes I hoped that he would just get fed up with me and leave me instead. But I knew he would never end it with me. I couldn't seem to break the terrible cycle.

Prison Breakup

One of my many failed breakup attempts occurred during college. Bob and I had an argument over the phone, and I spontaneously told him I couldn't take this anymore. It was too much pressure, he was still married, I felt terrible about it, and I was tired of feeling bad all the time. He clearly started to panic that he was losing his grip on me because he drove immediately to my school to see me. I remember feeling almost honored that he would drive "all that way" (an hour) to see me to try to make things right. Then I felt guilty that he was going out of his way to see me. And what about his wife? What would he tell her if he got home late?

Bob arrived at the school and picked me up outside my dorm. We started driving, and he was talking at a rapid rate. He was explaining all of the reasons why things were so difficult right now. He tried to validate how tough it all must be for me. It was very strange to see this side of him. He was being so kind and understanding, and it seemed to cloud all the other reasons I had been so upset. We just kept driving and driving, and I had been crying and listening the whole time; I didn't speak very much on that drive, and I certainly wasn't paying attention to where we were headed.

We ended up on a bumpy dirt road, and he pulled the car over and continued to talk. We were lost in discussion when suddenly five police cars surrounded his vehicle. We looked at each other and didn't say a word. I was convinced that I was going to be arrested. I felt *that* guilty and responsible.

One officer slowly walked to the driver's side, and Bob rolled down the window. The officer said, "Sir, do you know where you are?"

Bob apologetically replied, "No, sir, I don't."

The officer said, "You are on the grounds of Bridgewater State Prison."

Bob almost chuckled but said, "Oh my God, how did I end up here?!"

The officer gave him another look and then peered into the car and looked at me. It was clear I had been crying—my eyes were red and puffy, and I still had tears on my cheeks.

He asked, "Are you all right, miss?"

I just nodded and slightly smiled. He looked at me again and then looked back at Bob. He asked Bob what he was doing, and Bob told him he was taking me back to school. He said I was upset about something that happened at school, and he was trying to help me. The officer looked at me for confirmation, and I just nodded my head. The officer took Bob's license and registration and ran them in his system. The other officers got out of their cars and started talking to one another and glancing over at us.

What is a good adjective to describe my feelings right then? I think I need to create a new word! I was beyond terrified. *Was this really happening?!* I thought the police would find out that this man had sex with me when I was a kid, and that somehow it was my fault. I was convinced I had a role in that wrongdoing. Part of me wanted to throw open my door, run to them, start sobbing, and tell them everything. I wanted them to take him away in handcuffs and never see him again. I wanted them to rescue me. But this other side of me wanted to protect him. I just didn't feel justified in my pain to walk away. I felt like my insides were battered.

The first officer walked slowly back to Bob's car and handed him his license and registration. He told him to drive straight back to Bridgewater State College. Bob agreed, and we drove away.

I started crying again, and Bob laughed at me. He said, "Oh come on, it wasn't that bad. See? Everything is fine."

I felt so stupid right then. *Why was everything making me so upset? Why wasn't he having a reaction to this?* When he dropped me off at my dorm, he said, "Now don't let the little police thing affect your brain, okay? We are fine, everything is fine, and things will get easier, I promise. Just study and don't go out to any parties or anything, and I will see you this weekend."

I agreed and went back to my dorm. That was one of the loneliest walks of my life. I felt so isolated and knew that no one else in that dorm could ever relate to what I had just gone through. I couldn't make sense of anything anymore. I didn't know what I wanted or needed. My life wasn't my own. I fell asleep that night in tears. *Would this ever end?*

Breakup at Jimmy's

Several weeks following the Bridgewater State Prison incident, I was again determined to end it with Bob. I met him at his brother Jimmy's apartment. As usual, all the confidence and determination I had built up went out the window when I saw him. We talked for a while and then ended up having sex.

Afterward, we were lying on the bed, and I blurted it all out. I told him that I couldn't do this anymore. It felt so wrong that he was still married, and it made me feel really bad. I asked him if we could take a break until he left his wife, and then we could give it a go. So I was basically asking him for permission to leave him. It strikes me that I always used the excuse of his marriage as a reason to end things. It was never a valid enough point that he was controlling or mean or abusive. That never entered my mind because **I would never be able to convince an abusive man that he was being abusive.** It seemed safer to use the marriage card instead.

He went into rationalization mode. He explained all the reasons he couldn't leave his wife just yet, but that very soon he would be able to break away, and I needed to be more understanding for his circumstances. He and his wife had known each other since first grade, after all. One does not simply leave after everything they had been through.

The thing that stands out in my mind the most is that he actually thanked me for having sex with him that night. He thought it was a touching gesture that I had all this on my mind, but I was able to put it aside and still show him how much I loved him. That was the end of the discussion.

We left Jimmy's place, and I felt so defeated. I needed to learn a language this man would understand. Somehow, if I just said the right words, he would "get it" and let me walk away. I really believed that. I was waiting for permission that would never come.

In Too Deep

Another failed breakup attempt occurred sometime after college. I again spoke ineffective words about not being able to take it. Each breakup attempt seemed to get more intense reactions from him. I had simply shared my feelings of being overwhelmed. I wasn't even trying to end it. I thought I would just start a more open dialogue with him. He got angry this time. He always felt that he had done so much for me and had sacrificed so much, and this was the thanks he got.

We were headed to a pizza place at the time. We sat down in a booth, and he was giving me the silent treatment, which I dreaded. There was a mini jukebox on the table. I decided that some music might ease the tension a bit. Being the lyrics freak I am, I also wanted to find a song that would convey my feelings in a better way, and maybe it would appeal to his logical side, and he would magically understand and stop being angry.

So I put some quarters into the machine and searched for a song. He was pouting and looking off to the side. I decided on "In Too Deep" by Phil Collins. I really thought the song would reach him, but it had the opposite effect. He looked at me with daggers and said, "How can you kick me when I am down like this?" He sank down so low in the booth that I could barely see him. I let out a nervous giggle, and he sat up, looked at me, and walked out of the restaurant. People were looking at me, waiting to see what I would do. I sat there for a minute in a panic.

Do I let him walk? Do I run after him? I had no way to get home. Part of me wanted to just stay there and eat some pizza! I just didn't have it in me to kiss up to him and beg for forgiveness, which I knew I would eventually do. I wanted him to keep walking, and I just wanted someone to walk over to me and say, "It's okay, honey, I'll take you home and you never need to see that nasty man ever again."

Of course I left the restaurant and followed behind him. He got into his car and never looked at me. We drove in silence for quite a while. Something shifted in me, though, with this silent treatment. Normally, I would be sweating it out and racking my brain to think of the right thing to say to ease the tension. This time, I just let it be quiet. I figured I had said enough damaging things, and when he was ready to talk, he would talk, yell, whatever. This is when I learned that the silent treatment was a controlling maneuver for him. I had always thought he was too angry to speak. But now I saw that he used it to make me twist and squirm.

When he realized I wasn't going to speak, he blew up. "You don't have anything to say to me after that performance?!"

I just shook my head no.

"How could you play that song when you knew it would devastate me?"

I simply answered, "Because I didn't know it would devastate you. I knew you liked Phil Collins, and it was the only Phil Collins song there. It was a peace offering. I didn't think about the lyrics."

All lies. I wanted to say so many other things, but this anger was too much for me to tolerate, and I needed things to feel peaceful as soon as possible. He spewed out the most angry and ugly comments, laying on the guilt. He devastated and deflated me with his words. It took weeks to recover from this episode. I decided it really was not worth trying to break away because I clearly would never win this battle with him. He was too smart and quick-witted and frightening, and I could not stand up to him.

I resigned. Again.

Therapy

During my first year of graduate school, I had a great professor who taught a course called Human Behavior in the Social Environment. Her name was Deborah, and she also had a private practice. She would discuss some of her clients' issues in class and find a way to weave them into whatever topic we were covering. I remember feeling like I would love to have her as a therapist. She was so warm, compassionate, and skilled.

During the second year of graduate school, I was falling apart. There is no other way for me to describe it. I was depressed, suicidal, and making horrendous decisions left and right. I had the poorest of boundaries, and I was looking for any distraction out there to numb my pain. I was still hoping to be rescued because I had given up on myself and any hope of a happy life.

During that time and a few years later, I became destructive, both to myself and to some other people. I felt so terrible about myself and my life—so what else mattered? Would it really matter if I did anything immoral or unethical? Who would care? I lived such a façade. Not many would have guessed that I felt devoid of life or hope. I had become great at faking happiness and composure at every turn. Inside, I was no longer screaming. I had resigned.

One night, during my second year of grad school, I had a vision similar to the one in the car in sixth grade. I was driving and watching a large semi-truck come toward me. I was mesmerized by the image. Suddenly, I realized my car was veering closer and closer to the yellow line and actually started to cross the line. The trucker laid on his horn and swerved to his right.

I snapped out of whatever daze I was in and pulled over to the side of the road and started sobbing. Suddenly, I felt pressure on my shoulders. It stopped me in my tracks, and I looked around. No one was there.

I felt warm energy surround my body, and a sense of calm filled me. I knew I was not alone in that moment. And then a vision appeared to me again; me with a huge smile on my face and many people around me. I looked so happy, free, and confident. Then that vision faded away, and an image of Deborah, my professor, appeared in my mind. I knew what I had to do. I went home and called her to schedule an appointment.

Say what you will, but I believe without any doubt that I have been blessed by some pretty caring angels. They reached me at my darkest moments to let me know it would get better. I couldn't sit around waiting to be rescued. I had to rescue myself, and I had to learn how.

That first session with Deborah was interesting. I blurted everything out to her in about fifteen minutes. She had to slow me down a number of times because my mouth was on fast forward. I told her that I had so many issues to deal with, many including my father. But the thing I needed the most help with was trying to leave my boyfriend. I actually explained the true nature of how it all started with him. I said, "I know he is not good for me, but I just don't know how to leave."

She asked me if I had told him that I wasn't happy.

That question startled me. Hadn't she been listening this whole time? There was no way I could tell Bob that; he would die! She sat there and watched my strong reactions to the question. I remember telling her that if I could tell him that, I wouldn't need to be sitting there figuring out how to leave.

After she listened a while, she said, "Andrea, I get this strong sense as you talk about him that he is sitting here in the room with us."

She was right. I carried him everywhere, and not in a good way. His control was deep within my pores. I believed that if I thought something negative about him, he would know. If I told her in that therapy room that I was not happy, he would find out.

We planned to meet once a week. I did not tell Bob I was going to therapy. I would go every Tuesday night, and I would tell him I was at school studying. I would also "create" activities with family or friends for Tuesday nights, so I could reserve that time. I would drive so fast each week to see her.

Deborah became a very important part of my life. I can't imagine how frustrating it was for her to work with me sometimes. I was so battered emotionally, and I would go in there with the best of intentions to learn whatever I needed to leave this man. I would leave the session pumped up and determined to be that much stronger. I would see him the next night and just wither back down to the same controlled child. It drove me crazy. But slowly, I regained my drive to live the life I wanted to live. I desperately wanted Bob out of my life. I just could not connect the dots between her wisdom, my gut feelings, and my fear.

I was still with Bob when I graduated from BU in 1992 with a master's degree in clinical social work. Bob came to my graduation and sat in the back. My mother saw him there but said very little about it. I felt ashamed and angry that I still could not leave this man. I was twenty-four years old, so it had been about ten years at this point—*longer than I had been an adult.*

I got my first job as a therapist at Bay State Community Services, in Quincy, Massachusetts. I was hired to be a clinical therapist to help children, adolescents, and their families. Part of me felt very grown-up.

Secretly, I again felt like a huge fraud. Who the hell was I to even remotely help anyone else when my life was such a wreck? It was always easier to focus on other people and their issues. I loved working with the adolescents. I knew what it felt like to need someone to talk to at that age, and I loved providing that to others. The staff at this agency was fantastic. We all became very close, and, as I mentioned earlier, I started letting some of them know about the "relationship" with Bob.

I told a few close friends the reality of how it all began. Little by little, I became more honest about my life. They accepted me more than I had ever been accepted before. I would open up about a fight or argument and about his mean or hurtful words. Some of them would express their concern that this was an abusive relationship, but I always minimized it.

I put a lot of blame on myself back then. It was hard for me to admit that Bob was abusive. I knew he was a jerk, of course. But I had a hard time with the "abusive" classification.

Around this time, I started developing an eating disorder. I began eating less and less, and I exercised more and more. I was exercising three times a day. I would wake up and work out. I would exercise after work. Then I would work out when I got home late at night. It was a very empowering feeling to have that much control over my body and what I put into it and what came off it.

No one noticed in the beginning. But after a while, my coworkers questioned how much I was eating, which frustrated me. I would have what looked like a normal-sized lunch, but then I would throw it away after I had two or three bites. I could not get enough exercise time in. I would visualize yelling at Bob and walking out the door while I climbed countless stairs on the Stairmaster.

Gradually lots of people started chiming in with their concerns about my behaviors. But I just wanted the world to leave me alone so I could lose as much weight as possible. The eating disorder took on a life of its own. The pain I felt with Bob was slightly numbed because I would get such an adrenaline rush from seeing the scale go down a pound or buying smaller sizes.

Bob even started to notice that my eating habits had changed. He never seemed to express interest or concern about my health or safety. He would just complain that my boobs were getting too small. We had a few arguments about this, and he yelled at me one night, screaming that I needed to get some help. I felt my head spin with happiness. I pretended to object, saying that I was fine.

I was not actually concerned about the eating disorder at the time. I was just thrilled that he thought it was his idea for me to get some help. So I put up this great fake argument for about ten minutes and then agreed to find myself some help. He was very pleased with himself because he had won and was going to get his boobs back.

I waited a day and then told him I called an old professor of mine who had her own private practice, and that she could fit me in next Tuesday. He was glad I called and clueless about the rest. It was a nice little victory for me. I didn't realize how sad it was that I did not feel entitled to say, "Bob, I'm not happy so I am going to go to therapy." I was just proud that I received his permission.

I continued seeing Deborah Tuesday nights. As I got stronger and clearer, the eating disorder slowly started losing its grip on me. I would never quite be free of the body-image issues that have haunted me since childhood, but I was able to eat healthier portions and exercise a moderate amount. I stopped weighing myself eight times a day, and I started working on empowerment techniques with Deborah. She was my rock.

I would go in there, week after week, complaining about Bob's new way to shame me or control me. She would listen and then try to work with me to help me break free. Nothing seemed to crack my hard shell of victim mentality. I may have been in my twenties at this point, but inside I was still this fifteen-year-old child who was being abused and controlled by a scary, angry man who had been my teacher.

During a session, in the middle of one of my weekly rants, Deborah stopped me. She asked me to hold out both my hands, palms facing upward. I obliged. She placed her hands on top of mine and looked straight into my eyes. She said, "Andrea, I'm afraid that we are going to be sitting here five years from now, and you will be telling me these same stories week after week."

That shook me. I think she felt like we were at an impasse. I had been seeing her for over three years. I still felt lost after all those sessions, and she clearly felt lost, too.

Breaking My Silence

After working with Deborah for several years, she helped me realize that I needed to become more truthful in my life. I had too many secrets and lies to protect. She helped me see that if I removed this toxic deceit, one layer at a time, it would bring me closer to the life I desired. So I decided it was time to bring my mother into therapy with me and tell her what was going on.

I was pretty anxious about it. I had no idea how my mother would react to any of my news. I think I was more anxious about not knowing how life would be once she knew the truth. I had spent my whole life living a certain way—hiding in shame. I put forth so much energy into exuding this façade of happiness and independence, and I never felt the sense that my mother could help me, so why allow myself to feel vulnerable with her? It would only hurt more being disappointed. So how would my mother and I forge ahead?

Deborah and I decided together that the best thing to do was to tell my mother everything—my father's abuse, Bob's abuse, and that I was still with Bob and struggling to leave him. I felt sorry for my mother and what was about to hit her in the face. How does one process even a part of one of those messages, never mind all at once?

I called my mother, and we were just casually chatting. I kept stalling. I knew I needed to ask her if she would come to therapy with me, but the words somehow got stuck. I was acutely aware that once I asked her the question, everything would change and I could not go back.

My mother kept chatting away, never allowing moments of silence to slip past her. It was very easy for me to stall, and she would never have a clue that I had something on my mind. So I actually started to get irritated. I needed to ask her this life-changing question, and she was chatting about Lord knows what a mile a minute. It turned out that the irritation was a great motivator to spit out the question. I had to fight my way into the one-sided conversation. This fight would become a sort of foreshadowing of the fight that was needed to leave that man. I had never felt it before, and it felt strangely good.

I finally interrupted my mother and said, "Mom, I need a favor."

She stopped abruptly and said, "*Umm*, okay, what is it?"

I took a very deep breath and paused for what felt like an hour. "Would you mind coming to therapy with me next week?" There, I said it. My body started to shake, and my head felt like it was underwater. My heart was racing, my hands were sweaty, and my mouth went dry.

I was not afraid of my mother, and I really wasn't afraid of her answer, whatever it would turn out to be. My body was reacting to my world changing in that instant. I knew it. I felt it. The truth was being unveiled. It may have been a small sliver of truth, but it really felt like letting even a small amount of air out of an inflated balloon. The huge balloon of lies in my life just got a little smaller.

She, of course, asked why I wanted her to come. I so badly wanted to minimize the reason. That was my natural reaction to things, to make everything seem fine. I also did not want to get into all the reasons prior to the therapy session. That was the point of bringing her to therapy—to have Deborah's support through the tough stuff. So I just explained that I had been working on lots of things that I wanted to share with her and that it was important to me that she go with me. So she hesitantly accepted my answer and agreed to go to Deborah's with me the following week.

Waiting for the session to arrive was painful. So many thoughts ran through my head. My mother and I didn't talk about it. I was preparing myself for different scenarios of reactions from my mom. More than once I wished I could go back and erase the question I had asked her.

I kept doubting myself, wondering why on Earth I was putting myself through this. *Were things really that bad that I had to tell her everything? Yeah, they were that bad.* I would have conversations like this inside my head on an hourly basis.

Deborah and I had decided that it was best to hold nothing back from my mother. If I was taking this big step, why sugarcoat anything? I wanted a life of truth and honesty. **You can't have truth and honesty "a little bit." It took me years to master that one. You are either honest or you are not.** Since my foundation was based on secrets, shame, and lies, this would prove to be an especially challenging moral for me to learn.

A few hours before the session, Bob called me. I told him my mother was joining me for my therapy session. He asked why and what I planned to say. I told him I was going to disclose my father's abuse as well as my involvement with him.

Bob's only concern was that I not tell my mother when our relationship began. I told him I planned to be completely open with her.

He freaked out.

"Andrea, how many times have we been through this?" he shouted. "No one can know how long this has been going on! What part of this do you not understand? How the hell can you do this to me after everything I have done for you and sacrificed for you? You're just going to piss that all away because *you* feel a need to be honest? That's great—where the hell does that leave me? Why don't you think a little sometimes before you go and ruin someone's life?"

Well, *that* I didn't expect. I tried to reassure him that it would all be fine. My mother was not a dangerous person to share things with. It is not like she would run and tell anyone at the school, I assured him, so what difference did it make?

His argument was that if it made no difference, then why did I need to tell her anything about when things started between us? He understood my need to tell her about our present involvement since I was tired of lying to her, but insisted I say no more. He was clearly feeling threatened about being exposed for the child molester he was. (I didn't frame it that way until much later. At this point, I still didn't think of him as that.)

He quieted down a bit when he realized I had not yet agreed to curtail the "truth" I was going to reveal in a few short hours, so he tried a different tactic. "Andrea, just think about it, okay? Think about what you would want if you were me. Okay?"

I agreed to think about what I would want if I were him.

We hung up, and I panicked. I called Deborah immediately, one of the maybe two times I had ever called her with a problem outside our sessions. I usually felt in control enough to be able to handle things, but this talk with Bob really got me mentally unbalanced. She heard the panic in my voice.

Bob had ordered me to not reveal the truth to my mother. How could I . . . disobey him?

Deborah listened and then asked, "Andrea, why did you tell him all this right before the session?"

I'm sure she was worried that all the work we had done preparing for this moment was at risk of being wiped away in one conversation. I just told her I felt like I was supposed to tell him so he wouldn't get mad at me later for not informing him.

Deborah was steady and consistent with me. "You have the right to say whatever you need to say in this room tonight. He will not be there; you will. This is your chance to speak your truth, and you have earned this. It is yours, and no one can take that away from you."

I thanked her and hung up. When the time came, I headed to Deborah's office, where my mother would be meeting us. (I didn't want to drive over with her because I would not have been able to handle the small talk. Plus, I wanted time to prepare with Deborah before she joined the session.)

During the drive over, I felt like I was in a movie. Everything seemed so surreal. I still remember every detail about what I wore and how I dressed that night, so great was my awareness at the time. I knew this was a huge moment for me. I didn't know where it would lead, but I knew my life would never be the same.

I sat down with Deborah and took a deep breath. She checked in with me and asked what I planned to disclose. I told her I honestly didn't know.

She looked concerned, but she let me work through it. I was afraid of the possible consequences of telling my mother that Bob was "with" me in high school. I wasn't focusing on how wrong it was. I just worried that she wouldn't understand, and he might get in trouble. Deborah and I talked a bit, and I started relaxing a little. She always had this way of soothing my anxiety with a caring look. She could phrase things in such a crafty manner that the deep parts of my psyche really understood. I decided I would tell my mother everything and deal with the consequences as they came. But it was time. It was my time.

Here We Go!

The doorbell rang, and we both went to the door to answer it. My poor mother looked like she was walking into a shooting range! She had a fake smile going, and she chatted some small talk all the way into the room. She sat down and kind of looked around the room, gathering herself.

I looked at Deborah, pleading for some guidance on how to start this thing. Deborah looked at my mother and said, "Big day, huh?"

I laugh about that now, but at the time, I cringed. It was very strange. We all knew why we were there—something big was going to be addressed. Yet, I was secretly hoping the not knowing part could last just a little longer.

My mother said, "Well, I guess so, and I am having muscle spasms in my back because I have been so stressed about what this is all about."

Poor Mom. I would have been a wreck, too. I just didn't know how to approach any of this alone. Deborah began speaking, explaining that I had been meeting with her for a long time, trying to work through some really tough issues. She went on to say that I wanted to bring her here to tell her what these issues were so that I could move forward. So my mother just readied herself in her chair and waited.

All eyes were on me. I wanted to run. I wanted to escape so badly. I wanted to turn around and pretend everything was fine. But I knew there was no way out. There was a great song by folk singer Lui Collins that I used to listen to over and over called "Baptism of Fire." The last line in every chorus is "The only way out is through." That line suddenly came to me.

I faced my mother and took a deep breath. I looked at her and said, "Okay, well, the first thing I need to tell you is. . . . " And I stopped. *How could I get those words out? How could I tell her this? Why was this my life?* I was so frustrated. I thought once we got to this point that I would be solid in my attitude and approach. Instead, I felt like a wimpy, pathetic child who was confessing to breaking a precious china doll. It was such a struggle because I did feel like I was confessing things. It felt like these were my secrets, not someone else's. I carried so much shame around, and I didn't even know it. So I tried again.

"The first thing I need to tell you is . . . I think that Dad abused me."

My mother just looked at me. "What do you mean? Like physically abused you?"

I said, "No, sexually."

She said, "What?"

I started to explain to her that I had flashbacks of his penis and strange memories and bits and pieces of being in his room when she wasn't there. I told her many of the things I had been working on regarding my father.

She took it all in and just said, "What a bastard."

I'm sure she could not even begin to process that information. She asked a few questions, but really, it was too big a topic for her to attack. She couldn't even begin to wrap her head around it. Then it was time for the next disclosure. I asked, "So are you ready for the next one?"

We laughed a bit, and she said, "I guess so."

I took another deep breath and said, "Well, Bob Baker and I are, like, together."

She wasn't as shocked by this admission. After all, she had confronted him back when I was in the eleventh grade that he was spending too much time with me. She had asked me on more than one occasion following high school if I was seeing him. I always denied it in the same, cool way. Here I was, telling her the truth. She said she always wondered and things just didn't add up sometimes, but I was always so insistent that nothing was going on.

I explained to her that it was very important to him that no one know the truth. She asked a few questions, and I told her everything. I told her about how this whole crazy mess began and why I had to lie to her all those years. I spelled it out for her that I had been with him since the ninth grade in some respects. She listened and seemed to calculate some of these facts. And then she said, "Well, as long as you're happy now, I guess that's all that matters."

I remember feeling so relieved by her response. As I am writing the response, I have a very different reaction, but I will revisit that later.

So when she said that, I got choked up for the first time in the session and said, "But I'm *not* happy."

My mother looked at Deborah. Deborah asked her if she could tell that I was upset. My mother said she could tell by the way my voice sounded. It was an awkward moment. I told her that I was trying to find a way to leave Bob but was really stuck.

She sympathized with me and validated how hard it must be to leave him after all those years. I'm sure it pushed her buttons. She had been with an abusive man for years and couldn't stand up for herself for a very long time. We talked for a little while longer, and the session was drawing to a close. Deborah warned my mother to not be surprised if the next few days she felt like her world had been turned upside down. She said that it would take some time for the dust to settle before she could really process all of this information. My mother assured Deborah she would be just fine.

I walked my mother to the door and asked if she was okay. She said she was, and she asked me if there was anything she could do to help me.

I told her, "You can go to therapy. I think it will help us be able to talk about some of this if you can look at some of your own 'stuff.'" I also said that she probably needed some support to make sense of all she was just told. I certainly was not going to be able to provide that for her—I had more than enough on my plate.

She agreed, gave me a hug, and said, "You know I love you, right?"

I said I knew this.

"I love you" was not a phrase that was spoken in my house growing up. Saying it to my mother always felt awkward. So I think she knew it was important to tell me right then. I waved good-bye and rejoined Deborah.

When I saw Deborah, her eyes were filled with tears. I asked her what she was thinking through that whole encounter. She said that she was just so aware that this was a huge moment for me, and she knew things were beginning to change in my world. I agreed.

We talked for a long time about my mom's reactions to things. I left there feeling exhausted but strong. It truly was a life-changing, empowering moment for me. I felt like I had reclaimed part of my life.

I never did tell Bob about my full disclosure. I realized I didn't have to tell him anything I didn't want to tell him. Some of his power over me was gone. **I felt like I was coming out of a strange hypnotic trance in a way. Perhaps this trance was part of the reason I hadn't been able to leave him yet. I just didn't realize I was the only one who could break the spell.**

Sexual Abuse Group

While I continued working with Deborah, we worked on issues concerning my father as well as Bob. I struggled with so many sexual abuse issues. So Deborah told me that she thought we needed to shift my therapy a bit. There was a therapeutic group that was forming, and the focus of the group was for sexual abuse survivors.

We both knew that something needed to shift in my work if I were ever to break free from Bob. I wasn't too sure about the whole group thing, though, and the topic frightened me a bit. I was not 100 percent sure that my father had molested me—I had no specific memories to point to—just a few flashbacks here and there, a familiarity when my teacher was inappropriate with me, and a gut feeling that things were not right. What if that wasn't enough "proof" that I belonged in that group.

Deborah seemed fairly certain I would fit in just fine, so I decided to meet with the two therapists for a prescreening. I was as honest as I had ever been—I told them all about my father and what I believed in my heart had happened. I also told them I had no proof and would understand if they didn't allow me into the group. Near the end of the meeting, I also mentioned this kind of controlling guy who had been in my life for a really long time.

They asked me a few questions about him, so I told them the truth. I was half expecting to get in trouble for this. They ended the meeting, telling me that they had to meet with other women and determine the right mix of people. They were going to contact me one way or another.

I had to wait two weeks before I would hear that they felt I would be a good fit in that group. If I described what those two weeks were like for me, it would be a whole other book! I experienced the whole gamut of emotions during that waiting period. I had a feeling that this group could be my ticket to freedom. I had no clue in what manner, but something deep inside me knew that the answers I had been seeking for so many years lie in the work of that group.

When I got the call that I was, in fact, being asked to join the group, I was initially thrilled. But as the first group session approached, my anxiety began to rise. What if my life and my issues didn't fit in with theirs? What if I was just one big baby, and the other women looked at me like I had no problems compared to them? Dozens of thoughts like these went in and out of my mind.

I showed up to the first session, and the other women were waiting in the waiting room. It was so awkward. We all knew why we were there, and it felt very exposing and vulnerable. We all just sat there pretending not to size each other up. Then one woman reached into her purse, pulled something out, and said in a silly fashion, "Would anyone like a Life Saver?"

We all laughed. It was just the icebreaker we needed. We started chatting about where we had just driven from and how long it took us to get there. The small talk was a relief for us all.

The group leaders came out and asked us to join them. It suddenly got quiet again. They explained the purpose and nature of the group. They let us know what to expect each week. This was a fifteen-week group dealing with survivors of sexual abuse. We were all going to choose a goal the second week—one specific, very measurable goal, to work on. That first session, we all took a turn explaining who we were and why we were there. We had to name our perpetrator. That sentence was made up of just six words: we had to name our perpetrator.

Should be simple enough, right?

That was one powerful sentence for me. When it came to my turn, I fumbled a lot. I apologetically said that I thought my father molested me, but I wasn't as sure as everyone else because my memories were so hazy. I expected everyone to point at me and tell me to leave. Instead, I was met with kindness, acceptance, and understanding. I wasn't the only one who doubted her memories.

I also mentioned that my boyfriend was controlling, and I had been trying to leave him for years, but I didn't know how. I was hoping that the power of the group experience could help me find the courage and strength to do so. I was tentative with my words and worried the others may have felt there was no place for that topic. But the women were incredibly supportive. I decided I was going to like this group!

We ended that first session with the goal of coming back the next week, knowing what long-term goal we wanted to work on. As I drove away, my mind was reeling. I could hardly believe how many strangers I just told about all of this darkness. I also left with a warm feeling inside. It wasn't just the validation and support I received. It wasn't just hearing the other women name their abusers. It wasn't just having two skillful therapists devoted to five women who they were determined to help and change. The warmth was something much deeper and broader than all that. I couldn't put my finger on it until I pulled up into my driveway. I opened my car door, deep in thought. Then, I opened the door to my apartment, stepped inside, and I suddenly knew what the warm feeling was. It was something I had never experienced before or thought I would ever feel: *hope.*

Fifteen-Week Goal

I arrived forty-five minutes early for the second group session. During the whole week in-between, I vacillated between hope/excitement over my new support system and anxiety/fear over choosing a goal and the painful work that was ahead of me. As the second session grew closer, a tiny voice inside me began to grow louder. I kept reviewing the stories the other women had told about who their abusers were. I recounted the things I said in there: my uncertainty about my father's role in it all, my controlling boyfriend, my need to leave him, and my complete inability to do so.

Why were they all so okay with my mentioning Bob and my need to leave him? This was a group for sexual abuse survivors. I was surprised not to be limited to just dealing with the issues concerning my father. These thoughts and questions bubbled and marinated in my head all week.

We entered the therapy room, and everyone chatted more comfortably than the session before. Then it came time to go around the room and name the goals we had chosen for the duration of the group. Some women's goals were to simply survive the group and have the experience of purging their stories for the very first time in a safe environment. Other goals included confronting their abusers. One woman was in the process of going to court and testifying against her perpetrator.

My turn arrived to state my goal. I was silent for a bit. The struggle I had all week came to the surface, and I got very flustered. Everyone, including the group leaders, supported and encouraged me, reminding me that I was safe and I belonged there. I took a deep breath because I knew that the following words were going to change my life. "I think I have to name another abuser."

They all just looked at me and waited.

"Bob. My boyfriend sexually abused me."

I was in shock. I did not formulate that conscious connection until that moment. I had some difficulty breathing. The group leaders validated the hell out of me, reassuring me that this was a huge and powerful realization and to take my time.

All those recent years, he was just a controlling boyfriend in my mind. I never made the connection that he had molested me when I was a child. I just saw the whole high school experience and this crazy thing that happened because he just happened to fall in love with me, and his controlling nature messed it all up. If people had tried to tell me that he, in fact, molested me, I never got it. Something never clicked. Now here I was, in a room with six others, getting it as I was speaking. It was overwhelming. I didn't cry. I started to shake a little and giggled nervously.

Once I regained my composure a bit, one of the therapists asked me if I was ready to write my goal on the large sheet of paper hanging on the wall. I stood up and walked over to the marker. Everything felt like it was in slow motion. I turned to face everyone, clueless about what to write.

The therapist asked me, "What is one thing you would like to be different at the end of this group, Andrea?"

I paused and looked down at the floor. I tried to visualize one small, measurable goal that would help lead me to a life of freedom. I looked up at her and said, "I want to tell Bob that I'm not happy."

She slightly grinned and said, "Then write it."

The following sessions were incredibly intense. They consisted of activities and lessons to help us all understand how abuse years ago could still impact us and the decisions we make today. One of the most powerful sessions in this group was when each woman had a chance to tell her story. It was as if we got to have personal witnesses.

There is something very validating about six other people listening to only me and my story. They had no other agenda other than to listen and give me feedback. Not only was it helpful to have my own session, but also listening to the other stories provided a sense of validation as well. Here I was, doubting that I would really fit in with the others. I downplayed my own stories, thinking that I had been through nothing compared to them, but each time someone would spill the details of a molestation, my mind and body would react.

One woman discussed being molested by a relative, and she described the experience of dissociating so much that all she could see were her bare legs and knees in front of her. At that statement, I started to shake. My face grew hot, and sweat began to run. I felt this panicky feeling inside and my stomach knotted up.

I wasn't reacting to her as if I felt terrible that she went through that. I was reacting as if I had been through it myself. My mind was usually able to shut down many conscious thoughts; my body was not. I remember feeling like my body would often betray me. I was always a cerebral person who overanalyzed everything. But my body could not be fooled. It remembered everything—even if my mind could not.

Almost all the women shared stories of dissociating, eating disorders, or body-image issues. Everyone felt that the wrongdoing by others long ago stayed with them in the present. Relationship and sexual difficulties were common, as were substance abuse and career troubles. Some struggled with depression, anxiety, and suicidal thoughts. What struck me the most was how I could relate to just about everything every woman struggled with.

The woman who was in the middle of a court case during the group discussed the case, and, in my eyes, she seemed very strong. She had no problem going to court and testifying against her abuser. One session, the group leaders told us that she would not be attending because she was in court. I remember having a strong reaction to this, while no one else seemed phased. I remember putting it out there to everyone: "Isn't anyone else worried about her?"

Everyone looked at me, a bit confused. I continued, "She is in court today! That is huge! What if she is in danger? What if something happens to her and we don't know?"

I was so surprised that no one else seemed concerned. Some of the women called me out on my anxiety. They explained that she informed us all during the first group session that this was going to be occurring and that she was ready for it. *What did I think could happen to her? Why would she not be safe?* I remember the leaders just sat back, allowing the group to do the work that groups do so brilliantly and naturally.

I paused for a moment. *Why was I freaking out? They can't all be wrong or insensitive.* "I just can't imagine taking Bob to court and living through it without him trying to kill me."

There, I said it. I did not realize that was my fear. That was my fear all along, and I just realized it. It took someone else standing up to her abuser for me to realize why I couldn't stand up to mine. I did not realize the depth of my fear of Bob until just then.

They helped to reassure me that Bob did not have the power over me that I thought he had. I had every right to do anything I wanted, and he had zero rights in taking that away from me. It was quite the session that night. I left there with a full brain and weary body.

All that next week I focused on those thoughts. He had no rights over me. I had no desire whatsoever to go to court or anything like that. I knew, at the time, that just leaving him would be a dream for me and would take every bit of strength I could muster. However, something deep inside was bubbling and brewing and causing a general ruckus.

I think that when you have thought a certain way for years, and an opposing challenge to that way sets up camp in your brain, "ruckus" is the only appropriate term to be used! I was beginning to see, and, more important, believe, that I had rights. I was an adult now. I was no longer a child victim with no say in how I was treated. I was twenty-five years old. I had the right to live a twenty-five-year-old life, however I chose to live it, and I started to realize that Bob never had any rights to own me like I felt owned.

Bob abused me.

I felt entitled to remove my father from my life because he had treated me so poorly. I had no trouble justifying this in my mind. Why should Bob be any different? What a shift this was making for me.

When I had the opportunity to tell my story one session, I was uncomfortable, and I had the toughest time getting started. They all encouraged me in different ways to just tell something easy at first. So I started with my father. I told them what I knew and what I didn't know. I brought some photos and some drawings and shared them with everyone. I was struck at one point by how intent they were all listening, and I realized I belonged there more than anywhere else. I no longer questioned or doubted. I was a sexual abuse survivor, and the details were insignificant. I was abused, and that made a huge impact on me as an adult. *And* I could do something about it.

Once I got started, I got on a roll. I talked and talked and talked. I told them all about how things started with Bob in eighth grade, and how it progressed. I remember one woman said, "And you weren't sure if you had been abused enough to be here? Honey, please!"

It was a great moment for me. I needed this real validation so much. It helped move me forward and past the paralysis of doubt and fear. I ended my session with a song. I had been learning to play guitar, so I brought it in and sang for them. It was my symbolic way of showing them that I had found my voice. I'm sure the song was pretty lame, but it did not matter—it moved us all.

That group—the women, the leaders, the work, the fifteen weeks—it saved my life. **I am always in awe of the power that exists in our thoughts. What we believe, we create. I believed I was trapped, so I was trapped. Once I believed I could be free, I was free.**

If any women or leaders from that group are reading this, thank you from the bottom of my heart for your bravery, honesty, kindness, and acceptance.

The Note

During my first therapy session, Deborah had asked me if I had told Bob that I wasn't happy. I couldn't even imagine those words coming out of my mouth. It was this very statement—"I'm not happy"—that was the key to getting out of that abusive situation all along. It was as if I were wearing Dorothy's ruby slippers in *The Wizard of Oz.*

Remember when Glinda the Good Witch tells Dorothy at the end of the movie to click her heels three times and say, "There's no place like home," and poof—she'd be home?

The Scarecrow gets angry with Glinda and says, "Why didn't you tell her that in the beginning? That could have saved her all this trouble!"

Glinda simply replies, "She wouldn't have believed me. She had to find out for herself."

I believe life is truly like this. If someone hands you an answer, you don't really earn that answer and learn its lesson. You have to deal with all the muck and the mud and the scary witches and the flying monkeys, and sometimes even the creepy guy behind the curtain, and decide which path of the yellow brick road to follow. The lessons are in those parts of your movie.

There was a huge buildup to my telling Bob that I was not, in fact, happy. I went to the fifteen-week sexual abuse survivor's group and determined that my goal was to be able to tell Bob that I wasn't happy. The group ended, and I knew what I had to do. I was ready.

Shortly after the group came to a close my niece, Sarah, was born out in California. My mother and I decided to take a trip out there to meet her. I decided the time was right to confront Bob. *Right* after how many years? Eleven years of knowing this man, being groomed for all this crazy abuse, I was finally ready to put an end to it—by myself. I was not going to be rescued by anyone else or have him end it magically for me. I was ready. I was terrified. But I was so ready, and ready meant ready for any consequences that might ensue. **My pain finally outweighed my fears.**

He knew I was leaving for California for a week. He understood and was fine with it. I planned to end it with him the night before I left, but I couldn't bring myself to do it. The words wouldn't come out. I was stuck and so angry that I was chickening out. I ended up having sex with him that night, knowing that it would be the last time I would have to do that with him. It felt strangely empowering.

As he slept that night, my mind flooded with images over the past eleven years. I realized I was no longer wondering how my life ended up in such a sad and controlled state. I found this strange feeling inside of me, stirring things up. I could not identify it at the time because it was a new feeling for me. I had a really tough time falling asleep that night. I wanted it to be morning. I wanted to unleash my plan that minute. I wanted the façade to be over. I was ready. It was about to happen.

I was about to be free.

The next morning, Bob got ready for work. I was leaving after him. He wished me luck on the trip and told me to call him when I arrived in California. I said good-bye, and I know that my smile was brighter than usual. I was moving faster and had a spring in my step. He left the house, and I wrote him a note. These were the words I used:

"I hope you have a good week. I am going to use this time away to think about some things with us, and I just need some space to get my head clear. I will call you soon."

Now, I thought that this was the most well-crafted, clear, direct, and assertive note that had ever been written! I realize to outsiders that this was quite a meek attempt at breaking away. It doesn't even resemble a break away. But I knew that if I could utter those words, even if on paper, that it got the ball rolling because there was no backing out. I had never spoken words like that to him before. Any breakup attempt in the past had always related to hating the fact that he was married. Everything else I said to him had an agenda for keeping the peace. This was the first time, in eleven years, that I had insinuated I was unhappy with him.

I was on such an adrenaline high that day. My mother and I got on that plane, and I was almost manic. I told her what I had done, and she was happy for me. She sort of warned me that it didn't really sound "over" to her, but the farther we flew away, the more excited I felt. I was convinced that the dirty work was done and the rest would be easy. I have never been more wrong.

We arrived at the airport, and I saw my beautiful niece for the first time. I felt that she represented my rebirth, and, to this day, I mark her birthday as a reminder of how old I am *sans* Bob. As of this writing, I am nineteen years old, free and clear of abuse and control.

My mother and I had a great visit with my brother and his family, but the thought of Bob waiting for me to call him loomed overhead the whole time.

I decided to head to a pay phone to call him. Luckily, this would be a short call due to how many quarters were required for a call across the country. I dialed his number, and I had that old familiar anxiety, but I also had that same strange bubbly feeling in my gut that I had the last night in his bed. He picked up the phone.

I took a slow deep breath and spoke calmly. When I told him it was me, he said nothing at first. So I actually just acted like everything was fine, which surprised me.

He said, "How could you leave a note like this, Andrea?"

My stomach got a little knotted up at this point, so I answered him honestly. I said, "Well, it's true, I have needed to do some serious thinking about some things, and it is really hard to think when I am with you, so I thought I would take advantage of this trip and clear my head."

He was furious. He spoke very slowly and quietly at first. "This was the most gutless thing you could do."

I stayed quiet.

"I don't even know you," he said.

I remained quiet.

Then he wanted answers. "What the hell do you have to think about that you couldn't tell me in person?"

I tried to avoid getting into it as much as possible. "I don't know, just lots of things that I want to sort through. We can talk about them when I get back."

He yelled a lot and then got quiet. He tried to guilt me a bit, asking why he should ever trust me again. "What difference does anything make now? How will I ever believe you are even coming back home?"

I reassured him I would, and I got the little signal that meant the time was about to run out. I let him know that I would call him when I got home, and then I hung up.

I was in shock. I hung up on him. He had done that to me many times. I had never done that to him or to anyone. It felt GOOD! I still had a fear of the unknown. However, I now had experienced taking some control back. I knew what it felt like to say no. I had never, ever learned *no,* and here I was, teaching it to myself.

When you don't know what no feels like, it is really difficult saying it to a big, scary guy. I knew that I would have to deal with him when I got home, but I was across the country, and, unlike my Disney internship, it didn't feel like I had to check in with him. He was no longer in the room with me. I had stripped him of much of that control that he had over me since I was a kid. I had this faith that when I faced him, as scary as it got, I could handle him. And if he did try to hurt me, I would die fighting rather than cowering.

This felt really GOOD!

O.J. Simpson

During my actual break away from Bob, interesting things were happening in the world. While I was in California after I left Bob that note, O.J. Simpson had been accused of killing his wife, Nicole Simpson. The media was in a frenzy, with the car chase, the evidence, and, more important for me, all the discussions about abusive relationships. I remember listening to one news report during which they discussed how frightened Nicole had become of O.J.

An expert was speaking about the dynamics of abuse, and how fear played such a large part in the abusive cycle. I heard the 9-1-1 tapes from the past where Nicole called in and sounded terrified, and O.J. Simpson could be heard yelling in the background. I felt like these were all signs from the universe that I was getting out just in time. I could relate to certain aspects of the abusive cycle that were discussed. This story fueled my courage to face Bob head on when I got home. I needed to protect my life—physically and emotionally. Along with my niece's birthday, the O.J. Simpson case always triggers a reminder of how long I have been free.

Las Vegas

I extended my California trip and went to see Andrew, my old boyfriend from the Disney internship, in Las Vegas. He was working at the Luxor hotel, getting it up and running. I still had a sense that I was free and done with Bob. I knew there was work waiting for me when I returned, but I was really able to enjoy feeling like a free spirit while I was gone.

I wasn't waiting by a phone to talk to Bob or making up excuses about why I didn't want to go somewhere, just so that I could be available if he decided to call. Nope—my day was my own. It was the first time since tenth grade that I felt this way.

When I met Andrew in Vegas, he was so happy for me. He showed me the sights, and I had a fantastic time. Everything felt a bit surreal. I felt like I had landed on another planet, and not just because it was Vegas (which could make anyone feel that way). The world looked different to me. Everything—the sky, the trees, the cars.

Andrew and I decided to take a trip out to the Grand Canyon. We didn't have much time, but I didn't care. I thought it was all too fitting that after I finally broke free from this man that I got to see one of the Seven Wonders of the World. My joke with Andrew was that my breakup was the Eighth Wonder. It was a long road trip, and we played a lot of music along the way and talked about anything and everything.

I enjoyed being with Andrew, but part of me wanted to be doing the trip solo. My soul was reeling. It was hard for my mind to catch up to the rest of me.

We got to the Grand Canyon late and checked into a motel. I'm sure Andrew had thoughts of intimacy that night, but it was the furthest thing from my mind. I felt like I needed a purification of some sort. The thought of being close to someone like that was not a comfort, to say the least. Andrew was very understanding, and we ended up playing gin rummy!

We woke up the next morning and went to the canyon to watch the sunrise. I could not believe I was there. I was amazed by the glory and beauty that surrounded me, and that I had just accomplished something, which for years, I believed was impossible. I was excited about the life that was ahead of me, just waiting for me to grab. My heart, mind, soul, and emotions were full. I felt free.

I'm Not Happy

When I arrived home, Bob had left twenty-seven messages on my answering machine, varying in tone and content. Some were calm, checking in on me. Others were angry and threatening. Still others were pitiful. I truly did not expect to come home to that. I had to call him. I was ready—for what exactly, I wasn't sure. I knew this was the fight of a lifetime for me, and I knew in my heart and soul and cells that I had the right to do this. It was time to stand up for myself and claim the life I deserved.

I called him up. His voice was shaky. I said, "Hello."

Right away he asked, "Are you okay?"

I kept my answer simple and just said, "Yes."

He asked to see me right away. At this point he was acting respectful and concerned. I had the visual that I was a butterfly he was trying to catch by tiptoeing softly up to me. Then he would try to slam his big net over my head and keep me in a jar on the shelf. I kept the call brief, agreeing to see him the following day.

I went to see Deborah and told her all that had happened. I told her about the note I left, the trip to California, the phone call to him, the twenty-seven voicemails, and how I needed to meet with him. Her head must have been spinning because I had been seeing her for over four years, and it all went down!

She advised me to meet him in a public place if I truly felt I had to see him. I wasn't sure why she was suggesting that at the time. Now I completely understand—there are so many violent stories out there of someone turning a gun on another person because of a conflict or breakup. Bob was unpredictable on a good day—how would he react now? I was convinced I could handle him, but I heeded her advice.

Bob and I met at Nantasket Beach and walked for a long time. He went through many emotions as he talked. I mainly listened to him. He kept telling me that he was shocked that I left the note and asking how I could put him through a week of hell the way I did. He wanted an explanation.

I took a really long pause, and I swear it was like the clouds parted, and for the very first time in my life (and I really mean that), I found the way. I found the answer to every situation I had ever been in. It was on that beach that I found the truth. This had been building for years.

Sometimes in life, I think we can hear words of wisdom, read inspiring quotes, love amazing people, and know in our minds the answers. But when you truly integrate that knowledge within you, you can't unlearn it. It becomes a part of you, and you are forever changed.

I realized in that moment that all I had to do with him was be honest. It really came down to that. It sounds so simple. But I had never, ever learned how to be honest. Honesty felt dangerous to me in the past. Now, it was my only way out.

"You want to know why I left that note?" I asked.

"Damn straight I do," he said, fuming like an angry dragon.

I took a deep breath and mentally high-fived myself for what I was about to say. "I left that note because it was the only way I could get out any words of truth to you. I have tried to tell you for years now that I don't want to be with you anymore, but I have always been too intimidated by you to do it. So, the note allowed me to start this without backing out."

Once I revealed this, he no longer argued about the note. He moved on to arguing about my feelings, and the beautiful thing was, it did not matter what he said or did or yelled or cried—I was done. I patiently allowed him to have closure, and somehow, I would know when I could walk away. I didn't know when that time was, but I knew the hardest part was over. I could finally handle anything he threw at me.

I got in my car and drove home. I was feeling incredibly strong and lucky. I was seeing everything through new eyes. My body felt different. I walked differently. I felt lighter. I felt like George Bailey at the end of *It's a Wonderful Life* when he shouted, "Merry Christmas, you old building and loan!"

Shortly after I walked into my house, Bob called me. He asked to see me again, and I asked him what more we could talk about. He asked me to give him a chance to think about everything so he could ask me some questions. I said that would be fine. I had been with this man since I was about fourteen—I was now twenty-five. I didn't think it was fair to deprive him of this process.

We arranged to get together about a week later. While waiting for that day to arrive, he left me more messages. One message was particularly disturbing. He sounded depressed and distraught. He threatened to kill himself—by driving up to the top of a mountain in Maine and then just driving off. It sounded so ridiculous and dramatic. I was starting to see him in a whole new light. He wasn't an all-powerful man . . . he was a weak, insecure, abusive, manipulative coward—a big baby who wanted everything his way and wanted to pay no consequences for his actions.

I blew off his suicide threat at first, but as the day progressed, the thought sat in my head. I started to worry about him doing something crazy. I also started to worry about my safety a bit. If he was threatening to kill himself, anything was possible. This was an unstable guy. I had just torn his world apart, and he was crumbling.

I called his friend Mike and told him about Bob's threats. Mike assured me that Bob would never kill himself and that he was just trying to do whatever he could to get me to change my mind. Mike also reassured me that Bob would never hurt me. I tried to find solace in his words, but I found myself looking over my shoulder for a few days.

I went to work the next day. I had filled in a lot of people about the breakup, and I swear they wanted to throw me a party. I now filled them in on his latest threat. Everyone seemed to react more seriously than I did. Then, at one point, I looked out the third-floor window of our office, and I saw Bob's car outside in the parking lot. It felt like someone had punched me in the stomach.

Bob eventually drove away, but my coworkers urged me to tell the director about it. I didn't want to share this information with her because it embarrassed me. I hadn't talked with her about any of this before. Where would I start? But I agreed to talk with her because I didn't want anything crazy to happen, and I felt like I should warn people just in case. So I told her the gist of the breakup and that he's "a little upset right now."

She remained calm and said, "A little upset? Andrea, he's stalking you."

I never thought of it that way. Her words got me unhinged. All this empowerment was getting me nowhere. How could he take anything away from me when I worked so hard? So she discussed this with all the staff to make sure he was not allowed in the building and for the receptionist to not accept any calls from him. Someone would walk me to my car at the end of the day. I found myself looking over my shoulder everywhere I went. It felt lousy. I didn't want to feel this way. I wanted to feel freedom. Instead, I felt a different kind of weight on my shoulders.

I met Bob one final time. I still felt sure of what I needed to do and say, but I was a bit anxious over what his reaction would be. I decided to meet him at his house to diffuse his anger a bit. I figured if he wanted to hurt me, the location would not have mattered.

He was very serious, as if he knew this was his last shot. He asked me a few basic questions about how I was doing and if I still felt the same way about ending our relationship.

I just said, "Yeah, I'm sorry it hurts you, but my feelings have not changed."

He started to pull out the guilt cards. He asked me how I couldn't have come over or called him when he told me he was going to kill himself.

So I answered honestly, "Well, I really hope you don't do anything to hurt yourself, but there is nothing I can do to stop you if that's what you make up your mind to do."

His manipulation wasn't working, and he got angry, very angry. He started to get louder and red in the face. "So you don't give a shit about me or if I live or die?!"

I paused for a long time. He calmed down a bit, and I could tell that he knew the anger wasn't working, either.

I said, "I care about you. I hope you go on to live a happy life. But I am not happy being with you."

I said it!

That big scary sentence Deborah asked me about years ago—I said it and felt entitled to say it. They were my feelings, and he couldn't take them away. He froze and looked at me as if I said I just murdered his dog—a reaction that had paralyzed me for so many years. Now, it was expected, and I was prepared.

"You aren't happy? What the hell was Waterville Valley and tennis and hiking and the beach and all that crap then?!"

I answered, "I know we have had some good times through the years, but I am not happy being in a relationship with you. This whole thing started when I was a child, and you were my teacher. That is *beyond* wrong, and we would never be able to be on equal footing—we never had a chance."

He kept insisting that he never meant for it to happen, that he just fell in love with me because I was so special. Then he said, "You told me you loved me."

It's true; I did tell him over and over that I loved him, right up until that May. I was afraid not to tell him.

So I took a long breath and said, "I lied. I used to love you, but I don't love you anymore. And I lied because look at the reaction you are having. I wasn't strong enough before to deal with this. So, no, I don't love you anymore."

That was it. He was done. He took a few steps back and went white. He looked at me with an empty stare. He said, "So everything is a lie. Waterville Valley was a lie. Every kiss was a lie. This chair is a lie."

At the chair comment, I made the grave mistake of allowing a slight smile to emerge. It was a tad dramatic.

He said, "And now, you're laughing at me."

And somehow I knew to just shut up. I knew if we continued to play a tug-of-war with our words, this would never end. And I truly was done. I had said the final words that needed to be spoken.

He saw that I was done speaking. He walked in a slow and exaggerated motion toward the stairs. He turned off the light and started to walk upstairs. I sat there for a few minutes, wondering what to do. I heard him lay down in his bed upstairs. I realized that it was my cue to leave. So I walked toward the door and looked up the stairs at the dark hallway. I felt like I needed to let him know that I was leaving. So I said in a very weird, awkward, and tentative voice, "Okay, um, bye. . . . "

And I LEFT!

I left, I left, I left!

I ran to my car and drove about 80 miles an hour (not really, but it felt like it!) and laughed and cried the whole way to my apartment. I knew I was done. I would not visit him or talk to him again. I was done.

I got home and called Andrew. I said, "It's over! I did it!"

He cheered for me and wanted to hear the whole story. Then a beep sounded, indicating another call was coming in, and I clicked over, and it was, of course, Bob.

He said, "How could you just leave me like that?"

I said, "Bob, it's over, and I'm not going to talk to you anymore. I am hanging up now."

And I hung up the phone.

I clicked back over to Andrew and told him what happened. He coached me to not answer the phone anymore. Just let the call go to voicemail, and I would be able to screen my calls that way. And that's exactly what I did for many months until his calls finally stopped. I got very little sleep that night. I was full of brand-new emotions. I had a new lease on life. Whatever the future held for me after that, I knew I would never be back in that hell again.

FOR YOU, THE READER
CONSIDER THIS . . .

I was finally able to leave Bob. No one in my life believed I would be able to do it. I certainly didn't believe I would ever be able to leave him. I could never explain why I couldn't do it, but once I broke free, I knew that answer. I had no voice, no skills, and no truth to speak with him for a very long time. He found me at a time when I had been controlled and abused by my father, who had stripped away any voice I may have had. Bob just continued the control and abuse under disguise. I was a child who never had the opportunity to individuate and find my own voice. I had to learn how to tell the truth, plain and simple. I had to tell the truth to myself first before I could tell it to anyone else. Once I found that voice of truth, everything became clear to me.

For all readers . . .

- Do you see any similarities between my experiences and that of a battered woman?

- What are some cycles of abuse you recognize in this chapter?

- Do you know someone who is trying to leave an abusive person? What prevents her from walking away? How can you help her safely make the break?

- How much do fear and control contribute to abusive situations?

- Do you know of a child who may be in an abusive relationship? What steps can you take to protect that child from the abuser? What if it is your child?

- If you are trying to leave someone but find yourself "stuck," what are some of your fears? Are they legitimate concerns, perceived difficulties, or a combination? Do you have a support system in place?

As a survivor . . .

- How did the abuse end?
- Did someone end the abuse for you or did you stop it yourself?
- Do you wish the abuse ended differently?
- Are there other things in your life that you are waiting to end in a similar way the abuse ended?

Those who are in abusive relationships and situations need all the support and understanding they can find. Your timetable for them to break free from the abuse may vary greatly from theirs. If you are reading this and are currently in an abusive situation, gather as much support as possible. Know that you can speak your truth with the proper support and safety plan in place. Seize the life you were designed to live.

CHAPTER 8

Starting Over

————◄◦►————

My life was now my own. In my mind, the possibilities were end-less. I was so excited to create whatever world I chose to create. There were many things I did not expect as I forged ahead into my new world. I had to dive in and see for myself what this so-called free life was all about.

As excited as I was to begin this new chapter in my life, I quickly discovered that starting over was not effortless. I needed months of reminders that I was free, and I actually had to practice the art of independence. It would be a few years before I finally felt like I was really *in* my life.

Surreal Feeling of Freedom

I never took an hour for granted during those first few months of free-dom. Simple tasks were great achievements. Going to the movies, buying a newspaper, sleeping in late—they all felt like gifts. I still experi-enced that dissociative feeling of being in a movie, but at least this time I wasn't dissociating for traumatic reasons. I had been stifled and con-trolled for so many years that it had become an unexamined norm. For so many years, I had asked for permission to do basic things like going to the beach or meeting up with a friend.

From the time I was born until I turned twenty-five, I had answered to a controlling man—first my father, then Bob. *Twenty-five years.*

Once you've worn shackles for that long, the marks and pressure around your ankles and wrists are still evident even after they have been removed. I felt them for many years.

To this day, I still find myself checking in with my partner, William, about trivial things like running the dishwasher, or if I am talking too much, or if I have said anything to other people in front of him that might have upset him. The conditioning and brainwashing that I would be "in trouble" for saying or doing something wrong had lasted my entire childhood and for seven years of my adulthood. I needed to work hard at reconditioning myself, which is still a process for me. William was, and is, very understanding.

The beauty of it all was that each time I reminded myself that I was free to make my own decisions, it felt like opening a new present. If I checked my watch and automatically thought I had to call Bob, a little happy voice would sing, "Nope! No Bob here anymore . . . you may proceed!"

Making decisions like what trips to take, car to buy, or career to pursue was an interesting process for me. Upon encountering a decision that had to be made, I would first panic because, as controlling as Bob could be, there was some weird comfort knowing that my choices were limited to what he approved or disapproved of. I didn't have to think for myself. He had me convinced that I couldn't deal with decisions like that on my own. So after the initial panic, I would force myself to be still and listen for an inner voice.

What I initially found were two possibilities: either my inner voice was mute or I was deaf. I had a gut feeling early on that everyone, including me, had an inner voice. I knew my inner voice, as muffled as it was, had given me permission to go to the prom, had enabled me to go to college and graduate school, had helped me escape to Disney World, and ultimately had given me the strength to leave that sick man. I knew that voice was in there somewhere. However, when I had a conscious decision to make on my own, I would become panicked and paralyzed.

I believed Bob's central message to me: that I was an idiot incapable of functioning on my own. This belief went down to my core. Fortunately,

I also had a competitive fighter in me, and I was determined to prove Bob wrong and thrive in my life. I knew my inner voice was there, but sometimes I felt it was harder to hear it once Bob was out of my life. I certainly didn't expect this twist! Self-doubt and insecurity filled me at every turn. I needed validation from everyone in my life that I was making good choices.

Gradually my inner voice grew louder and my "hearing" became more acute. As more opportunities and decisions were presented to me, I literally practiced making decisions and choices on my own without going to others for that validation I had so desired. Not all my decisions were winning ones, but they were *mine*.

Harvard Square

One of the first Saturdays after leaving Bob, I woke up realizing that I had no plans. I didn't have to meet Bob anywhere, and all I had was time on my hands. I lay in bed for a while pondering this new experience of being able to do anything I wanted to do! My mind started spinning with ideas. I decided I would head into Harvard Square for the day and just see what the day would bring me. This had always been a dream of mine. I would look at people with such envy when they seemed free and easy, coming and going as they pleased. Now I was one of those people. It didn't feel real.

I drove into town and found a great parking spot, which I took as a sign that the heavens were smiling down upon me. Everything was some sort of sign to me back then. I bought a newspaper and a bagel, and sat outside a coffee shop and pretended to eat. I looked around at this busy world and took everything in. I couldn't focus on the paper or on my bagel. I was too happy that this was my life now. No one could take it away from me ever again. I felt like the luckiest girl in the world.

How many people get a chance to experience life this way? Most people go through their day-to-day journeys and get caught up in the little crises and victories. For me, I was reborn. I was seeing the world for the first time, and I loved what I saw.

I walked around Harvard Square and listened to all the musicians playing on the streets. They were so talented and passionate. I got choked up every time I listened to a new one. I kept looking at my watch, wondering what time I needed to call Bob, and then I would get a new adrenaline rush, realizing that I never had to call him again. It would take years for me to lose this feeling.

It started to get very cold in the afternoon, and I hadn't brought a jacket. My instinct was to head toward my car and go home. As I was walking, I saw an Express store to my left. In the window was a forest green jacket that caught my eye. I stared at it for a long time, getting lost in my thoughts.

I kept hearing Bob's voice in my head saying, "You idiot, why didn't you bring a coat? You knew we would be out all day."

I felt foolish that I wasn't prepared. I started wondering if maybe he had been right sometimes about my lack of common sense. Then a stronger voice echoed in my head. "You don't have to plan a thing today. You can do anything you want. He is not here. Buy the jacket!"

My eyes literally opened wide when I realized I could go in and buy that jacket.

I walked inside, found my size, and I tried it on. I looked in the mirror, and I started to cry. I was so happy and relieved, and tears were the last thing I expected. It was such an overwhelming moment for me. I gathered up my emotions and my cash and walked out of the store wearing my first purchase in my new, free life. I still own that jacket. I don't wear it often. But I look at it in my closet and smile. I will never get rid of it—what it represents is too powerful to discard.

Another part of that day that always stands out in my mind was the concert I went to that night to see one of my favorite folk singers: Lui Collins. Her music was therapy for me.

The line from "Baptism of Fire"—*The only way out is through*—rang in my mind any time I had to face Bob or deal with something brutally painful in therapy. So imagine my surprise when I was walking around Boston that day, and I saw a flyer announcing that Lui Collins would be performing *that night* in Boston. This had to be another sign! I kept checking myself, wondering if it was all right for me to stay out this late. I literally looked around and reminded myself that Bob was not next to me or behind me or on the other end of a phone. I could stay out as late as I wanted and be anywhere I wanted to be!

I made my way to the concert venue and bought a ticket. They had CDs for sale, and I bought one. I took my seat and read all the lyrics on the CD cover. The singer-songwriter whose music had gotten me through some of the most painful and trying times of my life was about to sing right in front of me. A lump formed in my throat and didn't go away.

Lui Collins walked on the stage, and I was mesmerized. She looked so grounded, peaceful, and strong. She sang beautifully and told wonderful stories. When her set was over, she announced that she would sign the CDs. I was determined to somehow let her know how much her music had saved me. I walked up to her, and she turned to me with a kind smile. I started to speak, but I got choked up and couldn't say a word. She did this really interesting thing next.

She could see that I was struggling, and she centered her stance and seemed to take in the moment. She clearly knew this was momentous for me. She placed her hand firmly on my shoulder, which allowed me to take a deep breath, and I said, "Just . . . thank you. . . ."

She smiled and replied, "It's absolutely my pleasure."

I wanted so badly to tell her what her music meant to me. But where would I start? How could I convey all of that in one or two sentences? I couldn't, so I simply thanked her.

Lui Collins's music can change lives, and I hope she knows that.

I drove home late that night happier than I had ever been. On the surface, the day had been filled with simple, even mundane components. I drove into town. I parked. I bought a paper and a bagel. I people-watched. I heard music. I bought a jacket. I went to a concert. But these commonplace activities held so much more meaning for me. They were symbols of freedom, and I drank in every ounce of them. I would not take any amount of freedom for granted for a very long time.

Stalking

After I made the final break from Bob, he would still leave me voice-mails that I would delete as soon as I heard his voice. Even this was progress for me. I no longer felt like I *had* to listen to him. I realized there was no point in listening to his words. His voice would "appear" on that machine, and my finger would hit the delete button faster than you could say "freedom."

As thrilled as I was to have this newfound life of freedom, I couldn't quite shake the fear that Bob would reappear unexpectedly. I awoke with a deep sense of gratitude each morning, yet I also had a nagging feeling I was going to see Bob somewhere. I never knew if he was following me or watching me walk into my office. He still had this presence in my world that I constantly tried to push aside. I would be in the middle of a party, and I would catch myself looking around to see if he was there. I found all new restaurants to visit, malls to shop in, and routes to take to work.

I didn't realize just how draining this behavior had become until my friends pointed it out to me. They knew how much Bob was still on my mind and how much control he still had over me. At first, I reacted to this defensively. After all, I had just gained the strength of 10,000 men in my mind! I had beaten him! I had walked away and swore to never look back. But, in reality, Bob's control over me had not simply vanished.

Shipping Off to Boston

My discomfort was magnified in and around my apartment. Coming and going, I would look over my shoulder to be sure Bob wasn't there. This very angry, unstable, and abusive man knew *everything* about me: where I lived, what I drove, where I worked, who my friends were, and so on. With the O.J. Simpson case being the big topic on the news, the talk of domestic violence was everywhere. The idea that Bob could do something to harm me was always on my mind. So, as much as I adored that little apartment, I just didn't feel safe in it anymore.

My cousin Kristin was moving into a cool apartment in Brookline, Massachusetts, with a friend of hers, and she asked if I would be interested in moving in with them. It took me about twelve seconds to gratefully accept the offer.

My very first apartment had been a symbol of my growing up and beginning to foster the strength to leave Bob. Letting it go was difficult. I also felt a bit defeated, as if Bob had won this battle. However, I knew that I had won the war, so I accepted defeat in this one instance. What mattered most was for me to feel safe—always. I vowed to never again feel fear in any place I lived or with anyone I knew. So, I packed up my things and moved to Boston.

We all had a great time living together, and I fell in love with Boston. Although I had gone to Boston University for graduate school, I never had enough time to explore the city. Once I lived in town, Boston seemed like a new world. I got into the folk music scene, and I met amazing people—singers and non-singers. I had a better sense of freedom since the environment was so different and fresh. However, I was sadly surprised to still find myself looking over my shoulder to make sure Bob wasn't lurking in some corner.

I could bury you, he had told me repeatedly during our ten years together, and, apparently, that threat had left a strong and lasting impression.

When would this feeling that I was being stalked by that disturbed man ever leave me?

Music

During a therapy session before I left Bob, I casually mentioned to Deborah that I used to love to sing. I had sung all through high school and tried to learn the guitar while in college. When it came to the guitar, I always likened myself to Phoebe from the show *Friends* because I knew about five chords and could only sing songs like "Smelly Cat" along with my playing. In any event, I only mentioned my love of singing in passing, but Deborah made me stop there and elaborate. I had no idea why she thought this was worth discussing in more depth, but she insisted.

She asked, "What did music mean to you?" And "Why did you stop singing?"

So I thought about my answers for a while. Music had always been such a soothing outlet for me, but I had become frozen and closed when it came to expressing myself in song. It had been a long time since I felt that joy.

Deborah encouraged me to find my voice again. I didn't realize how deep this went for me. So, shortly before I left Bob, I picked up my guitar again. There was a strong correlation between finding my singing voice and finding my assertive voice with Bob.

The first session following my final break away from Bob, I sat in Deborah's office and said, "Okay, so do we dive in and talk about all the shit that happened with my father?"

Deborah looked at me a bit bewildered and said, "Andrea, we have been working on you leaving Bob for four years. I think right now we look at who you should date and where you should sing."

She was right. I did need a break from all that intensity!

So I started playing my guitar daily, learning many of my favorite songs and playing in front of my friends. The experience was so liberating. My friends encouraged and supported me. I'm sure I sounded less than stellar back then, but they didn't care. They were all so happy I was finally free. They probably would have listened to me for hours and hours if they had to, no matter how I sounded.

My old college roomie Nilde was listening to me one day, and she suggested that I try singing at a coffeehouse or open-mic night, but I shut down that idea pretty fast. *Those people knew way more than five chords!* Still, she was persistent with this idea.

So, like all the other ideas in my life where I initially said no way, I signed up for an open-mic night! It was at this cool bookshop in Cambridge, Massachusetts, called the Book Cellar Café. They held open-mic nights on Sunday evenings. I asked the owner if it was alright for beginners to sign up, and he said, "Absolutely!"

I practiced all week. I kept yelling at Nilde for *making* me agree to this. Although I was a nervous wreck, I knew this was an important step for me—a symbolic occasion that would mark finding my voice.

Sunday arrived, and Nilde and I went to the café. Excited and happy for me, Nilde kept reminding me this was more about getting up there than about how I sounded.

"Just get this one out of the way," she encouraged.

I listened to a few singers, and my heart sank. They were so good! Plus they told funny stories between songs. Their picking was elaborate, and their voices were strong and beautiful. I decided my performance would be a disaster. That's when the host announced my name.

Holding my guitar, I bravely walked up to that stage and looked at Nilde, who wore the biggest smile on her face. She gave me a thumb's up . . . and I thought I was going to throw up. My hands were sweating, and I couldn't even remember the name of the instrument in my hands. I sat myself down on the chair and looked out at the audience.

I got this image in my head of Bob sitting in the back of the room, shaking his head disapprovingly. He would *never* have wanted me to perform in front of all these people and would have said he would be embarrassed for me. That would be his way of trying to control the situation and keeping me under his watch. A rush of adrenaline hit me.

I was free. I was alive. I was about to make a fool out of myself. But I didn't have to answer to anyone but myself.

I told the audience this was my first experience at an open mic, and they all clapped in support, which eased my nerves a little. I began playing and felt I had done a terrible job by the time I finished, but at least I had played. Everyone cheered.

I smiled and said, "Okay, this is *way* different from singing in my bedroom!"

Everyone laughed! They thought I was funny! I finished my next two songs, which flowed more easily, and that was it. I fell in love with performing, much like I had in the fifth-grade talent show.

I was so grateful to Nilde for pushing me into this amazing experience. Soon, I began singing at various open mics and coffee shops throughout the Boston area. Many amazing people shared advice and stories with me. I found my comfort zone on those little stages with those people. This was one of the most unexpected pleasures of my life. I felt like it was a true transition from bondage to freedom. I had found my voice!

Dating

About a year after leaving Bob, I felt it was time for me to start dating. I had never officially dated anyone without Bob in my life. Any "relationship" I had was based on secrecy and lies. It was all I knew.

I had no clue how to go about dating. I would also slowly discover that I had a deeper problem as well. I had incredibly low self-esteem. Yes, I felt immense pride in myself for finally leaving Bob and felt great happiness to have this new life, but the effects of being controlled and abused for so long were far-reaching. I walked around feeling like the fat, ugly kid in the room—always. All the exercise in the world could bring me peace and strength, but deep down inside, I did not believe in my own self-worth. I could not envision a guy "digging" me.

I talked with Deborah in therapy many times about my belief I would never find someone who would even want to go out on one date with me. She assured me that she had absolute confidence I would have plenty of opportunities to date when I was ready. I had zero confidence in her confidence.

I could write a separate book about my dating escapades! The title would be *You're Not Going to Believe This*. I would choose this title because this is what I said every time I reported back to my friend Lynn about a recent dating disaster.

I met some interesting men—that's for sure. I also met some great men. However, several themes emerged during this time that proved troubling. First of all, my lack of self-esteem wreaked havoc on my ability to logically decide whom to date. Quite simply, if a man showed interest in me, I would go out with him. I always felt beyond flattered if a guy found me attractive or interesting, not believing that could ever be the case. I did not feel worthy of anything. Thus, I would accept the invitation, and then I would let the relationship go on much longer than it should have.

I also had very poor boundaries in relationships. During childhood and beyond, I received the express message that I could be used for someone else's pleasure. My boundaries were whatever someone else told me they should be. I had no gauge to determine what my boundaries should be. This lesson took me many years to learn.

A terrible effect of my lack of boundaries, which I have difficulty discussing here, is that I made some very poor, hurtful decisions. It would be easy for me to skip this part, but I am determined to share my story with honesty and integrity. As a result of my low self-esteem and muddled boundaries, I would be with anyone who wanted me. When I say *be with,* I do not mean *sleep with.* I had sex with very few people in my life, but I would date, kiss, and fool around with almost anyone who seemed interested. Never was it about who or what *I* wanted. I had never experienced that, so I didn't even know what it was supposed to feel like. If a man were married and gave me attention, I would succumb. I had dissociated and compartmentalized my *whole* life. I would just be in the moment, surprised that this man wanted to be with me and believe I should just be grateful for his attention.

I look back now and feel disgusted by my actions. I am so much more whole and clear and strong that I cringe at the lack of insight I had. If I could go back, I would change it all, and I would apologize from the depths of my heart and soul to anyone I hurt along the way. I do not feel that I deserve a "get out of jail free" card just because I was abused. **There is no excuse for hurting other people, just because you may have been injured yourself.**

I now understand the reasons I had such poor judgment. And I have changed. And I feel remorse and guilt. I lingered in that place for a very long time, and it punished my heart in ways I cannot describe. I like to think that I have moved beyond this, but I am truly shaking a bit as I write these words. So perhaps it is still there. At any rate, it is important that I share this part of myself to educate people about the long-lasting effects of sexual abuse. The abuse can be stopped, but the effects linger.

Sexual Reactions

It should be no surprise that I had difficulties when it came to sex. A trusted teacher had sexually abused me. How could I *not* be affected in that arena? I always called these difficulties my "leftovers." Truthfully, I am still affected to this day, and there is much work still to be done. I worked so hard on the emotional abuse I endured, but there was, and is, a body of work still left to be done, and I am just now, in my forties, ready to focus on this.

Here are a few examples of the ramifications, or *leftovers,* of all the sexual abuse. Tears. Lots and lots of tears. I could be intimate and be absolutely fine and in the moment, and then one touch the wrong way or a perceived strange look or an aggressive move, and I would be reduced to tears in seconds. I can literally count the number of times I have had intercourse and not cried. I also found that if I drank alcohol, I could relax so much more. So, I started relying on more than a few drinks if I knew I was going to be in a situation that would lead to sex.

I would have panic attacks when someone would try to perform oral sex on me. I would feel so fat, vulnerable, and disgusting that I would require the lights off at all times. With hatred toward my body that I could not shake, I would actually apologize as my clothes were being removed, feeling sorry for the person seeing my body. My poor body had been through so much, and then it had to endure this self-hatred that makes me really sad now to think about.

Sometimes I felt like my body had betrayed me. We were definitely not friends. It would take years of self-talk and hours of exercise to forge a truce between us. I am kinder to my body now, but the ugly left-overs rear their heads once in a while, and I have to remind them that there is a peace treaty that cannot be violated here! They whisper a bit, but they stay at bay more often than not now.

Move to Florida

During the year following my break away, I took two trips down to Florida to see my Disney program buddies. My wonderful friend Missy let me stay with her for as long as I'd like. I had a lot of vacation time accrued at work, so I went for two two-week trips to Orlando. I felt utterly at peace the moment I stepped off the plane. The weather was incredible, and every person I met seemed filled with warmth, kindness, and acceptance. I would go to the beach, sunbathe in Missy's yard, go to the Keys with Andrew, and just . . . be.

During my first visit, I decided to seize the opportunity to sunbathe in Missy's yard. Missy came out of the house with a chair to join me. She had a look on her face that I had seen several times before. Something important was going to come out of that mouth of hers! I sat up and braced myself.

She looked at me and simply said, "Why don't you move here?"

I asked her to repeat herself. Utterly flabbergasted, I explained to her that I couldn't move to Florida. *Who does that?* Most people from up north stayed up north. They often didn't even leave their hometowns! They generally married someone from the same town and raised a family and lived out their lives there. No, you just didn't leave New England. Plus, all my music was up there now. I had found a great circle of musician friends who were teaching me much about life and music.

Missy listened to me for a while. When she finally spoke again, she said, "Andrea, all I hear you say when you are up there is that you are constantly looking over your shoulder for Bob at every turn. He is still *with* you up there. You just seem so much more relaxed down here. Imagine how much you could move forward if you weren't worrying about him all the time? You can sing down here. We will find you new music friends and places. You feel safe here. You should move here."

She was right, of course.

God bless good friends who sometimes know what's better for you than you could possibly know for yourself.

I went home after that trip with my head spinning. *Can I really do this? How do I leave a place I've never considered leaving? How do I walk away from the Boston music scene that I love so much?* My cousin Kristin would be sad if I left. But the image of the beach, the Keys, the sun, and the absolute peace I felt began to overshadow my ties to Boston. Gradually, it became a no-brainer for me.

I went to therapy the following week and told Deborah about this new idea. She was taken aback. She listened to all the pros and cons I tossed around, and then I asked her what she thought.

She was quiet for a moment. Then she said, "You know if you were considering this a year ago right after you left Bob, I would have encouraged you to slow down and not make any big decisions like this. But a year has passed, and you seem to be settling into your life pretty well. I think it makes sense."

I hadn't expected to feel an ache in my heart when she said that. I suddenly realized how much I was going to miss her. She had been there—*really been there*—through so much. I had been working with her for almost five years. My gratitude for her help and kindness overwhelmed me.

I went back to Orlando about a month after my last session with Deborah in full planning mode. Would I really be living in a place where I could wear flip-flops all year long? How could anyone have problems while wearing flip-flops? This planning period became one of the most exciting times of my entire life. I truly felt free. I knew in my heart it was the right move to make. Everything fell into place.

One of my other Disney buddies, Paula, was moving there the same time and needed a roommate—perfect! She found a gorgeous apartment for next to nothing in rent, and she had all the furniture, which worked out wonderfully because I owned a lamp and that was about it. So I had a place to live. Now I needed to find a job.

Lakeside

One Sunday, following my decision to relocate to Florida, I sat in Harvard Square poring over a newspaper and still pretending to eat my bagel. I was able to look for job ads in a Florida newspaper. This was before the convenience of online career sites. In the midst of my browsing, I came upon a want ad for a mental health therapist at an agency called Lakeside Alternatives in Winter Park, Florida.

I called the number on the ad the next day and spoke with the director of the agency. I told him that I was moving down to Orlando in three weeks and that I was very interested in the position. We had a great conversation about Boston and Orlando and really seemed to hit it off. He seemed unfazed by the whole timing issue and told me to call him once I arrived in Orlando so we could set up an interview. Somehow, I felt very confident that this job would pan out. I had such clarity about this whole move.

I told my friends and family about all my big plans, and I received lots of support and understanding. My loved ones were sad to see me go, but they all knew that I needed this fresh, new start. I packed my blue Mitsubishi Precis and headed southbound on I-95. I was so eager to begin this new leg of my journey that I left at 6:30 AM, stopped at 11:00 PM that night, left the next morning at 6:00 AM, and arrived at my new apartment at 2:00 PM. That drive was fantastic. I sang the whole way, and I teared up a bit as well, overwhelmed by the sensation of freedom and possibility that increased with every mile I traveled.

This was my life! I claimed it. I was moving to Florida. I wondered what new adventures were waiting for me, and knew that, no matter what I encountered, I would be able to handle it. I was so grateful to be free, and I said quiet prayers of gratitude when I crossed each new state line. Okay, they weren't *quiet* prayers. I would see a new sign saying, "Welcome to Virginia!" And I would shout, "Woo-hoo! Hello, Virginia!" I couldn't contain my excitement.

I called the director of the mental health agency the day after I arrived. I experienced a brief sense of disquiet that perhaps he would have forgotten our conversation, but he answered the phone as warmly as ever. We set up an interview for that week.

I felt relatively relaxed during that interview, knowing in my heart that this was how my life was supposed to unfold and this was the job I was supposed to have. Rarely have I had such clarity, before or since. It was as if someone else were leading me by the hand to all of this saying, "You have been through enough, my dear. Let me handle this." I really felt that God was walking with me in a loud and obvious way, like it was my reward for surviving, and I graciously accepted His help.

The interview went great, and I began my new job the following Monday. I met some fantastic coworkers and got to help lots of people. My new life had officially begun, and I felt great, never looking over my shoulder for Bob. *Why would he be in Florida? He didn't know where I worked or lived or ate.* It was very peaceful for me. This was when I really began to let go of him and move forward.

Andrew's Role in My Life

Andrew was one of the biggest cheerleaders in my life, and one of my biggest supporters as I tried to break away from Bob. Since Andrew now lived in Florida, he was thrilled that we could finally have a real dating relationship free from any obstacles or distractions. Unfortunately, I did not feel the same level of excitement about jumping right into another serious relationship so soon after my move. I had just received the biggest gift of my life—my freedom.

I explained to Andrew that, although I did care about him and wanted to date him, I wanted to experience life and all it had to offer. This meant I needed time alone, time to date other people, and time to heal. Something inside me knew that this time in my life was precious, and I needed to honor it.

I felt so pleased that I could listen to my heart and declare what I needed, especially knowing that he was not going to be happy with my decision. I felt like I was passing some sort of test to make sure I was living this new free life of mine correctly.

Andrew had a difficult time understanding this. He tried to be patient with me as always. He had done absolutely nothing wrong—he was a fantastic person who only showed me kindness and love, and I did my best to make sure he knew that.

We dated for a while, but I was always honest with him about all the happenings in my life, which included dating escapades. Andrew thought he could handle hearing these stories, but everyone has a breaking point. His abundant well of patience dried up, and we parted ways.

We left on good, friendly, loving terms, but it was sad for both of us. A few years later, we ran into each other at the gym. We spent a few hours catching up and decided that we had too solid a friendship to not be in each other's lives. We forged a friendship that is still strong to this day. I will forever be grateful for Andrew's role in my life, and I am proud to call him one of my greatest friends.

More Friends

I realized while working at Lakeside that I was meeting many enjoyable people. I found it strange how easily I could form real friendships. What a contrast from my childhood days when I felt like I hadn't a friend in the world! I also started realizing that people enjoyed being around me. It wasn't just that I met extraordinary people; I had something to do with this, too. *Maybe I'm actually a cool person to get to know. Maybe I have something to offer other people.*

My self-esteem had taken such a hit for so many years that I had always attributed people befriending me or dating me to a kind gesture on their part. Now that my life was clear of Bob's control and abuse, I felt like the dust had settled and I could evaluate myself more honestly.

One of the things I found was that I kind of liked myself! I was good at making friends, and I made them feel comfortable and safe. My wonderful friend Jenn says that I am like a safe place to land. I like that! Gradually, my self-worth started to increase.

I constantly noticed and evaluated the lessons I was learning and the growth that would take place. I also found myself getting angrier with Bob as my awareness grew. I saw what he had stolen from me. I could feel the self-hatred he helped implant in my brain, but the angrier I became with him, the kinder I became with myself, and the more gratitude I had for a second chance.

Key West Trips

My friends and I made a half dozen trips to Key West in the span of four years. These trips were more fun than I thought could be had. We would pile into one or two cars and drive eight hours to get to the southernmost point of the states. We stayed in a bungalow in the less-than-glamorous quarter of Key West and were happy as could be. Roosters would walk the streets and wake us up each morning with their loud calls. We would stroll around the island during the day, visiting Ernest Hemmingway's house, eating sandwich wraps, and sunbathing. At night, we would drink, dance, laugh, and people watch.

Each Keys trip, we would all swear we were going to move there for a summer, and, of course, we would return to our lives and forget all about it.

A very powerful event occurred during one of our Key West adventures, which occurred on my thirtieth birthday. I decided that since my birthday fell on December 30, there was no better way to bring in a new decade than to celebrate it with my friends in Key West.

New Year's Eve festivities were in full swing. We were dancing at a bar and having the best of times, and I had a giant smile on my face. Suddenly I froze.

I went into the bathroom because I wanted to get a good look at what I looked like right then, smile and all. And it hit me: I looked exactly like the vision I had had back in sixth grade as I sat in my mom's car, contemplating suicide. That vision showed me an older version of me (I had even guessed that I was around thirty at the time), and I looked happy and healthy with lots of people around me.

Here I was, exactly thirty years old, laughing and smiling, as happy as can be, surrounded by lots of people who cared about me. I cannot find the right words to describe the feeling I had as I looked in that mirror. It was powerful and comforting. I said a silent prayer of thanks and went back out to the dance floor.

Exercise

In my twenties and thirties, I fell in love with several types of exercise. Exercise became a key piece of the healing puzzle for me. It made me feel strong, both physically and mentally. I did not feel like a victim. It also helped my self-esteem. When I was in a good routine of doing some form of exercise daily, I didn't feel fat. I started believing the motto "strong is the new skinny." I started accepting my body for what it was, and tried to strengthen it in a healthy, non-obsessive way.

Several forms of exercise found their way into my life. I began roller blading quite a bit, and it gave me a huge sense of freedom. I could skate for hours and let my mind roll with me. I took aerobics classes and fell in love with swimming laps.

Swimming is by far my favorite form of exercise. Besides the obvious benefits of working so many muscle groups and getting the cardio going, it is a very spiritual exercise for me. The water and breathing rhythm become hypnotic. I count the laps one by one, and the world can sort of melt away. I feel like I can solve the problems of the universe in one swim.

When I was about thirty-three, I was reading a magazine article about running. I had never been able to run a half-mile in my life, but the article stated that anyone could "learn" to run if they approached it the right way. This caught my attention, so I kept reading. The article explained that if you take small jog breaks, like fifteen to thirty seconds every few minutes during a walk, you can learn to run. I knew that I could jog for thirty seconds, no problem.

So, the next time I was walking, I tried it. I felt pretty dumb, but I discovered that it was a nice change. What started out as a 15-second jog break during my walks evolved into jogging for several minutes at a time. I felt surprised and proud to find that I did, indeed, enjoy running after all! If you are curious about this method, please visit www .jeffgalloway.com. It is the best website for safely learning to jog.

Running was another way I began to redefine myself and come to terms with my body. I always saw runners as amazing people who could accomplish things that were outside the realm of the possible for me. As I became a slow walk/jogger, my confidence increased a great deal. I was doing something I had never considered possible. My body also became stronger, and my self-hatred for certain body parts began to release its grip. I started to look in the mirror and not cringe. Rarely would I love what I saw, but I didn't avoid the mirrors. It was also nice to be able to run in a moderate way. I was not working out three times a day, and I wasn't running as fast a pace as possible. I was a healthy runner.

As I entered my forties, I thought the next logical event to add to my fitness repertoire would be triathlons. I had no idea I had the potential to be so goal-oriented until I trained for my first Olympic-distance triathlon.

My brother Ronnie called me up one January morning and told me that he was competing in an Olympic distance triathlon in Miami in

March, and that I should compete, too! At first I laughed at his suggestion. I hadn't really been on a bike since I was twenty years old, and the race was about ten weeks away. Just to clarify, the three stages for an Olympic Triathlon are a 1.2-mile swim in open water, a 25-mile bike ride, and 6-mile run—all in one day! We hung up the phone, and that same old voice inside me that knew what I really wanted to do came rushing into my head.

I called my friend Jillian, an amazing swim and triathlon coach. I asked her if it would be possible for me to train for a race like this in just ten weeks.

Her silence following my question worried me, as it was unfamiliar; anything is possible to Jillian. Finally she said, "This will be tough, but if you follow the training I set out for you, I think you can do it." Jillian created a detailed yet manageable training plan for me, and I followed it religiously.

The event itself was amazing—and the toughest physical thing I have ever done, so of course it was also the most worthwhile. As I approached the finish line, I thought that no one in that crowd could know what this meant to me. I was alive! I was strong enough to train for something like this. I had been so depressed and abused and had thought I was incapable of the smallest of things. That I could complete this challenge far surpassed even my highest estimation of my own potential. I crossed that finish line with pride, love, and gratitude.

I finished the race in 3 hours and 40 minutes—twenty minutes before the cut-off mark. Throughout the whole race I kept thinking about all the things I had overcome in my life, and how somehow, in my forties, I was tougher and stronger than I ever dreamed I could be. I was drawn to triathlons from that point on, more for the training than for the races themselves. Triathlons represent overcoming obstacles for me. Bring it on!

Joe

While working at Lakeside, I met Joe. Joe worked as a therapist at the access center for Lakeside. We became friends, and we would go out and play darts or pool together. He would show up to my performances to hear me sing, and we often had a lot of deep conversations about life and spirituality. Joe had had a tough childhood in some ways, so we would share and compare our stories. I felt like he really understood me.

We came together on a level of shared pain, and he seemed very kind and compassionate. He held this place of safety for me, which allowed me to tell him anything.

After a few months of building our friendship, we took a trip to Key West with two other friends. Key West was its usual blast, but all the while I wondered if Joe had romantic feelings for me, as mine were growing fast for him.

We drove back to Orlando and dropped off our two friends. On the way back to Joe's apartment, I couldn't take the tension anymore. I felt safe enough with him to blurt out, "So, do you like me or what?"

His jaw dropped, and he replied, "Yup."

I laughed, and he joined in. We both opened up about how we had been feeling throughout the journey of our friendship.

Joe and I dated for about eight months, and, although everything seemed wonderful, I became fixated on the length of our relationship, unsure of why it was so important to me. I was unused to an open relationship, and it felt strange to me. Basically, my relationship with Bob was all I had to compare this relationship to.

Joe was calm and quiet. He didn't raise his voice. We had fun together. These were qualities I had never truly experienced with Bob.

One of the criteria I developed for choosing a husband was that he would be a good labor coach. I thought that if a man could be a good labor coach, he would make a great life partner. Joe had the qualities of a good labor coach—reassuring, calm, and strong—so I had set my mind on marrying him early on.

After the first eight months, Joe began working two additional jobs. He became stressed out and was often tired. Because of the limited time, we started doing fewer activities together, and he was less patient than he had been in the beginning of our relationship. I always tried to be understanding, as I knew that his working so much meant that he needed to unwind at the end of the day. Plus, I had already made up my mind that Joe was the man I would marry. *Who else would be out there for me, anyway?*

Joe and I had so much in common on a spiritual level and shared common childhood issues, and we seemed to approach life similarly and with like-minded beliefs. I rationalized that he wouldn't always be working three jobs; this was temporary, and life would become easier for him and for us as a couple.

As time passed, all of his jobs and his stress remained. We would still have fun and enjoy time with friends here and there, but our differences were becoming more apparent. I was (and am) a very outgoing, talkative person. I love people, so I needed to be around them. A true extrovert, I drew my energy from being around others. But Joe was the complete opposite. He recharged his batteries by being alone and retreating into himself. We foolishly thought, back then, that we could bring out the other side of each other. I did not "like" the part of me that talked too much, and I thought it would be good to be a quieter person. So I believed that Joe could help quiet me down. He believed I could bring the extrovert out in him and help him to enjoy being with people more.

We had different communication styles at our cores. We went on a couple's retreat one weekend, and we learned the metaphor of the turtle and the hailstorm—the dynamic that we, and many others, engaged in for communication. The more I needed him to communicate, the more I would "hail down" on him, talking more and more, and the more I hailed, the more he would retreat like a turtle inside his shell. I needed to stop hailing, and he needed to poke his head out. We worked on these dynamics for years.

A New Life

I went through an annoying phase in which all I focused on was getting married and having kids. Many of my friends were getting engaged and married. During my time with Bob, I never thought I would have the opportunity to have a normal wedding or raise a family. Truthfully, I never believed I would live long enough. However, once I was in a stable relationship with Joe, I became fixated on weddings and babies. It took Joe some time to be sure he was ready to handle these new responsibilities.

After we attended that couples' retreat, Joe felt more confident that we could overcome any of our relationship difficulties. We flew up to Connecticut one weekend and stayed at his parents' home. His family was celebrating his mom's birthday and watching Notre Dame football. It was a beautiful New England autumn weekend. Joe and I went for a drive to the beach near the house. We got out of the car and strolled out onto the shore. He walked me to a large log and sat me down. He started telling me that he loved me and thought I was a great person, and he thought I would be a great mother someday. He got down on one knee and held out a ring. I was so surprised and delighted. I hugged him, and we kissed. After a few moments, we headed back to the car.

I started calling friends and family from the car to tell them the great news. We returned to his parents' house and told his family. Everyone cheered and celebrated. It was a beautiful and memorable day. I was really going to be able to participate in something that I had always believed was reserved for anyone but me. I felt so grateful that my memory of Bob would keep moving further and further into the background.

Once we were engaged, Joe decided to pursue his doctorate degree in psychology, which I fully supported. He was very smart, and I knew he could go far with such a degree. He researched schools, but he was coming up short finding a suitable one in Florida. He stumbled upon a school in New Hampshire and seemed determined to enroll there. I could never quite understand this—with all the schools available in Florida, why would New Hampshire even be an option? But again, as had become habit for me, I didn't question him.

The more Joe researched, the more excited he became about this school. The more he talked about it, the more anxious I became, until I started to feel slight panic whenever he brought it up. *Was he actually thinking of moving up there? Would I have to go, too?*

Despite my fears, I was determined to support him. He flew up to New Hampshire for an interview, and I wished him luck with a big smile. Later, when I was alone, I cried tears of anxiety and stress. Nothing inside me wanted to leave this beautiful place I called home. I felt so safe and had the most amazing friends and life in place. I did not feel like I had the right to tell him my true feelings about potentially moving to New Hampshire. **I felt myself revert back to the behavior of my Bob days, where I acted as if I had no right to express my true feelings. Without any other frame of reference, I was confused about what partners in a loving relationship do to support each other.**

Joe returned from his interview, brimming with excitement. I asked lots of questions about the program. We started discussing the logistics of moving. My heart sank more every day. This was a five-year program.

I worked myself up to tell Joe how I felt about leaving Florida. It took a while, but I got the words out. I diplomatically stated that I was happy for him to pursue his dream and wanted to be as supportive as possible. However, I reminded him that I had left New England for a reason, and Florida was now my home, and I felt safe there. Joe reassured me that if I would go with him and support him through the program, we would move right back to Orlando and never move again if I didn't want to. I took solace in his words and decided to support him full force. This was his turn to find a better future, and I would be there for him.

I threw Joe a big surprise party when he got his acceptance letter. This event was bittersweet for me, but I refused to show it. When people asked how I felt about moving, I would list all the positive reasons for the move while ignoring the gnawing in my heart. We were going to be married, and marriage was all about compromise, I thought.

Joe and I packed up our belongings and said our good-byes to all our dear friends. This felt much more painful than moving to Orlando four years earlier. We drove up north and moved in with Joe's parents for the first year. Our wedding was planned for that following summer in July 2000. That year was challenging in ways I can't even begin to describe, but I focused on my new career and on this big wedding we were planning.

Our wedding fulfilled every wish I had for that momentous event. I walked down the aisle alone, as I had chosen not to invite my father to the wedding. A few relatives expressed their displeasure over this decision, and it was one of the first times in my life that other people being upset with me didn't affect me. I had no expectations they would understand my decision. I felt entitled to feel safe at my own wedding. Walking down the aisle alone felt right.

Although I felt sure about my decision to marry Joe, not everyone in my life felt so sure about it. Years later, I learned that many of my friends had concerns, and some of them had tried to share them with me prior to the wedding. However, without realizing it, I wasn't at all open to their cautionary advice. I was getting married, and that's all there was to it. I got so caught up in the wedding preparations that I didn't think about the actual marriage.

My friend Missy actually shared her concern with me as a last-ditch effort as she was doing my makeup for the wedding. She stopped and looked at me with her "I have something big to say" expression. I knew that expression, so I braced myself.

"You know," she said, "you don't have to go through with this if you are unsure at all. It's not too late."

I replied assuredly, "I wish you guys knew Joe like I know him. You just see this other side of him where he is quiet and doesn't socialize that much. I see him at home, and he is different. He just gets stressed out from school a lot. Once he gets his degree, things will be much better, you'll see. Don't worry!"

It never occurred to me that it was a negative thing that my friends couldn't see the good sides of Joe. I spent years making excuses for him. I didn't see any of the problems others saw. He was so much better for me than Bob, so what else could there be to consider?

Career Transition

Around the time that Joe and I got married, my career path took a turn. Since 1992, I had been a clinical social worker, which was a noble career that I loved and continued to grow in. However, there was not much money to be earned in this career. Joe was about to dive in to full-time student status for five years, and we knew that two people surviving on a social worker's salary was not going to be the best scenario. I started considering careers that could generate a greater income.

A few of my colleagues talked about pharmaceutical sales as a great career choice. I looked into it, and it seemed amazing: great salaries, high bonuses, company cars, and working out in the field all day. This career was clinically focused, too, and I had always loved science and biology. I also felt that I would be able to communicate well with the physicians. So the week after Joe and I moved up to Connecticut, I applied for a position with a few different companies. I interviewed with two companies and landed a position with Abbott Laboratories. I was extremely excited to start this new venture.

I quickly learned that this job was nothing like I had expected. All of the training I received, which was about a month's worth, had little to do with what happened in those doctors' offices. This field had become inundated with pharmaceutical reps. I would get to a doctor's office at 10 AM, and I would be the tenth rep they had already seen that morning, and the doctors had no time to chat. There was so much pressure to get signatures from them for the drug samples I was leaving that I felt like a monkey could have done my job. When I did get a chance to speak with a doctor, I felt so intimidated and nervous that I would just ask how his kids were doing, get his signature, and bolt out of there.

I kept waiting for my nervousness to let up so that I could start enjoying my new job. The money was great and all the perks were a huge plus, but they couldn't make me feel happy or fulfilled. I started becoming anxious and depressed as the months passed. When I shared with Joe about how unhappy I felt in my career, he couldn't understand where I was coming from. He kept telling me, "Just hang in there for a few years. When I am done with this program, you won't have to do this anymore."

So I pressed on. I dreaded having my managers ride with me to doctors' offices because they would watch everything I said and did and took notes. After the sales call, they would review the list of everything I did wrong and write it all down in a report.

Honestly, I could not name a single quality about this career that I enjoyed. I desperately missed having a core group of coworkers whom I saw every day. I hated feeling like a "nudge," begging to see the doctor for twenty seconds just to get his or her signature. At times, I played the role of a glorified caterer, bringing in lunch for thirty people, just to get two minutes of time with a couple of doctors. Often they would scarf down their lunch, thank me, and be on their way.

I found myself waiting for Joe to release me from this way of life. It did not occur to me that I could put my foot down and say, "I'm not happy, Joe. This isn't working. We need to find a way together to make this work because it is important for me to enjoy my career." I reverted to my old ways with Bob, waiting to be rescued. I waited for Joe to give me permission to be happy or free. Although I was now an adult, I still had the mind-set of a controlled child who did what she was told.

I worked in pharmaceutical sales for a total of seven years with three different companies. Each time I would change companies or get a new manager, I would pray that I could find a way to enjoy this lucrative career. Each time, the joy eluded me. This was just not a job that was well suited for me or I for it. After seven years, I finally discovered an opportunity to work as an admissions representative at a university. I gladly accepted the position, was able to leave the pharmaceutical industry, and never looked back. Although it took me a while, I finally rescued myself again.

Tae Kwon Do

During our marriage, Joe started taking Tae Kwon Do classes. I watched him practice and take belt tests, and I felt envious. I had always wanted to study some type of martial art. When he started his classes, I was in the middle of a training program to run my first marathon. I decided that when the marathon was over, I would join his classes. And that's exactly what I did.

I fell in love with Tae Kwon Do. I loved everything about it—learning the forms, sparring, conditioning . . . it was the most empowering sport I had experienced. It felt really good to learn how to protect and defend myself, and I enjoyed taking the classes with Joe.

Unfortunately, we realized that our funds were a bit low, and we really couldn't afford both of us taking classes. Obtaining his black belt had been one of Joe's lifelong dreams, and I couldn't imagine depriving him of this goal, so I stepped away and cheered him on.

Inside, however, I resented it. I started to feel that I was continuing to make compromises and sacrifices for this marriage, but I couldn't seem to find the equality in the compromises on Joe's end. This was a confusing time for me, and I constantly struggled with the topic of "fairness." *Was it fair of me to need these things? Did I have the right to complain? How do I stand up for myself and make sure my needs get met? Are my needs reasonable?* All these questions puzzled me and caused me a great deal of angst.

Puppet Strings

So here I was: Working successfully, albeit miserably, in a great career. I was married and maintaining an active lifestyle. And, best of all, I was free from the "Bob chains," as I would call them. Referring to those chains as "puppet strings" would have been more apropos, however.

I was living what some might define as a picture-perfect life. The abuse had ended, the strings had been cut, and I no longer had to answer to Bob. I was no longer subjected to cruel, abusive treatment, and I was no longer living in fear. So why did I still feel unhappy?

I didn't know why I didn't feel a core sense of happiness. I would enjoy myself and the company of others, and I felt so much gratitude for this newfound freedom, but deep inside, I didn't feel the way I thought I should be feeling. I could not name it, but after all these years, I still felt the effects of Bob's abuse.

Here is the visual I would have: I had been a puppet for so long, and the strings had finally been cut, but I felt like I was walking around trying to get a grip on life, and the strings would drag behind me and get caught on things. I would walk forward, and I would get tugged back and stuck a bit. Some of the strings that would snag were things like an inability to make good decisions, problems establishing personal boundaries, issues with sexual anxiety, and an inability to stand up for myself. They would be constant reminders of the work that I still had left to do.

I would get so frustrated with myself. I kept feeling like I should be done with all the "healing crap"! *How long was it going to take? Would I ever feel whole? Just how much had Bob stolen from me, on top of my innocence and self-worth?*

Avoiding Sex

During my marriage, I consciously tried to avoid sex. I did not realize to what extent at the time. The intimacy between Joe and me had been declining through the years. I was feeling unhappy with work, and I also felt a bit resentful that he had insisted I keep working in a career that I had practically begged him to let me leave.

Joe clearly had issues of his own, and they were manifesting physically. He began to gain weight and drink more heavily. I enabled his drinking because I found that when he drank, he was more enjoyable to be around. He could tolerate my need to talk so much better. He was more patient and seemed to be able to roll with life's punches better when he was drinking. So I didn't discourage him. In fact, I would buy him a six-pack whenever I could, and I would also pick up some drinks for myself if I thought we were going to be fooling around that night to numb myself a bit before being intimate.

My anxiety gradually increased at even the thought of having sex. A complex combination of factors contributed to my avoidance. I always blamed myself completely for this problem. We didn't discuss it, and it made me so sad because when we first started dating, he had seemed so safe to me. I had thought I could work through a lot of my sexual difficulties with him. Now here I was, "grinning and bearing it," just muscling my way through sex, hoping I wouldn't hurt his feelings if he knew the truth.

Shame

Part of the problem with sex for me was all the shame I felt. I felt shame about my body. It was not just a modesty issue of being uncomfortable naked, either. It was shame, as if something was so wrong with my body that people might get angry if they saw it. I honestly felt like I could offend people with my naked body. When you feel this level of shame, just how sexy can you feel? I'd say not very much.

I mentioned earlier that I felt I was reborn when I left Bob, and that I marked my age by my niece Sarah's age. By the time I was married and having these troubles with my sexuality, Sarah was about six years old. When I started to see my "reborn self" this way, my anxieties made more sense to me. **I had no normal developmental period for growing up sexually. I had been abused for so long. Healing rarely takes place on our own timetable.** So although, on the surface, everything looked fine, on the inside, I was barely beyond childhood, still trying to learn how to walk through life. I operated like an awkward teenager who was supposed to be a fully functioning sexual being, and I wasn't even close to it.

I really needed a partner with whom I felt safe and secure. I thought Joe could be that partner for me, but I was wrong. I can say wholeheartedly that Joe had no bad intentions at all with me, and he wanted the same things I wanted. We just moved in different directions, and we dealt with our struggles in contrasting manners.

FOR YOU, THE READER
CONSIDER THIS . . .

I learned that starting over involved exploring exciting new experiences, as well as rediscovering dark truths about myself and how I operated in the world. The first six years away from Bob were the most exciting times of my life. However, as much as I tried to cast aside all of the Bob madness, I soon realized that pieces of my trauma remained no matter how much I moved on. The damage Bob had caused had fractured my self-worth and self-esteem. With a troubled marriage and a determined heart, I trudged along, wondering what was in store for me in my life without Bob. Little did I know that there was another battle waiting for me, and it would put to the test all the progress I had made.

For all readers . . .

- Why do you think mundane tasks were like big celebrations for me after I first left Bob?

- Do you think I could have experienced this time in my life any differently?

- How were my dating behaviors impacted by my experiences with Bob?

- What does it really mean to start over? What must be released? What must be accepted?

- What fears hold you back from beginning a new chapter in your life?

- Do you know people who constantly complain about being miserable, yet never seem to take the leap and start anew? Are you one of those people? If so, what prevents you from letting go of the things or people causing your distress or unhappiness?

- Can other things and people really make us unhappy? Is it more about how we choose to respond to these things and people?

- How do you know when you are ready to start over?

As a survivor . . .

- What changes occurred once the abuse stopped?

- Are there any "puppet strings" in your life that need to be addressed?

- Now that the abuse is over, do you focus on the past abuse or the freedom of the present?

- How can you acknowledge that you survived the abuse and are moving on?

I think most of us have "started over" at one time or another. Sometimes it's by choice; other times it's by necessity. In all cases, starting over is such an incredible opportunity to learn from and let go of the past and create the type of brilliant present and future that we all deserve.

CHAPTER 9

Pressing Send

◀◯▶

Deep into my marriage with Joe, I found myself realizing how much everything Bob had put me through still affected me, and I wondered what it would take to finally be rid of his influence over my life. I had moved, gotten married, and started a new career, and yet here I was still unsettled, which went much deeper than the surface things I thought weren't bringing me happiness. I wasn't sure what was missing or what I needed to do, but I knew in my heart that my work definitely wasn't finished.

A few pivotal moments and conversations, which I share in this chapter, began to heighten my awareness of the work that remained for me to do. This awareness progressed gradually, but once I realized what needed to unfold, I could not turn my back on the path that lay ahead.

Teacher Busted

One day while visiting with my sister-in-law, Cheryl, she informed me of a disturbing incident that had occurred at her husband's job at a prep school in Orlando. A well-respected teacher had been arrested for sexually abusing a student. Her husband liked the guy and was shocked that his colleague was capable of committing such a crime. This obviously brought up many issues and uncomfortable feelings for me, and Cheryl was sympathetic and kind, knowing many of the details of my abuse. I posed a question that would turn out to be a pivotal one in thrusting me forward in my quest for peace.

"Did the girl get in trouble for being with the teacher?" I asked.

Cheryl looked at me like I had five heads. "Why on earth would *she* be in trouble?" she asked.

I shook my head in disbelief that those words had actually come out of my mouth. I realized in that moment that I still carried around a sense of responsibility for what Bob had done to me. He had brainwashed me into fully believing I was as culpable as he was for the abuse.

Cheryl and I talked for a long time that day about how Bob reminded me over and over that it was my responsibility to protect his secret. I thought about this young girl who unfortunately had to go through so much with someone she was supposed to trust and admire.

This conversation with Cheryl gave me a new perspective on Bob's abuse and the lingering beliefs in my mind that I had not yet called out as false and unjustified.

Lifetime Movie

Another event that propelled me toward the work that was ahead of me was a movie I watched on the Lifetime channel. It was a true story about a high school student who was sexually abused by a coach. I watched the movie by myself one evening, and I cried the entire time. Shaking at the thought of it all, I was surprised by how many feelings and thoughts got triggered inside me.

This coach used grooming and controlling techniques that were all too familiar to me. The girl had the same conflicted feelings I had, and it was so clear to me how helpless she was in the situation. She had been taught to look up to the coach because he was a teacher and mentor, and he completely took advantage of that trust for his own gain and pleasure.

Then, the movie took a turn I did not expect. The girl testified against the coach in court. I watched this scene, feeling as if I were right there in the courtroom. I could not imagine having the strength to stand up to my abuser the way she did. I was still protecting Bob, just as I had done in high school and beyond. *How could such a young girl have so much conviction at such a young age? Would I ever have that much strength?*

Dinner with Missy

A few months after watching the Lifetime movie, I had dinner with my friend, Missy. As usual, we talked about everything under the sun, and the conversation got around to Bob. She asked lots of questions like she always did, and I answered them one by one, like I always did. Then she got that inquisitive look, yet again—and asked me the big question, the one that really stuck with me.

"Is Bob still teaching?" she asked.

I simply replied, "Yeah, I think so. Why?"

She continued, "Do you think he would ever do this again to someone else?"

I paused for a moment before replying. "No, he's not that stupid. This went on for so long, and when I left, it destroyed him. He wouldn't go through that again."

Missy just sort of looked at me and then out the window. We transitioned to one of our other dozen topics for the evening, finished up our dinner, and I made my way home.

The following week, I felt uneasy. Missy's words kept ringing in my head: *Is he still teaching? What if he did this again?*

I couldn't shake these thoughts. I argued with myself day and night that week. *There was no way he would do that again.* But the thought that wrestled with all that rationalization was, *What if . . ? What if he did something again? What if some poor girl was the victim of his wrath, and I never told anyone?*

This thought quickly overpowered the other, rationalizing ones. Once I was fixated on this concern, I couldn't sleep at night. I tossed and turned. By the end of that month, I knew I had to do something. I could not sit on this information, knowing that there was even a remote possibility that he could abuse someone else, but I was filled with fear. In my mind, Bob had been this scary, unpredictable, abusive man who was capable of much harm.

What would I open myself up to if I reported him? If he found out, I would surely be dead. My mind raced with all sorts of dangers and repercussions, but the thought of someone else enduring what I endured was much more oppressive. I was an adult. I could make choices. I had an ability to put things in place to prevent Bob from harming me.

But if another young girl were under his controlling clutches, she would have nothing to defend herself against him. The choice felt like it had been made for me.

I had to do something.

Call to the Principal

Joe and I decided that the best thing for me to do was to try to contact the principal of the junior high school where Bob was teaching. I wasn't sure about contacting police because of the possible statute of limitations. I thought I could start with the school system, hoping that they would handle it from there.

Through several phone calls and emails, I finally got in touch with Mr. C. He had been the principal of the school when I was there all those years ago. It turned out that he had just retired that past summer, but I was still able to get his phone number.

The anxiety that threatened to overwhelm me prior to my call to him was indescribable; nothing could cure it. I was practically dripping with sweat. I hardly believed what I was about to do. I didn't know if I was ready for all the unknowns that lay ahead of me. **The only thing that drove me to pick up that phone was fear—fear that some other child may be suffering the same abuses I had suffered. That fear brought the realization that I might be the only one to stop it from happening again.**

I retreated into my home office and closed the door. I needed to do this alone. I knew Joe was right on the other side of the door, but something in me knew I was the only one who could fight this fight. I stared at the phone number on the sticky note for a long time, and I said a little prayer. "Please protect me, God. Please let this be the right thing to do."

I picked up the phone and punched in the numbers. I took a very long, deep breath, closed my eyes, and pressed "Send." I wanted to cry. I wanted to hang up. I wanted to run away. With each ring, my frightful feelings intensified. Then, the ringing stopped and a deep voice answered.

"Hello?"

In an instant, I experienced the strangest shift in emotions. It was as if someone else took over for me. I explained to Mr. C that I was calling to report abuse by one of his teachers from many years ago. I told him that the teacher was currently still working in this school, and that I didn't know where else to turn, so I wanted to tell him. I just wanted to make sure no one else got hurt.

He listened intently and then asked who I was. I paused and then replied, "I'm not sure if you remember me, but this is Andrea Cieri." My last name had been changed to Clemens, but I thought he might remember me by my maiden name.

"Of course I remember you, Andrea," he said. He paused before continuing. "It was Bob Baker, wasn't it?"

I stopped short. He sounded so sure that it was Bob. "How did you know that?" I asked, dumbfounded.

"Well, he spent a lot of time with you," he responded. "I mean, he spent a lot of time with a lot of kids, but you seemed pretty special to him. Oh my God, did he seriously abuse you?"

"Yeah, he did, and it went on for years."

He proceeded to ask me a lot of questions, ranging from where the abuse took place, when it started, and when it ended. I told him that Bob would give me rides from school, and he sounded very surprised to hear that. We talked for about thirty minutes. I asked him what he was going to do with the information. He asked me what I wanted him to do.

What did I want him to do?

Honestly, I wanted him to go kick Bob's ass! But I told him he needed to do what he thought was appropriate to keep the kids safe. I told him this wasn't about me; it was about the students who deserve to be safe and protected in school.

Mr. C told me that he was going to tell the new superintendent and that they would take care of it from there. I told him that anyone was welcome to call me if they needed any information or assistance.

When we hung up, I sat there for a while. I did it. *Again.* I broke through my fears and did what I needed to do. I felt strongly that the school would investigate this situation and would call me with anything they needed. I felt strong and prepared enough to handle whatever Bob threw my way.

Voicemail

After I made the call to Mr. C, I went about my life, feeling pretty satisfied. I was proud of myself for taking a leap of courage and telling the school about Bob. I felt my part was done. I would let the school do what it is supposed to do to protect their students.

Eight months after the call, I received a voicemail that changed my life: "Andrea, this is Peter, and I'm a detective from the Norwood Police Department."

My heart raced. *I'm in BIG trouble,* I immediately thought. My mind raced so much that I couldn't focus on the rest of the message. I listened to the message five times. It went something like this:

"Andrea, this is Peter from the Norwood Police Department. I am currently conducting an investigation on someone, and we think that you could have information pertaining to this case. Would you please call me as soon as you get this message."

I sat in shock. *The police are contacting me?!* I still had a fear that I had done something wrong and that I was being called out for it. After all those years of therapy and healing, I still felt I could be held accountable for what Bob had put me through.

I did not call Peter back immediately. I talked with Joe about the message, feeling like a complete wreck. Joe couldn't quite understand why I was so anxious. *Hadn't I made the call eight months earlier? Wasn't I prepared for this?*

What I was prepared for was for the school to take over and my part would be short and hopefully painless. The fact that the police were now involved shook me to my core, and it somehow woke me up to just how severe the abuse I suffered was. I had minimized the level of horror that had been done to me. I was aware of the terrible effects the abuse had on me, but I never really put two and two together that it was, in fact, a horrendous crime. A crime had been committed against me—one that would affect me for decades.

It took me twenty-four hours to call Peter back. I vacillated between wanting to vomit and wanting to run and hide. I never really considered the possibility of not returning his call, of course. I knew this had to be done. I just didn't want to be the one to do it! **All those years of wanting to be rescued, and, in the end, I was the only one who could rescue myself.**

"It's not about me."

When the time came to make the call, I sat on the couch with my phone, a pad of paper, a pen, and Joe's hand in mine. Joe and I had been having our difficulties, but he was so supportive though all this mess. I will always be grateful to him for patiently supporting my process of healing and confrontation.

I took a few deep breaths and dialed Peter's number. My body showed every possible physical symptom of anxiety. Here I was again, ready to press "Send." I never expected to revisit that feeling, yet I knew that my whole life was about to change—yet again. I looked at Joe, he nodded, and I pressed "Send."

The phone rang twice, and Peter answered. When I identified myself, Peter let out a huge sigh of relief.

"Andrea! Oh thank God! I was so afraid we wouldn't be able to find you!"

Thank God? Was he grateful for something? My mind couldn't quite comprehend this. I hesitantly asked him what was going on, resistant to put everything out there to him without hearing from him whether I was in trouble.

Peter said, "Andrea, we are investigating a case and think you could help us a great deal with this. Are you aware of a Robert Baker?"

I looked at Joe and then closed my eyes. "Yes" was all I could say.

"Well," Peter continued, "he is in our custody right now, and we heard that you have information that could help put him in jail."

Coming a bit unraveled and not fully comprehending, I asked, "Under arrest? But I haven't even given a statement or anything. You haven't even spoken to me yet!"

Peter said, "No. He is under arrest for statutory rape of two fourteen-year-old girls."

Have you ever seen *The Matrix*? If so, you know the scenes where a person is in the middle of an awesome karate move, practically flying in the air, and everything freezes for a few seconds before the move is completed. That's exactly what happened to my world when I heard the words "two fourteen-year-old girls."

I stopped breathing, seeing, hearing . . . being. My mind could not process this information.

After what seemed like a very long time, I came to my senses with Peter on the other end of the phone saying, "Andrea? Hello?"

I reassured the officer I was still there, and I looked over at Joe. "It's not about me," I whispered.

A wave of overwhelming relief washed over me. Until that moment, I didn't realize just how concerned I had been on a deeply subconscious level that I was "in a lot of trouble." However, as Peter continued to recount the details of the case, the relief began to change shape.

Peter said the school contacted the police just that week. A girl had reported to a school counselor that two of her friends had been molested by Bob. *Two girls had been molested.* The school *just* called the police. I tried to piece this together. I asked Peter twice to repeat exactly when the school had contacted him. He patiently explained himself as many times as I needed him to.

I had been mostly listening until this point, but now I asked him, "Did you know that I went to the school eight months ago and told them about Bob?"

Peter replied, "We never heard from them until this week. Once they reported the allegation, they told us that someone came forward a few months ago and mentioned something about him as well. That's how I got your name and number."

Peter said that the school brought Bob in and informed him of my allegations. Bob denied them, of course, and that was it. They did nothing with the information. They did not notify the police. I don't know what I expected them to do exactly. I guess I just hoped they would fire him on their own and everyone would be safe. Peter wasn't concerned at that moment about what the school did or did not do. He had a tough case on his hands, and he needed my help.

I was ready for the cause. He asked if I would be willing to travel to Massachusetts to give them a statement. I agreed. Peter thanked me several times, and we settled upon a date, time, and location for the statement.

I hung up the phone and stared across the room. Joe watched me quietly. That relief I had felt was gone. Now, I felt sick, guilty, and responsible.

How could I have been so naïve as to think that Bob would never do this again? Why had it taken me so long to come forward? How could I be so selfish and self-absorbed to not protect the other kids out there? Two girls' lives were forever damaged and changed because I was silent. How could I be so thoughtless? What if I came forward right when I left him? Could I have prevented this?

I asked myself questions like that for hours. Joe tried to reassure me that I *did* come forward—when I was ready. The school had done nothing that had made a difference. That was not my fault. Joe tried to console me, but to no avail. Nothing could convince me that I was not at least partially responsible for what those girls went through. This fueled me to do whatever it took to make sure Bob served jail time.

My Statement

A week or so after the call with Peter, Joe and I found ourselves driving to Mansfield, Massachusetts, to meet with Peter and another detective at the home of one of the detectives. They asked me some open-ended questions to get me started. I began to tell them everything, starting with what happened in eighth grade. I told them as much as I could, as accurately as possible. Disclosing the truth to them felt empowering. I felt like I was finally doing the right thing.

Periodically, one of the detectives would look at the other and just shake his head. I would look over at Joe from time to time while I was speaking, and he usually had his head down, deep in thought. I felt bad that he had to hear these dark details, many of which I hadn't really talked about with him. I am sure it was difficult and painful for my husband to hear just how much abuse I suffered.

When I felt I had caught the detectives up on all the relevant information and events, Peter asked me more specific questions, including one that actually surprised me. He wanted to know if I could name any identifying marks on Bob's body.

I gave him a puzzled look. *Is he doubting my story?* I wondered, feeling defensive.

Peter astutely clarified his question, explaining that asking certain questions was standard procedure when taking statements such as mine.

So I began to search my memory for visuals of Bob's body. As I did so, I felt my anxiety level rising. Until that question, I had felt fine, telling the stories I had told lots of people many times. No one had asked me anything remotely like this before, and I had cleverly blocked out most thoughts and images of Bob's body. Now I was accessing part of my memory that was most unpleasant.

I struggled with an answer, and then I began to panic. I worried that they wouldn't believe me because I was struggling so hard to remember. The panic made me panic even more! Joe helped me calm down a bit, and I eventually slowed my breathing.

I closed my eyes and reminded myself that I was safe. I was not a child. I was an adult, and I was trying to help these girls. These girls needed me to pull it together. Finally, I remembered something about Bob's body. He had a large appendix scar, which he used to show off to me with pride.

When I told them, the detectives smiled at each other. This must have been an important piece of information for my statement.

They also asked me intimate, embarrassing questions, like if he had ever forced me to engage in phone sex or if he ever made me name parts of my body like my breasts.

As the questions came at me, more details surfaced. I realized that the more specific I could be with them, the greater the likelihood Bob would go to jail. I mentioned that he often said to me, "I could bury you." They told me that a phrase like that could possibly lift the statute of limitations. I also found myself explaining why it never really dawned on me until recently to come forward.

When we were finishing up my statement, I asked why they kept looking at each other and shaking their heads. They told me that the details I provided: the gifts he gave, the places he took me, the threats he made . . . they were identical to what the girls had experienced.

That was a tough one for me to take in. *How could he be so stupid and even lack resourcefulness?* Twenty years later, and he was pulling the same maneuvers, only he seemed to get worse and more daring. He ended up kissing one of the girls in her own house, in her bedroom, when her parents weren't home. She was fourteen years old at the time, and he was in his fifties.

The detectives told me that Veritas and Anastasia, the two girls, were friends. What was interesting to me was the fact that, apparently, neither of the girls had come forward to disclose the abuse to authorities. Veritas and Anastasia had told their mutual friend what was going on, and this friend came forward and disclosed the abuse to a guidance counselor. This was another indicator to me that there were similarities in our stories; I never would have disclosed the abuse to the authorities either.

As it was explained to me, Veritas and Anastasia would both go to Bob's house and hang out to watch TV and play video games. He would take one of them upstairs while the other stayed downstairs. This continued for months. Veritas seemed to grow strong feelings for him, yet she was also very feisty and wouldn't succumb quite so easily to his controlling maneuvers. She would defy him, doing things like hanging up on him and fighting with him.

Bob apparently had been dating another teacher at the time as well. Veritas would call up this woman's house and hang up on her. She felt like Bob was cheating on her. She did report that his anger frightened her a great deal, and that his anger was the reason she started to back away from him by the end of tenth grade. As she backed away, Bob started to move in on Anastasia more. It wasn't clear if he did this to get Veritas jealous or not. Anastasia did not seem to have the same kind of feelings for Bob as Veritas did. It also wasn't clear how much the two girls were communicating with each other. He made them music tapes. He gave them presents. He took them to the same Friendly's restaurant he had taken me. He threatened to kill himself if anyone found out about what was going on.

Listening to the detectives describe the statements given by the girls felt surreal. I could not fully process everything I heard. I was surprised to discover that a part of me felt hurt that Bob was carrying on "relationships" with other girls; this was a feeling I had no idea existed for me.

Although I knew in my heart that this man had abused me and how terribly wrong it was, there was still a part of me—that young innocent girl inside me, not the adult I had grown into—that had felt as if I were a special case. Bob had been able to lure me in at such a young age because he made me feel *visible,* as if I mattered to someone. What transpired was crazy, but he had me convinced that it was only because I was *so* special to him. I had truly believed him when he said he had never felt that way before and that he would never feel that way again. *I must be extraordinarily special to make him act in ways that were so foreign to him,* I had thought as a young girl.

Now, listening to all the similarities twenty years later with two teenagers, it was clear that Bob was just an ordinary pedophile.

Anger, outrage, pain, and betrayal all mingled inside me. That man was my teacher and mentor. He was a father figure and friend. I gladly handed over my trust to him, and he twisted it and turned it into his toy.

The pain I felt for these girls was immense. I couldn't imagine how they were feeling.

Peter told me, "Now, the girls are not really happy that you exist, Andrea."

This confused me a bit at first. How could they not be glad that I was going to back them up? I could potentially prevent this whole mess from going to trial.

Peter said, "They both felt that they were special to Baker."

I loved how he referred to Bob by his last name.

He continued, "They wouldn't believe me at first when I said someone else had come forward from twenty years ago. When I started sharing some of your details, they broke down crying."

Then I understood all too well. The hurt I felt was only a fraction of the level they were experiencing. It brought me back to the days when I truly believed I was in love with that man and would do anything to protect him. If anyone had tried to break us up, I would have fought to the death. I lived with conflicting feelings all the time. Even though I wanted to leave him at times, I was always protective of him and his job. And again, he made me feel special. I can't imagine how I would have felt as a junior in high school if some woman came forward saying that Bob had done the same things to her.

These poor girls were so mixed up, and I felt my heart breaking for them.

The other mind-shifting part of this experience for me was the detectives' impressions of Bob. They said that everyone at the station referred to him as "the worm." They viewed him as a wimpy, mealy guy. His house looked disturbing with outdated furniture, and he had a room full of Beanie Babies.

The detective informed me that when they arrived at his house, Bob had been welcoming. He told them he had been expecting them and willingly showed them around. He showed them notes Veritas had written him, "love tapes" she had made him, and so on. He painted a picture that he was the victim in this mess. He said the two girls would just show up at his house. He acknowledged that they would go upstairs to play video games, and that demonstrated some poor judgment on his part, but he absolutely denied he had any sexual contact with either of them.

The detectives shared with me that they seized his computer and the notes and tapes, and then they took Bob into custody.

I can picture his face as this was all going down, and, in his mind, he probably did not believe he did anything wrong. I'm sure he believed his own lies, and I cannot begin to imagine the rage he felt toward Veritas and Anastasia.

As our meeting concluded, the detectives thanked me several times for sharing my story with them. I asked that they please keep me posted on the proceedings. They assured me they would stay in touch with me and let me know of any court dates.

We all shook hands and drove our separate ways. The entire way home I replayed every single sentence the detectives had spoken. It took me a long time to process this information, as well as all of the feelings bubbling inside me. *Was my work done now?* I had spilled my guts to those detectives, and I felt depleted. I wasn't sure what lay ahead for me, but I knew deep down that it wasn't over.

In the Media

The day after I spoke with Peter, word spread about Bob's arrest. Segments were being run on local news stations, and articles were being printed in various local newspapers. I found it difficult to believe that I was actually reading about Bob in the paper and even more so when I saw him on television.

That was the first time I had seen his face since the night I ended things. He looked older and furious. The camera showed him being arraigned in court, his hands cuffed in front of him, looking downward, shaking his head and snarling his lips. I began to shake and sweat at the sight of him. I felt a combination of anxiety and anger. I had the hardest time looking at his face, realizing that he had violated two young girls. My stomach turned and my head grew dizzy. This was all too surreal for me to comprehend.

When the newspaper articles first ran, there seemed to be a spin on the story. The articles were written in a tone that favored Bob. They discussed his colleagues' shock and sadness, emphasizing how well liked he was by students and teachers alike, and how he had such a clean record for thirty-one years. It was a reminder to me for years to come to not believe everything I read.

Here is one of the first articles that was published in *The Daily News* transcript:

School Staff Express Dismay over Colleague's Arrest on Rape Charges

Mar 14, 2002 @ 07:00 PM

WALTHAM–NORWOOD—Acting Superintendent Ed Quigley said teachers and administration were "shocked and saddened" yesterday by the arrest of Norwood Junior High School science teacher Robert Baker.

Baker was arrested Wednesday by Walpole police and charged with six counts of statutory rape and seven accounts of indecent assault and battery on a person over 14. He pleaded innocent to the charges yesterday at his arraignment.

Quigley said he first learned of the serious allegation against Baker Tuesday afternoon and promptly granted Baker an administrative leave of absence, which Quigley said is standard practice.

Quigley said Baker is on leave with pay, but that discussions will be ongoing with the teachers association as to whether that status will continue.

Parents will receive a letter today explaining the situation, Quigley said.

"We want parents to know their children are safe," said Quigley. "And that there are people working swiftly on this, so that we can put it behind us."

Due to the nature of the ongoing investigation, Quigley said he could not offer many details, but he did acknowledge that a student told a school counselor about alleged incidents on Monday.

"It worked its way up the chain of command to me," said Quigley, who then contacted Norwood Police.

Quigley said the allegations were serious enough to put Baker on administrative leave as of Tuesday.

"I knew this was something that had to be checked into further," said Quigley, who said it was standard practice to get the teacher out of the classroom immediately and deal with details later.

"It is an allegation at this point, and we certainly hope things work out for the best," said Quigley. "But the safety of our students is the primary concern."

Baker is a veteran educator who has been teaching for 31 years, his attorney said yesterday. He also coaches several sports, is well-liked by his colleagues and has a good reputation.

John Quinn, president of the Norwood Teachers Association, attended Baker's arraignment yesterday.

"I've met him before. He's a very mild-mannered person," Quinn said. "He's a well-liked teacher. Everybody's shocked."

Quinn said teachers were not discussing the issue.

"We don't talk about it," he said.

Thomas Guiney is one of Baker's defense attorneys and also is outside counsel to the Massachusetts Teachers Association. Yesterday he said Baker has no prior disciplinary items on his record. A few teachers went to see Baker Wednesday night at the Walpole police station after he had been taken into custody following his arrest.

In his experience as an attorney for teachers, he has seen similar circumstances in the past.

"It's becoming a real threat to the profession," Guiney said of such allegations. "In this climate today, teachers are really at risk. Students know they can take a teacher down by making allegations. I'm not saying that's what's happening here but it has happened in my experience."

Quigley said crisis teams have been put in place at the junior high and throughout the school system to help students deal with the situation.

Furthermore, Quigley said a substitute with a science background has been placed in Baker's classroom, and will remain there for as long as it takes to resolve the situation.

As acting superintendent since August, Quigley said he only knows Baker on a professional level, but that the 31-year teacher has enjoyed a good reputation among colleagues and students.

"He was very well liked by students, and he got along well with his colleagues," said Quigley. "We were all totally shocked."

Reporter Jennifer Kovalich contributed to this report.

* * *

Reading this article admittedly got me unhinged. Did Guiney really state "It's becoming a real threat to the profession," and that "teachers are at risk"? I felt concerned that because of Bob's strong reputation and clean record, he might be cleared of all wrongdoing.

Several articles were published, however, that announced a third former student (me) had come forward, exposing Bob for the perpetrator he was. They also got into more detail about the accusation against him.

Third Student Accuses Teacher Norwood Case Seen Expanding
[Third Edition]

Publication: *Boston Globe—Boston, Mass.*
Author: *John Ellement, Globe Staff, and Ray Henry,*
   Globe Correspondent

Date: Mar 15, 2002

NORWOOD—As a Norwood Junior High teacher pleaded not guilty yesterday to statutory rape charges involving a 14-year-old student and charges he sexually assaulted her underage friend, a prosecutor confirmed that a third former student has come forward with allegations of sexual misconduct against the 53-year-old educator.

Norfolk Assistant District Attorney Lisa Beatty said the third former student, who is now an adult, contacted Norwood police Wednesday night after seeing news reports of Robert L. Baker's arrest in Walpole, where he lives. In Norwood, where Baker has worked in the town's school system for 31 years, police said they expect more allegations against the teacher.

[Robert L. Jubinville] said that Baker has never been charged with any other crime and that he has never been disciplined by the Norwood School Department during his career. He said Baker, who is divorced and has no children, wants to bring the case to a trial so he can clear his name.

The next morning, [Edward P. Quigley] met with Baker and suspended him with pay until the investigation is complete, a move Quigley took before Baker could return to the classroom, he said. Baker will remain on the payroll but out of the classroom until the case is resolved, Quigley said.

* * *

I felt both unnerved and yet empowered reading about myself. It was interesting to me that they reported my coming forward to the police after I had heard the news about Bob. Nowhere was it mentioned that I had gone to the school eight months prior to any charges.

The following article described more details about the nature of his encounters with the girls:

Former Norwood Teacher to Be Arraigned Next Week

Posted Jun 03, 2002 @ 08:00 PM

WALTHAM–DEDHAM—A science teacher at the Norwood Junior High South will be arraigned next week in Norfolk Superior Court on charges of rape and sexual assault.

Robert Baker, a 31-year biology teacher, now on administrative leave, was indicted last week by a Norfolk County grand jury on four counts of rape of a child and two counts of indecent assault and battery on a person over the age of 14.

Baker, 53, of Walpole, pleaded innocent to the charges at his March arraignment in Wrentham District Court where he was released on $2,000 cash bail. At Norwood Junior High South he also coached several sports.

Baker, who taught eighth-grade science, was arrested after school officials learned of the allegations a student made to a school counselor. The case involves former students of Baker. Police said at the time of the alleged offenses, the girls had graduated from the eighth grade and were heading into their freshman year of high school.

After his arraignment in district court, his attorney had said Baker denied any sexual activity and said his client repeatedly said he used "bad judgment" in having the girls over to his apartment at 35 Burnes Ave., East Walpole.

Lisa Beatty, the prosecutor, earlier said one of the girls started calling Baker after she took his class and fell in love with him. She and her friend used to visit with him after he picked them up at a park around the corner from his house, she said.

Police recovered cards one of the girls and Baker had exchanged as well as tapes of love songs one of the girls had made for him. Police also seized a personal computer from his home. Police said he and one girl used to e-mail each other with Baker using a handle of "L6WWI2" which he told police was made up of his middle initial and some of his favorite numbers. Beatty said police learned the letters were code for "I want you. I wuv you, immensely squared" Á or "I love you immensely."

The assistant district attorney also said Baker threatened to throw himself in front of a train if anyone discovered his relationship with the first victim.

Baker is also accused of inappropriately touching the second victim, whom he also kissed after a tennis match in the summer of 2000, Beatty said.

* * *

The fact that Bob acknowledged showing repeated bad judgment in having the girls over to his apartment gave me a greater sense of hope that justice would be served. It was also strange and eerie to read his handle, "L6WWI2." We always used the term "immensely squared" when describing how much we had loved each other.

The following is an excerpt from an article that was more sensationalized and racy than others:

Pupil Reports Affair With Norwood Instructor

Publication: *The Boston Herald*

March 15, 2002

A well-liked Norwood Junior High biology teacher carried on a torrid three-year affair with a former student that started when she was 14, authorities said yesterday.

"He told her that if she ever told anybody about the relationship he would kill himself and it would be her fault," prosecutor Lisa Beatty said of 53-year-old Robert "Mr. B" Baker.

The divorced Baker would drive the teen and her friend to his Walpole bachelor pad, where he had sexual trysts with the girl in his bedroom while her friend waited downstairs, authorities said. Baker, a teacher and coach for 31 years, has been put on administrative leave.

Baker touched the girl's breasts, . . .

* * *

It's difficult to describe the feeling of reading about myself in the newspaper. Something that had been a secret for so many years was now exposed for the world to see. There was something very liberating about this. As shaken as I was reading the paper or watching the news, I was also keenly aware that I felt strong in my stance. I was ready for whatever was about to unfold.

Baby Time

There was a very exciting reprieve during all this drama. Joe and I had decided that we were ready to bring a baby into our little family equation. The thought of being a mother was daunting and exciting. I wasn't quite sure I would be ready to deal with pregnancy while all of the legal issues were in play. However, I figured that it would take me a while to become pregnant, so I felt it was a safe time to give it a shot.

Two months later, on Father's Day, I quietly went into the bathroom at 6:00 AM and took a pregnancy test. When that second line showed up, my heart filled with a kind of joy I had never experienced before. I slipped out of our apartment, went to the store, and bought a card for Joe. A few hours later, Joe woke up, and I handed him the card.

He looked at it with a puzzled expression and asked, "Happy Father's Day?"

I just smiled.

His eyes flew open wide and said, "You're pregnant?!"

I just grinned and nodded.

He said, "Man that was fast."

I'm not sure if he was slightly disappointed that we weren't going to get to "try getting pregnant" any longer. However, we were both thrilled to enter this new phase of our marriage, and we eagerly awaited the birth of our son.

Court

Several months after giving my statement, I received a call that Bob was accepting a plea bargain. The court date was set for September 27, 2002.

I was told that I was allowed to attend the court hearing, but since this case involved Veritas and Anastasia, I would not be able to speak to Bob or give an impact statement. I was both relieved and disappointed. I really couldn't believe that Bob had accepted a plea bargain, and I was eager to find out the details. But I would have to wait until September 27 to find out.

Joe and I drove to Massachusetts again to the Norfolk courthouse. My cousins Kristin and Donna were meeting us there, and I was so happy to have their support. It felt important to have some family members by my side. My anxiety was pretty high that day, which surprised no one. I think Joe and my cousins were anxious as well. I didn't know if I was going to see Bob walking around the courthouse. I didn't know if I would bump into one of the girls or if I would even know who they were.

Prior to entering the courtroom, the district attorney approached me, asking me if I were Andrea Clemens. I just nodded, not sure of what was to follow. He extended his hand and thanked me. "Andrea, you don't know how psyched we all were that you got involved. We were really going to have a tough time getting this guy. He kept claiming he was innocent until I walked in and told him you had stepped forward and told us everything. He just put his head down on the table and gave up. It's the only way we got a plea bargain out of him."

I started to respond, but he interrupted me.

"Now, the girls aren't too keen on you being here, I just want to warn you. They're pretty upset about this whole thing, but after the sentencing, we're all going to get a chance to gather in the family meeting room and discuss what has happened. Sound good?"

And before I could respond, he was off. I just stood there thinking about everything he just told me. I couldn't picture Bob hanging his head in defeat. I just couldn't. He was this big intimidating guy, but everything these men had been telling me said otherwise.

I couldn't imagine what went on in his head when he learned that I was cooperating with the police—*that I had told them everything.* I have to admit it was both unnerving and empowering.

Bury this, Bob! I let out a little chuckle at that thought. But, there I was, looking over my shoulder just like old times. I kept expecting to see his face around a corner. But he was nowhere to be found. I had no desire to see him but wanted to be prepared if I had to.

Seeing the Girls

When it was time to enter the courtroom. Joe, Kristin, Donna, and I slowly followed many others into the large room. To my surprise, many people were already inside. I tried hard to take a mental picture of all the small details. I was completely overwhelmed. It was hard to believe that I was in a courtroom about to watch Bob get sentenced. I thought back to my sexual abuse group. I had made such a fuss about my fellow therapy group member testifying against her perpetrator, thinking I would never, ever have the strength to do that. I smiled proudly. Here I was, being thanked by a district attorney for helping to put Bob behind bars. How did all this turn around? **It just goes to show that you should never underestimate your ability to grow and change. You may not be able to accomplish something in a particular moment, but it absolutely does not mean you are doomed to remain at that level.**

The attorneys led us to a row near the back of the room. I do remember one detail: the window next to me was cracked open, and someone was mowing the lawn outside. I was so frustrated because I knew that would make it difficult for me to hear. Once we got settled in, I looked around again at my surroundings. In the row right in front of me sat Veritas and Anastasia. My heart started racing when I realized who they were. They were sitting with their parents, and they had tissues in hand and were crying. My brief feeling of victory and growth melted away at the sight of them.

These girls looked so young. It hit me that we all sort of looked alike. We all had straight brown hair and brown eyes. I nudged Joe and my cousins and sort of tilted my head toward the girls. They all nodded as if to say, "Yeah, we scoped them out already."

I kept staring at them, thinking how young they looked. Neither of them had graduated from high school yet, and they had already gone through so much turmoil. Then it hit me. *Oh my God. That's how young I was!*

I sat with that feeling for a few minutes. Until that very moment, I had continued to carry some level of responsibility for Bob's abuse of me. It had been ingrained in my mind from the start. But once I saw those kids, I placed complete responsibility on Bob. This was a shocking moment for me, really. I had kept telling myself that it wasn't my fault, and most of me believed it. But clearly not all of me was listening or buying it because I could not stop looking at them, thinking about how young they looked.

I had been that young. I had been that young when Bob told me he was in love with me. I had been that young when he was having sex with me when I was too afraid to say no. "I was that young" rang over and over in my head. What a new perspective I got in an instant. The only thing that pushed that thought out of the way was, *Why didn't I think about coming forward sooner?* I kept shaking my head, wondering where my mind had been all these years. Why did it take me so damn long to wake up and realize that, of course, he would do something like that again?

I was deep in thought when I felt Joe poke my arm. I looked up, and Bob was entering the courtroom. My heart raced yet again. I saw everyone in the room turn to look at him. I would love to say that I felt strong and sat up straight and tried to get him to look me in the eye, but that's not how I felt. I wanted to feel that way, but I didn't. Honestly, I felt myself shudder and turn my head away slightly. I'm not sure why. His presence in that room felt so powerful to me. I had not seen him in nearly eleven years. He walked in with his eyes straight ahead, and he was not in control of a thing. He looked old, and he didn't look as scary as I remembered. He was just an ugly, old, guilty man walking toward his doom.

His lawyers sat him down at a table in front of the judge. His handcuffs were removed; he took off his glasses and stared down at the table. The judge was talking quietly with some staff up at the bench. The judge called Bob up to his desk. Bob put his glasses back on and approached the judge. The judge must have asked him if he was taking any medication because Bob started pulling out pill bottle after pill bottle. He seemed to be naming the medications he was taking, rolling his eyes the whole time that he was explaining them, as if to say, "Look at what these girls are putting me through."

This was my first glimpse at his attitude toward his court appearance. I could tell that he was still claiming to be the victim in all of the drama. As I watched Bob, I looked to the other side of the room to see if anyone was there from Bob's circle of friends or family. I leaned over and spotted his brother, Jimmy. He looked like he had aged so much since the last time I saw him. He was looking down, and he looked so sad. No one else was there for Bob. This brought me great satisfaction. He had to face this on his own.

Impact Statements

As I mentioned, it was very difficult for me to hear with that lawn mower blasting right outside the window. The judge started reading some documents, but I could not hear what he was saying. He instructed Bob on some things that again, I could not hear. It never occurred to me that I could shut the window. Perhaps some things don't change. This was yet another reminder to me that I wasn't always able to advocate for myself or get what I needed. I just followed the rules.

Any time the judge spoke to Bob, Bob would put on his glasses and answer politely. When the judge finished addressing him, Bob would remove his glasses and look back down. Bob had terrible vision without his glasses. I think it was his way of having some control. He refused to look at anything he wasn't forced to look at in that room.

The judge offered an opportunity for the girls to come forward and read their impact statements. They started crying again and asked their parents to speak for them. Their parents went up to the front of the room. Veritas's mother was the first to speak. She was blasting "Mr. Baker" for breaking/betraying their trust and stealing their daughter's innocence. I have included, with permission from Veritas's mother, the impact statement.

My daughter is the victim of a horrendous crime. I stand before you today to express my feelings toward the accused.

I have always had what I considered to be a good life. I am married and the mother of two children and two stepchildren. When my children were born, my life became complete and there was nothing in the world I wouldn't do to help them or protect them.

When I learned of this crime and horrific action against my daughter, I was shocked and sickened. This type of crime did not happen to my family. I was a stay-at-home Mom, working just part time once the children entered junior high school so I could ensure I would always be there for them. Little did I know that junior high school would be a significant turning point in my sweet daughter's life.

Your Honor, Robert Baker used his position as my daughter's eighth grade science teacher to control and manipulate her. Over a period of time, he slowly gained her trust, and after he was confident he had gained that trust, he jumped at the opportunity to take advantage of a young, impressionable teenage girl.

He was so sly and conniving to keep control and power over her that when her grandmother passed away two-and-a-half years ago, he attended her memorial service. Let me say this, Mr. Baker, my mother would be heartbroken to know you did what you did to her darling granddaughter, and then for you to have the audacity to show up to her service looking like a nice, kind, and caring person.

Mr. Baker, there are more than two victims of your actions. We are all your victims. The girls, their families, your own family, your friends, your colleagues, your former students, and the teaching profession itself are all your victims. Think how many lives your selfish, despicable actions have touched and, in some cases, ruined.

I ask Your Honor that your sentencing of the defendant include a period of time to be spent incarcerated at a state facility along with an extensive probation period to follow. Due to Robert Baker's abuse of his authority as a teacher, I ask you not to allow Mr. Baker to ever teach again or work in the presence of people under the age of eighteen.

Mr. Baker, I want you to sit in a jail cell and think day in and day out about why you are there. I do not want you to ever to be able to hurt another person the rest of your life.

Thank you, Your Honor.

* * *

It broke my heart to hear this impact statement. I could hear the anger, pain, and betrayal in her words. However, I also felt validated, realizing again that I was a teenager who had been manipulated and abused. The weight of responsibility I had been feeling about the abuse was lifting in that courtroom. Veritas's mother's impact statement validated much of my experience with Bob. She was very strong to be able to read this in front of him. I am extremely grateful that she has allowed me to include her statement here.

Bob's Sentence

After the impact statements were read, the judge went through some formalities of making sure Bob knew all of the charges against him. The judge would read a charge and ask Bob if he understood. Bob would simply reply "yes." This went on for a while. The judge made a short statement to Bob about keeping the schools safe for our children. He sentenced Bob to two years in jail for two counts of indecent assault and battery on a person aged fourteen or older and four counts of rape and abuse of a child. Because he accepted a plea bargain, his sentence had been greatly reduced.

Two years.

Let that sink in for a moment.

Two years was less time that I went to therapy to help me leave him. Two years was less time than he spent with these girls. *Two years.* It made me sick.

However, along with the jail time came probation and registering as a level-three sex offender—the worst level. He also lost his pension and could never teach again. This pleased me most of all, I think. Though not impossible, it would at least be much harder for him to have access to his victims in the way he preferred and found most comfortable.

Handcuffs

Once the judge finished announcing the sentence, Bob was placed in handcuffs. I couldn't take my eyes off the handcuffs as he walked toward the back of the room. I knew in my heart that he had earned those handcuffs. I got a lump in my throat. Something about the handcuffs jolted me. I had no sympathy for him. I suddenly felt like screaming and crying at the top of my lungs. I had felt handcuffed for so many, many years. I felt as though I had restraints over my mouth, my hands, and my soul. It was intense to see his freedom stifled like this.

He was escorted out of the room, and I watched him more directly this time. I sat up a little bit straighter and looked right in his eyes. He didn't look back. I don't think he ever saw me that day. He looked straight ahead, his face expressionless.

As he passed, I felt a growing need to talk to him. It felt stronger with each step he made toward the door. I wanted to confront him and let out a giant scream. Multiple thoughts and emotions went through my mind. I thought about how he stole my innocence and the innocence of those two girls. I felt anger and betrayal, and I wanted him to know it. I heard the girls in front of me, sniffing and crying louder as he left the room. The moment carried a great charge, and I could feel it with every fiber of my being. In the end, I was able to refrain from any outburst because I just did not want Bob to have the satisfaction of evoking any reaction from me.

Meeting the Girls

After Bob left the courtroom, the DA invited me to head back to the conference room, where I would have the opportunity to meet the two girls. Joe, my cousins, and I followed the DA around the corner and down the hall. He opened the door, and the girls and their parents were sitting around a table. The girls were crying and would not look up at me at first. Both sets of parents smiled at me. I was suddenly a complete nervous wreck. I had no idea of what was about to occur or what I would say—to any of them. I hadn't prepared for this moment.

I had been consumed with what would happen inside the courtroom.

The DA explained that this would be a great opportunity for everyone to have a chance to express any thoughts about the case. He also stated that the girls were upset right now and may not feel up to speaking with me. I nodded, trying to show them all that I understood. The parents started speaking first. They were pretty emotional. I expected them to be angry with me. After all, I was aware that this man, capable of sexually abusing children, was still teaching, and I didn't stop it. As they began to speak, I watched them with a guarded look.

What they said took me by surprise. They thanked me. I was a bit flustered. *What were they thanking me for?* If I had only come forward sooner, perhaps their girls could have been saved. Instead, they expressed deep gratitude toward me. They felt that it took courage for me to come forward at all. They were convinced that had it not been for my statement, a trial would have been necessary. No one wanted to deal with a trial.

Next, it was my turn to speak. I took a deep breath and started. I addressed the girls first. I told them that I understood if they did not want to talk with me or look at me. I also told them that I was humbled and sat in admiration of their courage. Never could I have been truthful at their age and sat through a court proceeding the way they did.

I then spoke to the parents, and this is when I got choked up. I apologized. I told them how very sorry I was for not coming forward sooner. I understood their relief that no trial had to be conducted. But I insisted that if I had only realized the possibility of Bob repeating this abuse at an earlier time, perhaps the whole thing could have been avoided. I told them that it simply never dawned on me until recently that he would ever do such a thing again. I spent so many years of my life just trying to get away and then forget about him. The girls' parents were so supportive and understanding, and I couldn't understand why. They tried to comfort me, saying that I did whatever I could whenever I was ready. I was so grateful for their understanding and kind words. It was more than I felt I deserved.

The girls were given a chance to speak. Veritas just cried and looked down. Anastasia, through her tears, looked up at me and said, "We're just not ready to talk to you yet, but maybe soon we will be."

I smiled at them both and told them that I completely understood, and I wasn't sure if I would have wanted to talk to me if I were in their shoes either.

Veritas's mother then asked me if I would like to come back to their house for coffee. Of course I wanted to jump at the offer, but I looked at Veritas and said, "I would love to, but honestly, I don't want to make Veritas uncomfortable, and I can understand if she doesn't want me there."

Her mom looked at her, and Veritas shrugged her shoulders at first and then nodded with approval that I could come over. They gave me the address, and we were on our way.

When we arrived at Veritas's house, we sat in the dining room, and Veritas stayed in her room with the door open. As I engaged in some small talk with Veritas's parents, Veritas slowly made her way from her room, to the hallway, and finally to the living room. She sat on the couch and listened to what I had to say.

When it was time for me to leave, I asked for a piece of paper. I wrote down my phone number and email address. I walked over to Veritas and said, "This is for you. I can completely understand if you never want to see or hear from me again, so don't ever worry about that, but I want you to know something. I am the only one in this world that knows what you and Anastasia just went through with this man. If you ever change your mind and need to talk about any of it, get a hold of me, okay?"

She smiled slightly, took the piece of paper, and nodded her head. I was pleased by her response. I didn't know if I would ever hear from her, but that little grin and nod lightened my heart.

Joe and I got in the car and drove back to Connecticut. My mind went through a sort of movie-like process during the drive. I reflected on so much of what led up to this drive home. Things had come full circle. I also had a strong sense that something shifted in me that day. This was the work that had remained. And it was done.

FOR YOU, THE READER
CONSIDER THIS . . .

Now what? I thought. *What do I do with all of this?* One thing was certain: I was strong. I survived. I never needed to fear anyone. I knew how to speak the real truth, no matter how tough it seemed or what the possible consequences could be. Not all of my life was perfect, and there were still some loose ends hanging out there, but now I understood the process of tying strong knots.

For all readers . . .

- What dangers might arise in delaying a report of suspicions?

- Why do you think it took me so long to realize that Bob might have been abusing other students?

- What would have been the best first step for me to take when reporting his abuse?

- Why do you think the girls were so upset to learn about my involvement with Bob?

- Has a teacher ever made an inappropriate gesture toward you (i.e. prolonged touching, brushing against your chest)? If so, did you ever tell anyone?

- Is there a limit on what type of misconduct should be reported?

- What protocols and training should be in place at schools to address prior or current suspicions of abuse by an educator?

As a survivor. . .

- Did you ever report the abuse to anyone? If so, who did you tell? If not, why not?

- How can you ensure that this teacher never abuses another student?

There is risk and danger in not reporting inappropriate, abusive behavior by an educator. Tell someone in authority who has the power and jurisdiction to investigate the allegations and carry through on disciplinary action and police involvement.

CHAPTER 10

Closure

————◄○►————

Phases and stages, lessons and tests—life is comprised of all these things. I had found myself at a point in my life cycle surrounded by strength and awareness. The past had been put to rest, and the time to move forward had arrived.

I survived the day I never dreamed could possibly come. I sat in a courtroom and watched Bob get sentenced to jail time and be required to register as a sex offender. The courage and strength I needed to make it through that day came from years of pain, suffering, and, ultimately, the decision to survive and be free. I could not have arrived at this place of strength without the undying support and encouragement of those around me. I watched Bob walk out of that courtroom in handcuffs, knowing in my heart that I could conquer anything. There were still lingering issues in my life that needed attending to, but none felt insurmountable. I now had the skills and tools to deal with any obstacle in my life.

Relationship with the Girls

When we left Veritas's house the day of Bob's sentencing, I didn't expect to hear from her again. Although she had gifted me with that little grin, she also seemed hurt and angry with me. I understood her bitter stance, but I also hoped I could reach her and ease even a fraction of the pain she was enduring. We had had similar experiences with the same abuser. I felt a connection with Veritas and believed I could help her.

To my surprise, later that evening following court, I got a long email from Veritas. Shocked to see her name pop up on my computer, I hesitated before opening it. I had to brace myself for anything I was about to read. I expected an angry, teenage email blaming me for putting Bob behind bars. What I read was quite different.

She started out by apologizing to me for being so resistant to talking to me. She tried to explain why she was so upset, admitting that learning about my existence and my involvement with Bob, so long ago, rattled her. She felt hurt and betrayed that she was no longer "special." She also shared that if it weren't for her friend Janie, she and Anastasia would never have come forward with the truth. She felt that she was still in love with Bob. Although she had backed away from him, it pained her to see him get sent to jail, but on some level, she knew he was wrong. She told me she was extremely confused and upset, and asked if I would be willing to write back to her. She thanked me for listening to her and said she hoped to hear back from me soon.

I was dumbfounded. I read and reread that email dozens of times. It was as if my teenage self was face-to-face with my "post-Bob" self. She even worded things in a manner similar to how I would have.

I replied to her email almost immediately. I tried to validate everything she wrote. I reminded her that my own experiences with Bob made me one of very few people in the world who might truly understand what she and Anastasia had gone through. I also let her know that, although it probably sounded strange to her, I, too, had felt hurt and somehow less "special" when I learned that Bob had two other girls in his clutches. I told her that I didn't even know how to put those feelings in writing. I also told her that nothing would please me more than to continue corresponding with her.

I knew there was a possibility they could cry, yell, and even blame me, but I wanted to be open to hearing the girls' thoughts and feelings. I felt that if I could be there for them in any way, it would serve as a sort of penance for not speaking up sooner. I also could tell from Veritas's email that talking with the girls might help all three of us heal. It would be a healing that no amount of talking, singing, therapy sessions, group sessions, workout, triathlon, or magic wand could ever produce. I needed these girls as much as they needed me.

Veritas and I exchanged a few more emails over the next few days, and I looked forward to each one. I could see her opening up and trusting me. We connected on a deeper level with each email. Then Veritas asked me if I would be willing to meet up with her and Anastasia. I jumped at the opportunity immediately. We all agreed to meet at a restaurant in Dedham, Massachusetts. I was really excited to have an opportunity to sit down and listen to their stories. I was amazed to see events coming full circle like this.

I was not alone in this bizarre story. Two other people had shared in the pain and trauma. **When you find people who share a common tragedy or circumstance, knowing that someone understands what you've gone through can lessen the pain.** Even so, I can never release the regret that these two girls had to share in my pain because I didn't come forward sooner.

I arrived at the restaurant where we had agreed to meet to find that the girls were already sitting at a booth waiting for me. I took a deep breath and walked toward them, knowing this conversation could turn in many different directions. I silently prayed for strength to handle wherever it went. I greeted them in the warmest, friendliest way I could. They both stood up with nervous smiles and greeted me.

I immediately liked them both. I felt like I was sitting with two younger versions of myself. Once again, I was struck with the thought that we all looked alike. It was tough for me to focus on the conversation in the beginning, as I had so many thoughts popping in and out of my mind. I tried to shake myself out of my head and focus in on the girls. They needed me to be present for this.

The girls filled me in on how the whole situation with Bob began. Interestingly, they had both decided to call him "Kevin." They said that calling him "Mr. Baker" felt weird and "Bob" seemed creepy. They didn't disclose very much about the details of their involvement with Bob during this meeting. Instead, they asked lots of questions about my situation. I found myself opening up to them and watching their reactions.

They hung on my every word. When I noticed one of them starting to seem a bit overwhelmed with one of my stories, I would lighten up the conversation a bit. I was painfully aware of their still-fragile states of mind.

By the end of the conversation, we all felt so much closer. It was a completely different feeling from a week earlier, staring silently at each other in the court's family meeting room. We all agreed to stay in touch, and I encouraged them to call or email me with any thoughts or feelings that arose.

The three of us talked often and got together many times following that day in the restaurant. We gradually started talking about things other than Bob. I would hear their crazy dating tales and college escapades. I met their friends, their boyfriends, and their pets. We forged the most unexpected bond. I would often reflect back on that day in court so long ago when they could barely look at me. After a while, we rarely spoke about Bob—not because we were avoiding the subject, but because life marches on, and a whole slew of new stressors and adventures always present themselves.

Several years after that meeting in the restaurant, I received an envelope in the mail from Veritas. It contained what looked like a beautiful poem that she had typed up, and I wasn't quite sure why she was sending this to me. I read it, and a wave of emotion washed over me. Veritas was getting married. Her poem was asking me to be a bridesmaid, and she told me that she could never have been able to stand up at the altar and pledge her vows if it weren't for me.

I put down the letter and cried. The tears surprised me. I actually said to myself, out loud, "Talk about closure." I was going to be the oldest bridesmaid in history, but there was no way that I would miss that opportunity to be there for Veritas. Anastasia was her maid of honor, and it was an indescribable gift that I would be reunited with these two for such a special occasion.

It was a gorgeous wedding, and I was emotional the entire time. There is a picture of us bridesmaids watching Veritas say her vows, and the expression on my face in that photo sums up all of this. That something so tragic could unite the three of us in such a beautiful way still amazes me. **The possibility of beauty emerging from tragedy has been one of the greatest lessons life has ever taught me.**

I have changed both of the girls' names to protect their privacy. They both are fully aware that I have been writing this book, and I offered them the choice—use their real names or come up with a pseudonym. Veritas chose her name because it is Latin for the word "truth." Anastasia chose her name because it sounded cool!

Deborah

As I was driving home from Veritas's house after the hearing, I decided to call my former therapist, Deborah. When she answered the phone, I asked, "Guess where I just came from?"

She had no clue. I told her that I just watched Bob get sentenced to two years' jail time. I told her about meeting the girls and their reactions to me.

Deborah was rather quiet during the call, and I always wondered what she really thought about the whole thing. It felt wonderful, telling her about this great outcome after such a long and miserable journey. She deserved to hear the good things, too!

Later, I would find myself wondering if Deborah ever questioned her clinical approach with me. Should she have forced the point with me that Bob had, indeed, committed a crime? I would recall that first session with Deborah, where I had finished telling her about Bob and she had said that he did some things that were "inappropriate." Many questions would arise in my mind: Should she have reported him to DCF? Would she have lost me as a client if she did report him? I never considered anything of the sort back then. It took me years to realize that he was not just an abusive boyfriend; he was a sexual predator.

All I feel, as far as Deborah was concerned, is gratitude for a woman who hung in there with me through it all. She never gave up on me, no matter how frustrating my "paralysis" became. I do wonder, sometimes, how different things might have been if, in that first session, Deborah had said, "Andrea, Bob has committed a terrible crime against you. What's to stop him from doing it again to someone else?"

But I am a firm believer in things unfolding the way they are supposed to unfold. We are placed on this planet to learn the lessons life has to teach us and put them to use. It may take a lifetime to figure them out, but that is what we are meant to accomplish. I left Bob when I was able to leave him, and Deborah never left my side. We both learned from the experience.

I am forever grateful for Deborah.

Divorce

Once Bob was sentenced and the dust had settled a bit, I was able to focus on my marriage and the upcoming birth of my son. I could write two separate books on both of those topics, but I will have to settle for a few paragraphs for both.

On February 17, 2003, my son, Zachary, was born in the middle of one of the worst blizzards New England had seen in decades. At the time, I was afraid it was a sign of his personality to come! He was a gorgeous blond baby, and all seemingly went well.

Joe and I spent a while trying to adjust to this new family dynamic, but, as time went on, our differences became more apparent. Going through all the "Bob stuff," as I often called it, made me much stronger and clearer about who I was and what I needed. I eventually realized that I was still finding myself during my marriage, and the personal growth I should have undergone years before had been stunted while I remained under Bob's control. I started to become more direct with Joe about what was and was not okay with me. I was learning to establish my boundaries.

Joe became more distant and would simply "check out" of the relationship for long periods of time. He became less engaged with me as time progressed, and I drove him absolutely crazy with the amount of talking I could do. I had a very hard time stifling my comments, ideas, and processing things aloud, now that I had truly found my voice. I would try to time myself if we were driving somewhere. I would look at the clock and say, "Okay, I am going to wait five minutes before I say anything else. Then he won't be so overwhelmed."

We were just so different. All those amazing spiritual talks when we first met so long ago were obsolete now, and trying to navigate through life as a couple just wasn't working.

The agreement we had made before we left Orlando was that we would put in the five years up north Joe needed to get his degree, and then we would return to Florida and remain there forever. After Joe graduated from school, he changed his mind. He had no intention of returning to Florida. We had a child now, and he didn't want to have Zach participate in the Florida school system. It was true that Florida's public schools were rated forty-eighth in the country in terms of quality of education, but I was convinced we could find either a private school or some school district that could provide a good education for our son.

This was a huge struggle for us. I could not understand how the decision to move back was even optional, and Joe could not understand how he could be expected to leave New England and raise a child in Florida. Against Joe's will and better judgment, we moved back down to Florida in 2005. Joe and I had built up so many resentments through the years that we just couldn't seem to shake. We saw several different couples' therapists because we really wanted to make this marriage work, and nothing seemed to help. I got very down on myself, and I was left with the feeling that I was a complete failure.

We separated in October 2006. The separation and divorce were as tough as anyone would expect, but we always had Zachary's best interest in mind and managed to work out shared custody where we each had Zach for half the week. We still do Christmas mornings together with him and throw a joint birthday party for him every year.

After several years of adapting, Joe and I became pretty good at communicating with each other and co-parenting Zach. It took a lot of work, but it was worth it. It is unfortunate that Joe and I could not work through our core differences, as divorce was not something either of us imagined would ever happen to our relationship. In the end, I am glad we are able to communicate well so that Zach knows we are both on the same page and will always be there for him.

As time has passed, Joe and I have both come to realize just how different we are and how much happier we are living separately. I also realize that I spent most of our marriage waiting for permission to be myself. I did not take responsibility for my happiness—I put that responsibility on Joe's shoulders. Now I no longer leave my fate in anyone's hands. I have finally learned to create my own happiness, and if something isn't working, I am the one with the tools to fix it!

Single Mom

Raising Zach as a single mom was challenging, to say the least. Ask any single parent—there are struggles and obstacles you just cannot prepare for. But little by little, day by day, I found my way.

I discovered that certain issues that would arise would trigger reactions in me. I was overprotective—even neurotic—about so many things. I was hyper-vigilant about protecting Zach from being around strangers. I found that I looked back at my childhood and adolescence very differently once I became a mom. I will do anything to protect my child, and I would constantly question why I didn't receive that same protection. It's funny that, although I am comfortable enough now to write about all of this, I still struggle with some of these things. It amazes me how much I still carry with me.

One strange trigger for me is the idea of family dinner. To this day, I occasionally have to force myself to have dinner with Zach at the table. I am not proud of this, but there is a deep, ingrained aversion I have to dinnertime because of my father's raging outbursts at the table. I just don't like sitting down for dinner. Breakfast and lunch are no problem. But dinnertime comes, and I want it to be as casual and fun as can be. I have occasionally found myself serving Zach first before retreating to eat my dinner over by the sink. This is not how I want to raise Zach, so I have to push myself to remember that I have created a safe environment for him and can control what goes on in that environment. No one is going to be hurt in that environment.

I also found that, once Joe and I were apart, I became a much stronger parent. I could see things much more clearly without the cloud of a failing marriage in front of my eyes. I now only had to juggle temper tantrums of a then four-year-old. I became more and more confident in the decisions I made and the limits I set with Zach.

Through the years, I believe I have gained the most strength when I have had to fight my way out of tough situations on my own. I was no longer waiting for someone to rescue me in anything, including the whole single parenting issue. Once I accepted this, I became the mom I needed to be. I make many mistakes on a daily basis, but I take the opportunity to learn from each one and forge ahead. I am truly blessed to have a son who teaches me so much about life, parenting, and myself.

Very recently, Zach has begun to ask questions about the contents of *Invisible Target*. I have had multiple age-appropriate discussions with him throughout the years about personal safety and boundaries. In explaining *Invisible Target,* I have chosen my words carefully, and I have been honest with him about who I am and what I have been through. Zach needs to be aware that unfortunately there are some people in this world who have bad intentions. Above all, I want him to know that he can tell me anything, and I will absolutely listen and respond. Once he grasped the concept of the book, Zach's most special response was, "Wow, this is really important." I'll always be grateful for Zach's patience and support through the writing of this.

Dating Patterns

For a long time, I made pretty bad decisions in whom I would date and for how long. I had very low self-esteem, and I held this notion that if someone showed any interest in me, I was required to date him. I would always be flattered. I did not feel like I had the right to pick and choose whom to date. If there was someone I felt an attraction for, I was certain he would not be interested in me. I would end up with people who were unavailable—either because they were married or simply because they were not at a place in their lives where they were ready to open up and be vulnerable and communicative with me.

Some were alcoholics. Others were self-centered. Some were just in love with being in love and did not really see me in a true light. Others were married and would justify to me why it was acceptable to cheat. I would get caught up in justifying the situation to myself and wouldn't think about the ramifications.

As I write this, I wonder where all my logic and morals went during those times. These dynamics just felt so familiar to me. Bob was married most of the time he was with me. I was accustomed to not having full access to a person, and I felt that was all I deserved. I was used to compartmentalizing everything. I did not really think about anyone really being married. This person or that person had chosen me over their spouse, and that was the end of it. I never had a picture in my mind of being in a happy, healthy relationship. That was something reserved for other people. So if I got to experience a little bit of pleasure, it was a sweet surprise for me.

The drama that sometimes ensued with these conflicted relationships was also familiar to me. I didn't enjoy it, but I expected nothing better for myself. It wasn't until I got divorced that I realized the pattern I had been repeating for so long. Joe was also unavailable to me in certain ways. When I finally realized I wanted and deserved more for my life, I woke up. My choices started to improve. I would date a new guy and be surprisingly optimistic in the beginning. I always gave him the benefit of the doubt, expecting he would be wonderful. However, the moment I realized he wasn't good for me, I would end the relationship. At first, I attributed this pattern of behavior to my becoming bored very easily. But it wasn't boredom; I simply hadn't met the right person.

I fully realized this once I became involved with William. He was good for me in every way. I warned him in the beginning that I had a terrible pattern of what I thought was "getting bored" in relationships, and I didn't want to hurt him. He took in that information and proceeded, knowing that clearly this "thing" would never last. The weeks turned into months, and we both became closer and happier. This is by far the healthiest relationship I have ever experienced. Through the clarity and peace of mind that William brought me, I have reached a better understanding of my past choices and experiences. I dislike writing about this so much, and yet if it helps enlighten someone else who is making the same bad choices, then it is worth it for me. Again, to anyone out there I may have hurt along my route to understanding, I am sorry from the bottom of my heart. I wish I could take it all back. Please accept my apology.

I feel strong in saying that I have learned so many lessons the hard way. My relationship with William is one of the most beautiful gifts in my life. He has accepted my relationship with my son in such a loving and patient way. Zachary adores William, and that touches my heart. I have no doubt that William and I were supposed to meet at the exact point in both our journeys and not a moment sooner. He has helped me heal in ways I cannot begin to describe.

My "leftovers" still rear their ugly heads at times. Luckily, William understands and patiently reminds me that he is neither my father nor Bob, and the check-ins and apologies are unnecessary. I finally found a healthy, strong, and honest relationship in which I am cherished for exactly the person I am—no more, no less. This is more than I ever expected.

Current Relationship with Mom

My current relationship with my mother is good. She lives forty-five minutes away, and she has a wonderful relationship with her grandson. She has helped me out quite a bit through the years with watching Zach when I needed to work strange hours or needed to get away for a little vacation. We are able to talk easily about many lighthearted topics, and I find that she is the one who comes to me seeking advice rather than vice-versa.

I think my mother has had a difficult time adapting to many of the changes I have gone through. In order to escape from Bob's abusive control as well as leave my marriage, I had to change in a big way. I used to have a hard time speaking my mind confidently. I was timid about everything and seemed to be in a constant state of asking for permission and apologizing.

Now, it is a very different story. I have a difficult time holding back my feelings and opinions. I still tend to be apologetic more than is probably necessary. However, I am a strong-willed woman who will never be taken advantage of again. Part of that means I will no longer allow people to shame me into keeping things inside that need to come out. **They say that when you change yourself, other people sometimes fight that change and want the old you back.** I don't know if anyone wants the old me back, but I can tell that some people are not accustomed to my new strength, and my mother is one of them.

I don't think my mother quite knows what to do with me sometimes. Her demeanor also changes when we start talking about deeper topics such as my father, my childhood, or Bob. She appears fragile to me, and she is content with discussing only the surface, superficial things. It doesn't make me love her any less. I have just accepted my mother for who she is and what her limitations are.

When I began writing this book, I found massive amounts of support from nearly everyone—except my mother. I think it felt dangerous to her. She would never say, "Don't write it!" but I think she wished that it would all sort of just go away. Being truthful about ugly things is not her favorite arena. I'm sure she also didn't want to be shown in any light other than that of a fun and spontaneous mom, who just happened to suffer through a terrible marriage and now has a happy life. She definitely was fun and spontaneous—I think I acquired those parenting traits from her. However, there are some other, less positive traits that had to be mentioned here as well for me to tell the whole story.

As I was finishing up the writing of this, my mother was able to rally and show her support in the best way she could find. It has become a bit easier for us to engage in discussion about the past in a more truthful way. I'm sure the development of our relationship will continue to be a very interesting journey for both of us.

My Father

The last major encounter with my father I have shared thus far occurred when I asked him to help me pay for college. Several years later, when I was about twenty-four, I received a phone call, with a male voice on the other end of the line. I had no clue who it was.

"Hi, Andrea," the voice said.

"Hi, who's this?"

"It's your father," he replied.

My stomach dropped. I was active in therapy at this time, so I immediately practiced some of the techniques my therapist, Deborah, had been teaching me. I took a few deep breaths.

"Hey, what's up?"

"Well," he said, "I'm heading back down to Florida soon, and I just thought you might want to connect with me. Do you realize how long it's been since you have seen me?"

Normally, in response to a question like this, I would have stuttered a bit and said, "I don't know." But somehow, I was able to say, "Yes, in fact, I do know how long it has been."

This surprised him because it wasn't my normal, meek method of response. It certainly surprised the hell out of me.

Then, he pulled the guilt card. He said, "Well, I don't understand how you can be in that field you are in [which, at the time, was social work] and just leave a relationship like this just hanging out there like it is."

My response surprised me. It came from that healthy part of me that was finally starting to grow after such a long time of stagnation. It was the product of weeks—no, months—of intense soul searching and therapy and angst and sorrow and courage, facing my demons and myself. This was my response: "Well, I have been dealing with some things having to do with you, and I needed to not have contact with you in order to deal with them."

I have no clue how that sounds to an outsider, but, for me, it was the *most* honest expression of myself in my life up to that point. I spoke my truth. Something unlocked for me in that moment. As I write this, I have been sitting for some time, trying to think of ways to describe the moment. I just can't. Its power was beyond the scope of words. It is funny how something like that would truly be effortless for me to say now. But back then? It was huge and pivotal and courageous.

As soon as I made that simple, honest statement, his tune changed in a way that was unfamiliar to me. He started to talk fast, stutter, and really not make much sense.

"I hope you know I didn't abuse you or anything," he stammered.

I froze. *Did he just say that to me?* I thought. *"I hope you know I didn't abuse you?"*

If someone does not rob a bank, he has no need to tell someone that he did not rob a bank. My mother never abused me, and she would never have to clarify to me that she never abused me. So I froze.

I had been attacking this abuse question for years, and here it was, staring me in the face (or speaking right into my ear). So my response was simply, "What would make you say something like that?"

This is when he started talking really fast. "I don't know. You are talking about not having contact, and dealing with me. I just want you to know I didn't abuse you."

At this point all therapeutic breathing techniques went out the window. "Well okay then," I said sarcastically. "Glad you cleared that one up."

He finished up the conversation by saying how long he was going to be in town and if I wanted to meet up with him, I had a short window to do so.

"Okay," I replied. "Thanks for letting me know." I hung up and went into my living room and stared out the window for a long time.

Looking back, I have a hard time remembering what my thoughts were when I hung up that phone. I think I was somewhat in shock. I wonder what was going through his mind when he hung up. I'm pretty sure the call didn't go exactly as planned for him. He was so accustomed to manipulating and controlling me. When one player changes the game, it can be quite difficult for others to learn what the new rules are.

For many years leading up to that phone call, I had been content not having him in my life. I realized as I got older that I only wanted to allow kind people into my world. My father was not a kind person. I had already grieved the absence of a good father. I did not want to reconnect with him just to have a dad. I would rather be happy with the people who lifted me up, rather than forcing myself to make nice with the people who brought me down.

Recently, I had a surprising change of heart. There was something inside me that wanted to reach out to my father, to sit down and talk with him. I suppose being knee-deep in the writing of this book created a curiosity in me. Several people in my life questioned my reasoning. They wanted to know what my true intentions were. So I spent a lot of time asking myself what I would want to gain from this meeting.

I had no ridiculous expectations that he would have an outpouring of remorse. I never expected he would feel anything close to accountability for what he had done. I knew better than that. I don't think it would change anything anyway, even if that were his reaction. I had no need to hear him apologize or validate any of my experiences. I really just wanted to know, for myself, as an adult, that I was capable of sitting in the same room with him. I wanted to see what he looked like to me through my adult eyes. Much like when the police described their perceptions of Bob as being a "wimpy creeper," I wanted to see if I found my father less powerful and scary now that I had developed my own sense of self-worth.

My brother Ronnie thought this was a terrible idea. He thought my father was smart and incredibly manipulative, enough so as to make me cower under his will. Ronnie believed that he would find a way to inflict more damage on me. I wanted to see if this is the way my father still interacted with people. *Does he still see himself as a victim in life whose ungrateful children don't even talk to him anymore?*

I felt I could handle whatever he threw my way. I needed to find out.

As luck would have it, my father was on a similar path of wanting to contact me. In 2014, my brother Paul sent me a message on Facebook, stating that my father wanted my number, and he asked if it would be okay if I gave it to him. I paused for a moment, and responded that, sure, giving him my number was fine—I was ready. Paul left me a message later that evening wondering why I would put myself through this. Ronnie continued to think it was a bad idea, and William was even questioning why I would agree to speak with my father. But my determination and clarity were unwavering at this point, and it felt so wonderful to know my true intentions. I knew exactly what I needed to do and say to this man, and it really didn't matter what anyone else thought or felt. And if I made a terrible mistake in this decision, I was okay with that.

Ten minutes after Paul asked if he could share my number with my father, my cell phone rang. I let it go to voicemail, as I did not recognize the number. I listened to the message, and sure enough, it was "Dad."

"Andrea, it's Dad . . . give me a call."

It was strange to hear his voice after all these years. He sounded so old and gruff.

I was prepared for this call, and I decided that I really didn't want to engage in any superficial chitchat. I wanted to meet him near his house, face-to-face. Ronnie had told me that my father would in no way agree to meet anywhere outside his house. Paul and his family had visited him several years before, and apparently they had never left his condo —for days. My father's wife at the time took them to the mall, but he was clear that they weren't going anywhere. He had developed some mobility difficulties in these late years—he was obese, had developed diabetes, and was an overall unhealthy guy. So my brothers' expectation was that I would have to go to him. I firmly decided there was no way I would even set foot in that man's house, and if he would not agree to meet me somewhere else, that would be the end of it. I would walk away knowing I had tried and that he just wouldn't budge.

I waited for William to get home that evening so that I could call my father back. I dialed him, and my body started reacting similarly to the way it had when I had been about to call the principal and the police. I was aware that, as with all the other really big moments in my life, this moment required courage and clarity. They also required a confidence born of knowing that I had the right to do what I was about to do— strive for closure. That confidence had been missing for years in my life. Once I gained that confidence, things simply fell into place.

The phone rang a few times, and an old, frail-sounding man answered the phone. "Hello?"

"Hi, it's Andrea."

"Hi, hi, Andrea! Wow, you called me back."

"Yeah, how are you?" I asked, following up with a nervous giggle that pissed me off.

"I'm good, how are you?" He laughed as well.

"I'm fine," I responded.

And then he started small talking about how he gets emails from who knows where, claiming he knows nothing about the Internet, seeing my pictures on Facebook. He asked about Zach. "What's his name?" he asked.

I answered, and then he said he also saw a picture of me with someone who must be a boyfriend.

"Yeah, he has a nice smile . . ." he said.

At that point, I realized that he was grasping for things to say, and he sounded creepy and ignorant. I decided to take control of the call. I told him that I would like to drive down to where he lived (about 2.5 hours south of me), meet somewhere close to him, and talk some things over with him.

He sounded surprised. "Oh, you would drive down here to meet? Yeah, that would be great."

There you go—Ronnie and Paul were wrong. You never know how someone is going to react. Don't rule out things all the time. You never know!

I said I would try to find a free Saturday, and I told him to pick a place close by to his home, and we could meet. And then he said these words that still make me just shake my head and laugh every time I think about them.

"Yeah," he said, "and then you can stay over. . . . "

I seriously could not believe this man actually said those words. Was he in earnest or was he just fishing for a reaction from me?

"Yeah, no," I replied quickly. "I would not be comfortable staying over. But you just find some place for us to meet, and I will figure out a good day to head down there."

Now he sounded surprised. "You wouldn't feel comfortable? Really?"

"Nope," I replied again, "wouldn't be comfortable, but you pick out a place and I will meet you there."

"Huh, you wouldn't be comfortable," he mused aloud. "Wow, how 'bout that. Well, okay then, I guess we will meet somewhere."

It was difficult not to laugh or be sarcastic, but I remained calm and steady.

My father also added an assumption that I would be bringing Zach with me to meet him. I quickly stated that I would be visiting him alone and tried to move the conversation along. Nothing inside me could envision having my child meet this man.

He suggested meeting at a restaurant near his home, and I agreed. I told him I would call him in a few weeks once I had a good day picked out. He told me he was so glad that I called. All I said in reply was, "Okay, talk to you later."

I hung up, feeling great. That one brief conversation alone felt like a victory for me. I felt like I had been talking to a weakling, a man who was trying desperately to get me to engage with him but had nowhere to go. I was in complete control, and it felt amazing and empowering.

The day arrived when I was to drive down to West Palm Beach to meet up with him. William drove down with me. I experienced a moderate amount of anxiety, and we processed every possible thing my father could say to me during the upcoming meeting. I dropped off William at a bookstore and headed to Dunkin Donuts, where my father and I had decided to meet.

I arrived thirty minutes early. I went to the counter and nervously ordered a beverage. As the girl behind the counter rang up my order, I said to her, "So, in about thirty minutes, I am about to see my father for the first time in over twenty-five years."

She looked at me, confused, with an expression that asked, "Why the hell are you telling me this?" I just had a need for someone in that store to know that a huge reunion was about to occur. I couldn't be the only one who knew this! She simply replied, "Well, I hope it goes the way you want. . . ."

I thought for a moment, smiled at her and said, "So do I, so do I. . . ."

My father arrived fifteen minutes later. He walked in, glanced at me, and kept looking around. He didn't recognize me. After a moment, he looked back at me and made an exaggerated motion, acting surprised that I looked so different. When I saw him, I was surprised at how old and weak he looked. Here was another example of some scary, intimidating man from my past whose presence no longer had that same effect on me. He looked pathetic to me.

He sat down and launched into some small talk. I did not stand up to greet him. This decision not to stand and welcome him was important to me. I wanted to feel in control, and I did not want to embrace this man. After his ability to make small talk began to dwindle, he asked if there was anything I wanted to bring up.

I had heard from my younger brother, Paul, that he and Ronnie had started to confront my father recently about incidents that occurred in the past. His usual responses to them were that they were just misremembering things, and nothing had happened the way they recalled. They had both warned me of this, and I had no intention of confronting him on anything, mainly because I had no need for him to do or say anything. Nothing would have mattered at this point. I simply wanted to sit there and face him. And I was already doing that, so I had already achieved my goal.

When he asked me this question, I simply said, "Well, I was curious to know why you contacted me."

"Well, you were quick to agree to drive down here and meet me, weren't you?" he said.

"Yes," I replied, "because I was curious to see why you contacted me."

Right at that moment, I realized I was feeling incredibly pleased with myself. I knew that I could confront this person sitting in front of me with ease.

"Well," he said, stumbling a bit, "I really have no idea. One day, I just went into my office and started calling people. I called you. I called your brothers. I called other people, too, who I haven't spoken to in years."

So he just started randomly calling people? I was fine with that. He started talking about regretting calling some people because he realized they aren't very good people. One man, he insisted, was a bad person because he wasn't very kind to women.

I repeated his statement to him, and said, "Well, that's not a very good quality in a man, now is it?"

And this man, my father, who had abused me for so long, *agreed* with me. He certainly seemed to be putting forth some effort early in this conversation to convince me that he was a good person. This tune of his was all too familiar—he'd been singing it since I was a child, all those years ago. More small talk followed, and then he asked me again if there was anything I wanted to bring up or discuss.

It dawned on me that he was trying to lead me into naming things I was angry about, as my brothers had done, so that he could dispel them, one by one. I knew that my strategy here was to not bite at any bait he tried to feed me.

"Well, you know," I said, "I realized when you called that I was ready to have face-to-face closure with you."

He leaned forward. "Now, what do you mean by closure?"

"Well," I replied calmly, "we have not had a relationship in a very long time."

He nodded his head.

"And we're not going to have a relationship now either."

I felt such pride, strength, and clarity when I spoke to him.

His face fell. He looked down and said, "Oh we're not, huh? Well, that's too bad, but I understand. I understand."

"I want to explain something to you," I said firmly. "A long time ago, I made a very conscious decision of who and what I would allow in my life. I knew that I could only have kind, supportive, loving, unconditional people in my life—people I wanted to be like. And you didn't fit into that. You just didn't."

And he just nodded his head and said, "Good for you. Good for you."

He was acting supportive, as if he grasped everything I was saying, and I got the sense that he heard my words in a way that did not refer to him at all. We talked about a few other things, including my theory that everyone is on his own specific journey through this life, and people enter in and out of that journey to help him learn specific lessons. At first he agreed with an emphatic "Absolutely!" But as I continued, he said, "Oh, I don't think I am on any journey anymore."

I told him that we are all on a journey until we die, and then we have to face whoever is on the other end of that journey and will have some major questions to answer. I told him that no one could answer these questions for him—not even his grown children. He has to figure it out on his own.

He seemed so lost when I was talking about this. And he had such a victimized look on his face. The truth is, his actions and inactions have brought him to where he is today. He is all alone; none of his family wants to be around him, and he has only himself to blame for that.

When he knew that he was getting nowhere with me, he changed the conversation. "Can I give you some money?"

"No!" I quickly replied. "Why would you give me money?"

"Well," he said, "I have money and I thought you could use it."

I can't begin to explain how fantastic it felt to refuse his money. I told him that, although I appreciated the offer, there was nothing inside me that was capable of accepting money from him. He continued with his offer, stating that everyone needs more money when they are young.

I asked him another two times why he wanted to give me money. At that point, about five young teenage girls walked into the store giggling. He looked at them, sort of chuckled, and then got very teary-eyed. "I miss you kids," he said.

"I bet you do," I said coldly.

He added, "I missed out on a lot with you kids."

"Yep, you did."

"And I just feel like I should give you some money."

I explained that I would not accept anything from him, and he kept telling me that he didn't understand why. "Yes," I said, "I don't expect you to be able to understand this, and I'm really okay with that. I don't need you to understand. I'm good."

He hung his head again and tried to change the subject. Before we wrapped up, he said, "Just so you know, I wasn't going to give you a small amount, like $100. It was $14,000."

I just nodded and said, "Okay?" *And this,* I thought, *changes things how exactly?*

And he continued, "And the reason it is $14,000 is because there is no tax penalty to you or to me at that amount."

I told him that I thought the tax-free amount was $10,000, and he said that the amount had been changed.

"Oh well that's good to know," I said. "Yeah, no, no thanks."

I finally asked him if he had anything else to add.

He said, "If you ever need money would you give me a call?"

I leaned forward, a gentle smile on my face. "I won't be calling you."

He slowly nodded and looked down again.

With that, I stood up and said good-bye to him, and I walked out the door. I walked to my car, got in, sat down, and let out a happy yelp. I had such an adrenaline rush.

I picked up William at the bookstore, and we shared a celebratory lunch. Never did I feel as victorious or strong or, well, whole as I felt that afternoon. I had few expectations from that meeting, but the positive effects of facing my father are still manifesting to this day. I did not realize just how powerful this encounter could be. Although I understand the concerns that my brothers had about my well-being, I am glad I trusted my instinct and didn't let anyone else talk me out of facing my father.

My son, Zachary, finally asked me one day about my father. I never talk about him, and he really isn't in my consciousness at all anymore. Zach asked if I had a father and why I don't talk to him. I thought about it for a minute before responding.

"You know, Zach, my father wasn't a loving man. He was pretty mean to me as a kid, for a long time. I only let people who treat me nicely stay in my life, so I don't talk to him anymore, and I'm a lot happier."

I had always wondered how I would handle questions like that from my son when they were finally asked. I found that a simplified truth, such as the one I gave Zach, worked out well and hopefully taught him a lesson about how you should allow the people in your life to treat you. I'm sure we will have deeper conversations about things like this sometime in the future, but for now, it works.

My Brothers

As I began to allow my truth to speak for me while writing this book, I began to have an easier time talking with my family members about the past. My brothers and I had never really discussed my father or

Bob very much. Once I shared with them the fact that I was writing my story, it seemed to open a dialogue among us all for the first time.

I had included Paul in several outings with Bob throughout the abuse. Paul's younger age shaped how he viewed Bob much differently than how Ronnie viewed him. Looking back, Paul now understands the true nature of the abuse and is always willing to help me sort through issues that arise.

Ronnie's reaction to Bob's abuse greatly surprised me. Growing up, I never felt overly close to Ronnie, and I really didn't have a sense that he knew I existed half the time. He was busy trying to survive, just as we all were. However, I soon learned that he had very strong feelings about my parents, Bob Baker, and the lack of intervention from everyone. The statement Ronnie made that really got my attention was "We all have blood on our hands, Andrea."

He explained that they all knew, at some point, that Bob had sex with me while I was in high school. Ronnie had confronted my mother and me once he found this out, arguing fiercely that we needed to go to the police. My mother and I had both argued with Ronnie, claiming that there was no need to inform the police at that point, as I had finally managed to break away from Bob and I wasn't yet strong enough to face the issue.

Ronnie has said that there are defining moments in our lives—decisions that we make or don't make—that determine who we are. Not going forward to the police was a defining moment for him that he struggles with to this day.

Public Speaking

I began to experience a need to research the prevalence of what I had gone through with Bob. Was I really part of a very isolated and bizarre type of abuse, or were there many others that shared this experience? It became very important to me to learn about teacher sexual abuse on a grander scale.

I started doing some research on the Internet, and I stumbled upon S.E.S.A.M.E., Inc. S.E.S.A.M.E. stood for Stop Educator Sexual Abuse,

Misconduct, and Exploitation. The name alone brought me a sense of validation. I was surprised to find an entire organization dedicated to putting a stop to the horrible behavior I had been victimized by. S.E.S.A.M.E. is a nonprofit organization that is the leading national voice for the prevention of sexual exploitation of students by teachers and staff.

Once I discovered S.E.S.A.M.E., I realized just how much of a need there was for people like me to speak publicly about my abusive experience. The statistics were staggering, and yet public awareness seemed so limited. I felt I had finally heard my calling, and suddenly I knew what my purpose was: I was meant to speak out about the abuse, and not just for the purpose of sharing my story. Many people have stories worse than mine. My purpose in sharing my story was not just to experience closure, but to help prevent the same abuse from happening to other kids. I felt that part of the reason this had happened to me is because I was someone who could actually survive it, overcome it, and do something about it.

A strong need grew inside me to educate and inform others. I wanted them to understand the dynamics of abuse and what an abuser can look like. I wanted them to learn about what a victim can look like. I wanted them to learn what abuse looks and feels like. Most important, I wanted people to see the dangers of keeping quiet, of not trusting their instincts, and of looking the other way. I made those mistakes, as did many others in my life.

Things are rarely black and white in life. It would be easy for someone reading this book to say, "Wow, I wouldn't have done that—I would have done this instead. It is so obvious that he was molesting her. How could they not report him?" Things can get very blurry and complicated when a teacher sees another teacher as one of their peers—as someone they think they know. It has been my hope that by sharing my story, people can learn to listen to their instincts and tune their radar in on the signs of abuse before it escalates.

My first opportunity to speak publicly arose when Hofstra University in New York held a conference addressing the prevalence of educator sexual abuse. S.E.S.A.M.E. reached out, looking for survivors of educator abuse to speak about their experience. I eagerly jumped at the opportunity. I was a nervous wreck planning my speech, but the nerves were more about if I looked fat and what I should wear. I was ready to share my story with a large group of people who were there for the sole purpose of learning and prevention. It was a fantastic experience.

I also had the opportunity to speak on the *Montel Williams Show,* as well as two separate *Fox News* live interviews. All of these experiences were so valuable in teaching me techniques of getting my points across articulately and concisely.

Needless to say, this was a very emotional and passionate topic for me. Narrowing down my story into bullet point lessons proved challenging. It has been quite difficult compressing my whole experience into the chapters of this book. I couldn't imagine how I could compress this entire book into a five-minute segment. It was a process I had to learn and fine-tune with each new speaking engagement.

My favorite speaking engagements are in schools. I began speaking at Wellesley High School in Massachusetts. They held an annual seminar day, bringing in dozens of speakers from all walks of life. I commend this school for being so open and proactive and allowing me to speak about this sensitive and provocative topic to high school students, staff, and faculty. I gave three seminars each time I spoke there. Each seminar, kids and teachers filled the seats and lined the walls of the classroom.

While I felt a bit surprised there was this much interest, I felt comfortable speaking to them; it truly felt like I was born to do this. What was so healing for me were the questions they asked me during the Q&A session. These kids brought up questions I hadn't considered in years. One student asked if I had to act a certain way or hide certain expressions, so that people wouldn't know that I was "with" Bob. I had forgotten about that dynamic until she asked. Another student asked me what advice I would give kids in general to help them know if it is love or abuse. A third student wanted to know why Bob's wife never went to the police once she found me at home with him.

They were the brightest group of students I had ever met, and they were so sensitive as well. Their questions and comments helped propel me forward in my healing and growth in ways I could not have done on my own.

I continue to do public speaking on educator sexual abuse as often as I can and will for as long as I am physically able. I believe the more awareness that can be brought to the public about this crime, the better. It occurred to me one day that in all the times I have told anyone about my story, just about every person I told would recall some teacher from their middle school or high school "sleeping with" some student. I have yet to tell someone about my story and have a person tell me, "Wow that never happened at my school." I am sure there is a school out there that is clear of abuse. I just haven't encountered it yet. My ultimate goal is to help change this.

Decision to Write the Book

Following my experiences with public speaking, I knew that more awareness was needed in the general public about educator sexual abuse. I kept hearing one story after the next in the news about students being molested by their teachers. With each story, my stomach would turn and my heart would break. In October 2012, former Penn State University assistant football coach Jerry Sandusky was sentenced to thirty to sixty years in prison for his conviction in a child sexual abuse case. While that case hit the news waves, it felt like it was just another reminder to me of how much my book needed to get published. I was so sickened to hear not only of all the victims that were to forever be affected by these crimes but also of all the people who looked away for so many years. How many of those children could have been saved if people had stepped up and protected them the moment there was even a hint of wrongdoing?

I had toyed with the idea of writing a book about my experience for a few years, but any time I would start writing, my busy life would get in the way. I did not know how to balance work, parenting, exercise, race training, and book writing. I kept thinking the right time would just arrive and *poof!* out would come a book!

After a few years of this nagging feeling that I had something to say and teach, I met the love of my life! William entered my life at the perfect time. I could go on and on about how wonderful and brilliant this man is, but suffice it to say, William (among many other things) got me started writing this book. He helped me organize my thoughts enough to have structure in my days, evenings, and weekends. He also helped me organize the chapters so that this has almost felt like filling out a form rather than writing a book. My gratitude for his help with this book is endless.

The process of writing a book this honest has been complicated. Some parts felt liberating to write, while others felt painful. Some parts I could not write at all without the assistance of other folks who recalled more details than I did. I think the toughest part in writing this book was wondering how people who are still in my life are going to react.

How do you write about the things you lacked in your childhood and not worry how your mother will handle reading it? How do you write honestly about your failed marriage, knowing that your ex-husband will probably be reading about himself?

I have been determined to write honestly and fairly without trying to bash anyone. I have a natural tendency to protect people's feelings, sometimes at my own expense. William kept encouraging me to "just write it down—edit it later." I would get stuck often because I didn't know how to tell the truth in a way that wouldn't hurt someone's feelings. I had to work through this, and it was very helpful for me.

In the end, I wrote this book to help people. I didn't want to hurt anyone, but I felt that to help in the best possible way, I had to write the truth. If I didn't tell the whole story, it wouldn't accomplish the ultimate goal of the book, which was to try to explain how something like this could happen. I couldn't just write what was convenient to write. It all needed to be told.

FOR YOU, THE READER
CONSIDER THIS . . .

Is any chapter of our lives truly closed? Or do we simply gain clarity, forgiveness, and peace? Many actions, events, discussions, and so on have helped me to move forward in life. I am truly happy and fulfilled these days. I still carry my "leftovers" in certain areas of my life. I don't anticipate them ever leaving me. I am simply at peace with them.

Bob went to jail. He served, in my opinion, a very short sentence, but he did go to jail. He lost his pension. He is a registered sex offender and can never teach again. Veritas is married and has a successful career. Anastasia is engaged to be married and is also working full time. They both have their leftovers that they carry with them as well. But they are living and loving life.

I have a life rich in friends, family, and love. I am enjoying a career in speaking out against a terrible crime that can be prevented through awareness. I have a son who rocks my world and helps me grow. I have a wonderful man by my side I love with all my heart and who returns that love tenfold. I am happy, healthy, and strong.

If that isn't closure, I don't know what is.

For all readers . . .

- What is your perspective on my attitudes toward various people from my past (family, ex-husband, etc.)?

- How do you think the meeting with my father impacted me overall?

- How do early relationships in your life affect future relationships in your life?

- Do you have areas in your life that need closure? How does lack of closure affect you today? What prevents you from addressing those issues? How might your life be different if you did have closure?

As a survivor . . .

- Is there anyone or anything in your life needing closure? If so, what are you waiting for?

- Do memories of the abuse you endured affect your ability to function in a healthy manner?

- What are some positive things that resulted from enduring the abuse?

Closure can propel your life in directions you really can't imagine sometimes. We have one opportunity to live this life and learn the lessons provided to us. Ralph Waldo Emerson said, "Do the thing you fear, and the death of fear is certain."

Final Thoughts

—◀○▶—

People have asked me over the years how I can be so accepting of what happened to me. I have also been asked if I would change what happened if I could. I have consistently answered a resounding no. Although I experienced hell during and after that abuse, I would not change it. That abuse made me the person I am today. And today, I am a strong, outspoken woman who believes in protecting children and educating adults.

As I have mentioned, perhaps part of the reason I had this experience is because I am someone who can do something to stop educator sexual abuse. I am no longer a victim who feels she must remain silent to feel safe. I am a survivor and plan to live as such. I plan to continue to speak out and educate as many people as will listen. Who knows what path my life may have taken me had I never encountered Mr. Baker.

The main reason I wrote this book is to educate people. It is insufficient for me to merely spill out my story or create a personal memoir. I have a deep need to inform parents, students, educators, and administrators about educator sexual abuse. It is not enough for me to conduct seminars and speak occasionally on talk shows. While I thoroughly enjoy these opportunities to share information, my goal is to touch people on a much grander scale.

My hope is that this book will allow my story and message to reach every school system in the country. Consider how many cases of abuse could be prevented if every teacher in this country learns to recognize the warning signs that a teacher is grooming a student. My prayer is that if even one student is spared the abuse that I endured, this book will have been a success, and I did not suffer in vain.

Lessons from the Other Side
Red Flags, Advice, and Statistics

———◀○▶———

n my struggles to be free from the bondage of abuse and shame, I have learned many important lessons. It would be pointless for these lessons to end with me. I feel that I have resurfaced, in a realm rich in happiness, joy, health, friendship, love, family, and safety. Knowing what it took to get here, it became apparent to me that I could not take this other side of life for granted. I mentioned several times that I still deal with my "leftovers" occasionally, and the need for continued healing remains. However, I have also found that healing and pain can definitely coexist with living a vibrant, thriving life. I believe it is my duty to share some of the most important lessons that I have learned through this journey toward freedom and discovery.

In addition to documenting my story, I found it necessary to include the years of research that I have conducted on the topic of educator sexual abuse. What I found were common themes, statistics, and ideas that resonated deeply with my story and the experience of being abused at the hands of my teacher. My hope is that by sharing this information, you will be better equipped to deal with any potential scenarios that may arise.

RED FLAGS

In all the research and reviews I have conducted, several red flags seemed to be present in sexual abuse cases. Some red flags were similar to my situation; others were different. I've included a description of each of them here to help raise awareness of what to look for or to be sensitive to.

Grooming Period

The grooming process is a common dynamic in educator sexual abuse. Most of the cases I researched illustrate clear periods of time in which the perpetrators carefully gained the students' trust and affection prior to sexual inappropriateness. This period of time is critical in terms of interventions from parents and colleagues.

If someone had intervened prior to Mr. Baker's crossing the line with me, I would have been furious and confused. In my mind, he was doing absolutely nothing wrong, and he was just providing me with the care and attention I desperately needed. There was no way I could have known that this attention was a means to an end for him. However, young people need guidance and protection from the adults in their lives, regardless of how the child initially perceives this protection or reacts to it. Some type of intervention during Mr. Baker's grooming process of me could have prevented years of abuse and subsequent suffering.

Many abusers focus their energies on providing extra attention, complimenting the students, and talking more intimately about personal topics. Additionally, the misuse of technology such as Facebook and other social media outlets can contribute to a predator's ability to groom students.

It is important to understand that there may be a "testing of the waters" phase through nonsexual touch and physical closeness. Once the abusers sense they can successfully get away with an occasional touch or pat here and there, they will continue to create opportunities in which they "test the waters" on a more frequent basis, eventually leading to sexual touch and activity.

It is also important to understand that another reason abusers groom their victims is to prevent the victims from reporting the abuse. The more trust an abuser can instill/elicit/create, the more reluctant a victim becomes in wanting to get that teacher in trouble. I mentioned several times that I would have done anything to protect Mr. Baker. He stressed to me that people just wouldn't understand how special our "relationship" was, and, if he lost his job, the guilt would be on my shoulders for disclosing his secret. In this way, victims often bear the responsibility of protecting the adult, which can create massive amounts of confusion and turmoil.

Learning to recognize the signs of the grooming process could greatly decrease the incidence of sexual misconduct.

Extra Time Alone

One of the key reasons Mr. Baker had the opportunity to groom me was because I spent time with him outside class. I had lunch with him. I talked with him after school. He gave me rides home. We talked on the phone. He took me out to many places such as restaurants, arcades, amusement parks, the beach, and so on. It was during these times where he gained my trust and learned all he needed to place himself in a position to cross the line with me without my questioning it.

Be aware of teachers, coaches, and other school employees who spend time and attention with children outside their normal duties. Of course, there can be occasions when a teacher goes the extra mile to support a student. Many of us have that favorite teacher in mind who went above and beyond to make a difference in our lives. This can be a fine line at times. The difference in question is this: is the teacher coming out to see a student in a game or play where other adults are present, or is the teacher taking the student alone to the beach or an arcade? It is never appropriate for a teacher to have a student alone at his or her house . . . ever.

Gift-Giving

A hallmark red flag is the act of gift-giving. This is so common in cases of educator sexual abuse. Mr. Baker gave me a gift on the last day of ninth grade. I felt confused and as if he expected something in return. He made me music tapes, and he gave me bags full of gifts for Christmas and my birthday.

This is not acceptable! When a teacher gives a child a gift, there is a covert message associated with it. It feels conditional. It blurs the lines and confuses the roles between educator and student. The student will most likely feel incredibly flattered and special, thus creating more trust toward the perpetrator.

Gaining Trust with Parents and Colleagues

Much like Mr. Baker, many perpetrators are well-liked members of their staff and community. They often win awards for teaching and are known throughout their schools as dedicated professionals who care deeply about their students' overall well-being. It is this admiration and trust from colleagues and peers that allow the teachers to fly under the radar many times.

In addition, abusers are adept at gaining the trust of the parents in order to have more access to the children. My mother had Mr. Baker and his wife over for dinner. He attended my plays and concerts and showed all of the signs of a caring teacher who was supporting his student—all in the presence of my mother. All of these actions allowed him more access to me outside the classroom. If he seemed fine in the presence of my mother, why wouldn't he be fine on his own? I suppose we could say that Mr. Baker groomed my mother, as well. If a teacher seems to be too good to be true, I highly recommend staying alert and aware at all times.

Look for patterns. Watch for signs that are blurry and confusing. Trust your gut. If you sense that something is inappropriate, it probably is.

PROFILE OF A TARGET

What exactly does a target look like?

During a lecture at Wellesley High School, a teacher approached me with a request at the end of my talk. He asked me to please include a warning to high school girls about the way they dressed. He felt some of the girls dressed provocatively, and this would give the wrong impression to some of the teachers.

After taking several slow, deep breaths and collecting myself, I sat this teacher down and tried to explain a few things to him. First of all, no matter what clothes a student wears, a teacher's responsibility is to maintain professional boundaries. Attitudes such as this one perpetuate the mentality of blaming the victim.

In addition, many of the targets of educator sexual abuse are not the bold, provocative girls everyone sees. This is part of the reason I titled this book *Invisible Target*. I always try to explain in my talks that perpetrators target students much like a lion stalks its prey. Does the lion seek out the animals at the head of the herd, running fast and seen by everyone? No. It stalks the ones at the back of the pack that are slower and less visible to the rest of the group. Mr. Baker knew what he was doing when he "befriended" me. He knew that I needed to be seen. He made me feel so special that I did not question his intentions, and he had my inherent trust.

Many published articles discuss this dynamic. The teacher singles out the student as talented or promising, or on the flip side, very needy. The teacher will offer to spend more time and attention to make sure that child can thrive. Quite often, the parents are relieved to have this teacher's interest invested in their child. Many of the victims come from single parent homes. In almost everything I have read and researched about this type of abuse, my whole story fits in perfectly. I was the perfect target—the perfect, invisible target.

ABUSE

One thing I wanted to make sure to emphasize in this book was that I did not have a relationship with Mr. Baker. It was abuse.

I thought he was my boyfriend. He was *not* my boyfriend. He was my perpetrator. He gained my trust over a few years, he took advantage of that trust, and he abused me. The abuse lasted for over a decade. It may have had a different look from what our perception is of sexual abuse at times, but the scars it left do not feel any different to me from any ideal of "typical" sexual abuse.

It pains me when an abuse case is described as a relationship. Since when is an adult having sex with a child considered a relationship? The dynamics have to be in place for the abuser to groom the victim. This is what allows the perception of a relationship to be perpetuated. The child gets confused about the intentions of the abuser. It is important to understand that an abuser has his or her own motives for gaining the trust. There is an undeniable power differential. I got in touch with someone from high school a few years ago and mentioned the Mr. Baker situation, and I asked him if he knew about it. He replied, "Yeah, but I just thought it was consensual, so I didn't think it was a big deal."

This is also a common misconception. Just because a student may not fight the attention received does not make it any less abusive. If anything, it blurs everything. I would have done anything to protect Mr. Baker in high school. I thought I was in love with him. Obviously, I know now that it was not love. Statutory rape laws are in place for just this reason. Adolescents do not have the maturity or experience to fully understand all the dynamics involved in making the right choices in these situations. They can be manipulated more easily by someone who has power or authority over them. Also, some teenagers may tend to believe that they, in fact, DO know what is best and no one can convince them otherwise. This can be quite a dangerous combination that could lead to abusive situations.

It is also very important to note that abusive educators can have more than one victim at any given time. I have read multiple accounts in which an educator was grooming and abusing several students simultaneously. The predators keenly build up a student's belief that he or she is special. Meanwhile, three other victims can be experiencing the same treatment.

WHEN A PEER IS THE PERPETRATOR

When Mr. Baker was in custody, many teachers initially rallied around him. It was hard for them to believe that this beloved, popular teacher of thirty-one years was capable of committing such a horrible crime. This is understandable. Teachers who prey on students are generally very charismatic and put a lot of effort into being well liked. They often win teaching awards and are active participants within their communities.

An extremely important fact is that pedophiles gravitate toward careers in which they have access to children. Someone who has an obsession with children may not really be drawn to the world of, let's say, accounting—not a whole lot of kids are getting their taxes done these days.

Think about it: where do we hear many of these abuse stories taking place? Church, scouts, schools, sports, and so on—all the abusive professionals in these settings have the ability to gain trust, access, and use their position of authority to manipulate children.

It can be difficult to believe that one's peer would cross the line with a student. I believe that most teachers and administrators are in the teaching profession for all of the right reasons. It can be hard to imagine another teacher having less than worthy intentions. I can also understand having difficulty believing that a colleague could be guilty of misconduct when he or she is known for nothing but fantastic accolades and a history of popularity with adults and children alike.

Try to suspend your disbelief for a few moments and remember that everyone was initially shocked when Mr. Baker was arrested. Yet, with further investigation, many teachers quickly named me as a possible third victim. Something in them knew that he was inappropriate with me in some manner. I cannot emphasize enough the importance of trusting your instinct and reporting your concerns.

Report your peer anonymously if necessary, but report him nonetheless. It is not your job to determine the guilt or innocence of the teacher, as well as whether the student is telling the truth. Throughout my research, many teachers claimed that they had suspicions of inappropriate behaviors by a teacher, but they were so concerned with being wrong in their suspicions that they would never be able to forgive themselves. Again, there is no burden of proof on you, the bystander. It *is* your job and responsibility, however, to report any suspicion of wrongdoing. Teachers are mandated reporters, which means there is a mandate in place to report any suspicion of abuse or neglect inflicted upon a minor in the care of adults.

Dr. Charol Shakeshaft is an educational researcher who was commissioned by the Department of Education to review the available literature on sexual misconduct with students by public school employees, and she published her findings in 2004. Shakeshaft noted multiple teachers defending their stances against reporting possible abuse allegations for fear of ruining a teacher's career. A teacher was quoted as stating, "'If I reported and I was wrong, I would have ruined the life of another teacher.'" Shakeshaft's reply to this was, "I have never heard a colleague say, 'If I didn't report and this person had abused, I'd have ruined the life of a student.'"

Remember, teachers can be held liable for not reporting suspicions as well. Our children need you to speak up.

WHAT TO DO IF YOU SUSPECT

So many people in my life knew at one point or another that Mr. Baker molested me when I was in school. I knew this. My family knew this. My friends knew this. My therapist knew this. We all knew at some point that Mr. Baker, a teacher, had sex with me while I was in high school. Many teachers admitted to having suspicions about this. None of us—not a single person, including me—went to the police or the Department of Children and Families. It took me many years before I realized the implications of not reporting his crime. By the time I did, it was too late. Two other lives were ruined.

It is very difficult to act on a suspicion alone. Many of those teachers trusted and respected Mr. Baker. After all, he had invested many years in the teaching community, and he had no disciplinary actions against him. Mr. Baker was a well-liked teacher and coach. He helped out the kids who had a tough home life, and other teachers looked up to him.

How do you question all that, just because he is giving a girl a ride home? Here's the point: Question it. Speak out. Talk with the teacher in question about appropriate boundaries in and out of the classroom. Go to an administrator. Call the police. Call the Department of Children and Families. Talk to your colleagues.

Talk about it.

So many teachers seem to want to protect the teachers more than they do the students when it comes to accusations. You don't have to know all the answers or bear all the weight on your own. Parents also need to be informed that there is a suspicion of abuse regarding their child. The parents should also be informed of the reporting procedures that are in place in terms of who will be notified, regardless of whether they want this reporting to occur or not. My hope is that my story will make everyone stop and think about the repercussions of not trusting their instincts and not reporting their concerns.

SUSPICION OF GROOMING

The reason I have focused so much of this book on the grooming process is because I believe this is the phase where much of this abuse can be prevented. If someone had magically sent Mr. Baker away prior to the time when he crossed the line with me, I would have been very confused. In my mind, he was just being really kind and helpful. I would never have understood why someone thought his kind actions were dangerous in any way. The bottom line is: It doesn't matter what I would have thought about it. It would have prevented years of torture for me.

The grooming period can be extremely blurry, especially when viewed by an outsider. How do you differentiate a teacher going out of his or her way to make a difference in a student's life and a predator trying to gain a student's trust for his or her own personal pleasure?

Keeping the red flags that I have listed in mind, I believe people have to be on the lookout for patterns, not isolated incidents. One kind gesture from a teacher does not a pedophile make! A series of gestures with either one student or multiple students, on the other hand, should be questioned and expressed. Is the teacher spending a great deal of time outside class with the student(s)? Are the students getting out of other classes to help with a special project? Is the teacher giving children rides home? Is he or she meeting with them on the weekends? Are any gifts being exchanged?

Pay attention to the students' moods and behaviors. Are there any noticeable changes? Are their grades dropping? Are they becoming isolated from their friends and/or family? Look for patterns, and speak up. If enough people voice concerns, the administration will be more likely to investigate the matter. Don't be afraid to report suspicions to the police.

CONVERSATIONS TO HAVE WITH YOUR CHILDREN

When I was growing up, we never had to worry about walking to school or online predators. We didn't seem to hear much about domestic violence or bullying or alcoholism. There certainly was no mention of teachers molesting their students. Aside from the online component, can we really be sure none of these issues were so prevalent back then?

Maybe our awareness has just been raised. I talk to plenty of people who tell me they grew up in alcoholic households, but they didn't really have a name for it back then. I believe that teachers have been stretching the boundaries with students for a long time, and with the introduction of new technology and social media outlets, teachers and students have easier access to each other outside the classroom.

Good parenting involves educating our children about the potential dangers in the world without frightening them. We warn our kids about stranger danger, right? Well, far more kids are abducted and abused by adults who are familiar to them. In my research, I found that anywhere from 67 percent to 93 percent of sexual abuse cases involve someone the victim knows. There is usually a trust built up, which makes it far easier for the perpetrator to get what he or she wants.

Kids need to learn universal lessons about boundaries. It is okay to say no to an adult, even if it is a trusted teacher or coach. The fine line of no is a delicate one. It is one thing to be obedient and respectful about an assignment given or particular rule in a class. It is quite different to have to obey something that feels creepy or uncomfortable.

Children need to learn to trust their instincts. Teach them examples of the "red flag" feeling inside them. As they get older, they know the feeling of right and wrong inside their bodies. If they know something is wrong, their bodies let them know. Help them explore simple examples in which they can feel a red flag feeling inside. Help them tune in to themselves enough to get familiar with their own boundaries and instincts. I never learned to trust my instincts at home. So, when the crisis arrived, I had no skill set to discern what that red flag feeling was about.

Above all, please promote a spirit of open communication in your home. Make it normal to talk about the tough stuff. Your child needs to know 100 percent that it is safe to tell you anything. I believe this starts with the small things.

When your child comes home and has a bad day, don't try to just make it better by distracting him or minimizing it. Listen to your child. Let him or her vent. Validate like crazy. I always try to first validate my son before I try anything else. When he complains that someone cut in front of him in line at school, I always ask him how it made him feel. Then, I validate him. "That must have made you pretty mad, huh? I wouldn't have liked that at all!" That's it, nothing major, but he usually appears to feel heard. Then we move to problem solving or distraction once he's gotten it out. A little validation goes a long way.

If we don't build a foundation of safety and open communication when our kids are young with the perceived little things, how are they going to know how to open up to us when the big stuff hits? And remember, these aren't little things to our kids—line cutting is a very big deal in their world!

ADVICE TO SURVIVORS

I have been asked what advice I would give to survivors of educator sexual abuse. The first thing that comes to mind is, "It is not your fault, it is not your secret, and it is not your shame. Do not carry that around with you or it will drive you mad."

You can be ashamed of your actions as an adult, of course. I've got my own grown-up shame-filled actions, some of which I shared in this book. But things that happened to you when you were a kid—you are not allowed to believe any of that is your fault. It does not matter if you agreed with any of the actions or even enjoyed them. The body and mind have natural responses to emotional and physical attention. This does not give an adult the right to manipulate you for his or her own pleasure.

PLEASE . . . if you have not told anyone that you were abused, tell someone you trust right away. If you are a student reading this and something inappropriate has occurred, you need to tell an adult. I don't care how much you feel you need to protect that teacher or coach. I felt the same way, and I would have fought anyone who tried to expose the truth to me. Looking back now, I regret being so protective. I could have saved two other girls from being molested. You can prevent that, too.

If you are an adult, and the teacher who hurt you is still teaching, please call the police. I called the school system, thinking they would take care of it all, and they did nothing that made a difference. They asked Mr. Baker and he denied it, end of story. I should have gone to the police. Although I can't change that now, I can definitely encourage you to go to the police. Waiting for years to say something that could have prevented innocent lives from being harmed will haunt me for the rest of my life. Don't let the same happen to you.

Tell someone.

ADVICE TO TEACHERS

Boundaries, boundaries, boundaries. I know that most teachers have great intentions. It must feel frustrating to have to second-guess a hug you want to give a kid who looks like they are having a tough day. I agree that the landscape of education and teacher-student interactions have changed considerably, especially in the last few decades. An added concern these days that I didn't have to worry about back in the eighties is technology. Texting, instant messaging, and Facebook are all dangerous behaviors to engage in with students. The fact is, times have changed, and teachers simply must think differently about their classroom and the lives inside it.

Demonstrating clear and consistent boundaries with students is a very safe practice that can eliminate many concerns. I hear teachers voice their concerns about false accusations at times. If you are concerned about this, then safeguard yourself. Dr. Charles J. Hobson is a professor of management at Indiana University Northwest, and he is also a member of the S.E.S.A.M.E. advisory board. He recommends providing a safe place for students to talk with you that is visible to others. Do not put yourself in a position in which false claims can be made. Time outside the classroom needs to be limited to being spent with more than one student. I would not recommend giving students rides unless multiple students are present the entire time. Again, if you maintain stature that has consistent, appropriate boundaries, a false accusation occurring against you is less likely.

My advice for teachers who may have a concern about another teacher acting in an inappropriate manner: Approach the teacher first and speak to him or her about your concerns. I know most abusive teachers will not acknowledge any wrongdoing, but increased awareness by others cannot be a negative thing. Also, voice your concerns to administration. Make an anonymous call if you have to. Do not sit idly by with your concerns. As previously mentioned, many teachers have this idea that they have the burden of proof on their shoulders. Teachers do not have to prove guilt or innocence. What they are responsible for is reporting suspicious behaviors or activities. Once again, if it seems inappropriate, it probably is.

ADVICE TO SCHOOLS

I would love to see every middle school and high school have an annual training curriculum in place in which teachers and students learn about the prevalence of educator sexual abuse as well as what to do if suspicion arises. An expectation is often placed upon children to speak out if someone hurts them. Why is more focus placed on the kids than on the adults? How can we expect something of our children that we are not willing to do or do not understand how to do ourselves?

I enjoy lecturing in schools, but I always feel conflicted. I speak to hundreds of students, but they are not the only ones who need to hear my lecture—the teachers and staff do. I can encourage the kids to speak up, but it is the adults' responsibility to protect these children.

In his book, *Passing the Trash: A Parent's Guide to Combat Sexual Abuse/Harassment of Their Children in School,* Dr. Charles Hobson wrote the following suggestions of what parents can do on a school level to help insure the safety of our children:

> You can fight back at the school-level through the PTA/PTO or school board or your own individual actions. The goal is for the school system to adopt policies/practices that substantially minimize or eliminate the problem of educator sexual abuse. These actions could include:
>
> 1. Mandatory annual training on sexual abuse prevention and reporting for all students, parents, and teachers.
> 2. A policy prohibiting school employees from being alone with students.
> 3. A policy prohibiting or strictly limiting touching of students by educators.
> 4. Psychological testing in the hiring process.
> 5. Disciplinary consequences for employees who fail to report suspected sexual abuse.

I was surprised that the school did so little with the information I shared with them about Mr. Baker's abuse. The superintendent called him in and confronted him with my allegations. Mr. Baker denied the allegations, and they sent him back into the classroom. They never notified the police. Eight months later, two more victims were exposed, and *then* the police were notified. There was a clear lack of firm policy in place within Norwood that would ensure the safety of their students. This is why I am so determined to help schools develop training and procedures nationwide. We need to protect our kids.

ADVICE TO SCHOOL SYSTEMS

"Passing the trash" is a term frequently used in the topic of educator sexual abuse, referring to a trend in which a teacher gets dismissed from a school following allegations or charges of sexual misconduct. He or she is then allowed to work in another school system without that school system being notified of any allegations or charges. S.E.S.A.M.E., Inc. has been focusing on getting legislation passed where, state by state, a law would exist to prevent "passing the trash" from being possible.

School systems need to ensure they have a protocol in place to appropriately respond to accusations of abuse. The Norwood school system clearly had no reliable system in place to handle my accusations against Mr. Baker. Schools need specific criteria, guidelines, procedures, and protocol in place when a serious allegation, such as sexual abuse, arises. They need to know that a phone call to local police is imperative to successfully ensure that the child in question, as well as other students in the school, are safe. In addition, they need to develop school and district level policies that focus on the following issues:

- **Screening and hiring practices**—Strict background screening and fact-checking practices need to be implemented. Oftentimes, a teacher can have an offender record in one state and apply for a new teaching position in a different state, and his or her record may never be accessed/discovered.

- **Investigation policies**—Swift and succinct investigative procedures need to occur the moment a sexual misconduct allegation occurs. For the safety of the children, removing the teacher in question from the classroom needs to be immediate, until the completion of the investigation occurs.

- **Reporting procedures**—Every school employee in each school system needs a clear awareness of how to report suspicions or allegations of sexual misconduct. The school systems need to work closely with both local law enforcement and social service agencies to ensure proper reporting, fostering the enhanced safety of their students.

ADVICE TO STATE LEGISLATORS

There is an alarming lack of stringent policies in place in many states regarding consequences for teachers who sexually abuse students. Many states do not even require notification to the Department of Education when a teacher has been charged with abusing a student.

Dr. Hobson recommended the following at the state level:

> By contacting and lobbying state/national elected officials, you can request that executive orders (from governors or the president) be issued or laws passed to require schools receiving government funding to implement aggressive policies/practices, like those discussed in the previous section. S.E.S.A.M.E. is a national leader in these lobbying efforts and can help to guide/coordinate your individual efforts. Inaction allows sexual predators to continue abusing our children. We can't tolerate this and must join together in fighting back. There are countless ways to do this and many sympathetic, like-minded people to help.

Contact your local officials and request that aggressive policies be put in place to ensure the safety of our children.

NOT ALL TEACHERS ARE DANGEROUS

Most teachers are fantastic, and they only have the purest of intentions. They are motivated obviously not by their salaries, but by their drive to teach and make a difference. I had many teachers during my education who stand out in my mind as dedicated, wonderful educators. One teacher I recall was my high school English teacher Mr. P. It was obvious to me that he cared deeply about the craft of teaching and what his students learned. I remember watching him teach, taken in by his passion and enthusiasm for writing. He was a tough teacher, and I respected him from the first day of class until my final grade—which I would rather not broadcast. Ironically, writing was not my favorite subject!

By no means am I implying in this book that parents need to beware of every teacher out there. I am simply hoping to raise awareness of what to look for in a dangerous teacher.

STATISTICS

Throughout the chapters I have shared various statistics, but I wanted to include them again in this section to ensure that my message rings loud and clear about just how rampant this epidemic is in our school system.

Dr. Charol Shakeshaft noted all of the following statistics in her 2004 study:

"More than 4.5 million students are subject to sexual misconduct by an employee of a school sometime between kindergarten and 12th grade . . . nearly 9.6% of students are targets of educator sexual abuse sometime during their school career."

"10–15% of students in the U.S. will be sexually abused by a school employee at some time during their school career."

"90% of all child molestation is done by people who already know the child—a teacher, friend, trusted family member, or relative. That is significant—adults must remember that."

"One in 4 girls and one in 7 boys will be sexually abused before age 18, according to a 2005 report by the American Academy of Pediatrics."

"Nearly 7% of students have experienced unwanted sexual contact from an educator (from inappropriate touching to long-term sexual relationships and serial rape). Victims range in age from kindergarten to high school seniors."

"Only about 6% of all children report sexual abuse by an adult to someone who can do something about it. Fear of not being believed is the #1 reason kids don't report their sexual victimization at the hands of an adult. When it is reported, teachers, administrators, and some parents frequently do not (or will not) recognize the signs that a crime has taken place."

"Unreported Abuse. Educator sexual abuse is a widespread problem in American schools. Although more than 2,500 educators were punished over 5 years, most of the abuse never gets reported, and very few abusers get caught."

"Accused educators have consisted of teachers, janitors, bus drivers, librarians, school psychologists, principals, superintendents, and volunteers. Teachers are reported most often, followed by coaches."

"Many educators who abuse work at being recognized as good professionals and outstanding teachers in order to avoid suspicion and to gain a path to children. They are often popular and recognized for excellence."

"Perpetrators use powerful incentives to keep many victims silent, from vows of love to threats of violence from abusers."

"Sometimes the abuse is a result of bad judgment. Other abusers who prey on children often take jobs where children are easily accessible."

"Sexual abusers in schools use various strategies to trap students, such as isolating them, lying, and manipulating them into sexual contact. Often teachers target vulnerable or marginal students who are grateful for the attention."

"Most teachers who abuse students have a history of harming children, but do not have recorded criminal backgrounds."

Digital Journal (digitaljournal.com) reported that since 2007, over 2,000 separate sexual abuse cases have been filed against U.S. public school employees. This takes into account the relatively small number of cases dismissed outright, dismissed under plea agreement, or changed to other charges upon conviction, but does not include the many others that get swept under the rug, covered up, or never reported at all.

A 2007 *Associated Press* investigation, covering the period from 2001 to 2005 and reported in *USA Today,* found that of all reported educator misconduct cases, only about a quarter, or 2,570, of educators were punished for sexual misconduct nationwide. There were 2,625 cases that resulted in license suspension, revocation, denial, surrender or "other punishments," according to the report. Under current enrollments, this would represent a total of 4 to 5 million sexually abused U.S. public school students.

Resources

───────◄○►───────

This section includes various online resources concerning educator sexual abuse.

S.E.S.A.M.E, Inc. • www.sesamenet.org

S.E.S.A.M.E. (Stop Educator Sexual Abuse, Misconduct, and Exploitation) is the leading national voice for the prevention of sexual exploitation, abuse, and harassment of students by teachers and other school staff. Ending the practice of "passing the trash," a phenomenon where educators investigated for abuse are able to resign and get a new job at a new school, is S.E.S.A.M.E.'s top priority for ending abuse in schools. There are also great resources on this website for survivors, teachers, and families.

Dr. Charol Shakeshaft's full report (Educator Sexual Misconduct: A Synthesis of Existing Literature) can be found on S.E.S.A.M.E.'s site. This report examines the prevalence of abuse, ages of adults, how they select and groom children, where and how the abuse takes place, how they maintain secrecy, reporting of allegations, effects of the abuse on the victims, effect on other students, awareness of school officials and their responses, investigative practices, criminal background checks, false accusations, federal and state child sexual abuse laws, consequences for abusers, patterns of misconduct, and prevention strategies. Read the full report here: **www.sesamenet.org/supporters/links/29-educators/131-educator-sexual -misconduct-a-synthesis-of-existing-literature**

I have been a member of the speaker's bureau for S.E.S.A.M.E. for over ten years, and I could not feel more proud to represent such a wonderful organization.

KidSafe Foundation • www.kidsafefoundation.org

KidSafe Foundation is a nonprofit organization whose mission is to prevent child sexual abuse, bullying, and Internet dangers by providing education programs to children, seminars to parents, workshops to teachers and counselors, and trainings to all professionals working with children. I am a certified instructor with KidSafe, and I'm thrilled that I have the opportunity to empower children and educate adults through KidSafe's wonderful curriculum.

SHEARED • www.sheared.org

SHEARED (Spreading Hope for the Exploited and Abused through Resources, Education, and Discourse) is a nonprofit organization dedicated to spreading the hope of true healing to survivors of all types of exploitation and abuse, reducing further instances of abuse, and decreasing the harmful misunderstanding of trauma and its widespread effects among the public and professionals through resources, education, and discourse.

McGrath Training Systems • www.mcgrathinc.com/index.html

McGrath's programs are designed by nationally recognized education law attorney, licensed investigator, and Expert Witness in Bullying/Harassment lawsuits Mary Jo McGrath.

The Sexual Abuse and Misconduct training program is a three-course program designed to provide school personnel with the knowledge, skills, procedures, and legally sound tools to prevent harm and provide a safe school and working environment. The course is broken down into three key areas:

1. Awareness—What is sexual abuse and/or misconduct and how to detect the early warning signs?

2. Intervention, prevention, and the correct procedures for handling the complaint management process.

3. Investigation Process at site and district—Process information, procedures, and legal requirements for site and district personnel.

Darkness to Light • http://www.d2l.org

Darkness to Light offers programs that raise awareness of the prevalence and consequences of child sexual abuse by educating adults about the steps they can take to prevent, recognize, and react responsibly to the reality of child sexual abuse.

RAINN • www.RAINN.org

RAINN (Rape, Abuse & Incest National Network) is the nation's largest anti–sexual violence organization and was named one of "America's 100 Best Charities" by *Worth* magazine. RAINN created and operates the National Sexual Assault Hotline (1-800-656-HOPE and online.rainn.org) in partnership with more than 1,100 local rape crisis centers across the country and operates the DOD Safe Helpline for the Department of Defense. RAINN also carries out programs to prevent sexual violence, help victims, and ensure that rapists are brought to justice.

Survivors and Friends • www.SandF.org

Providing hope, information, and support for survivors of sexual abuse, for their friends, and for their families.

Male Survivor • www.malesurvivor.org

Provides critical resources to male survivors of sexual trauma and their partners in recovery by building communities of hope, healing, and support.

Childhelp • www.childhelp.org

Childhelp® is a leading national nonprofit organization dedicated to helping victims of child abuse and neglect. Childhelp's approach focuses on prevention, intervention, and treatment.
Childhelp: 1-800-4-A-Child (1-800-422-4453)

U.S. Department of Education, Office of Civil Rights • www.ed.gov

ED's mission is to promote student achievement and preparation for global competitiveness by fostering educational excellence and ensuring equal access.

Andrea Speaks Out • www.andreaspeaksout.com

Andreaspeaksout.com is the website I have created to share my experience and educate and guide others. My primary goal has been and will always be to prevent educator sexual abuse.

A Note from My Mother

———◀○▶———

A s I was completing *Invisible Target,* my mother became interested in contributing to the book. She felt an urgency to discuss her perspective of the abuse I endured. She also wanted an opportunity to caution other parents based on the lessons she learned from it all.

As a mother, I think your worst nightmare is the fact that you haven't protected your child from the painful years that my daughter went through. Why didn't you pay attention more closely to those little signs that things just weren't right? Why didn't you speak up more than you did?

When Andrea was in junior high school, it was unthinkable that a teacher (just as a priest, coach, scout leader) was anything more than what you had grown up believing—an adult with the intent of helping your child. I started to notice her teacher paying an unusual amount of attention to her—rides home, presents, phone calls in the evening, etc. I brought it up and her adamant response was always that "He's like that with everyone. Everyone loves him." There came a point that I thought, "I am the adult here and this isn't right."

I met with Mr. Baker and told him I felt Andrea was getting the wrong impression and was reading more into his attention than he intended. (I was still under the impression that, as the teacher, he was just trying to bolster Andrea's self-confidence.) Of course, his response was that he had "no idea." I asked him to please back off and keep things a little less personal. I also asked him to please not share our conversation with her. That afternoon, Andrea flew in the house, slammed her bedroom door, angrily yelling, "Thanks, Mom, for making me lose my only friend."

I was furious that this man had first of all broken my request for confidentiality and had put it on me that he couldn't see her anymore. I called him and he, of course, played the innocent—never intending to go against me. My biggest regret is that I didn't pursue this with the principal. In all honesty, I was afraid of risking my relationship with my daughter even further. I felt she would probably never forgive me.

Things seemed (to me) to quiet down after that, and I was lulled into the false belief that my worries were over. Little did I know that he would teach her how to keep everything secret. I had no idea how they would escalate. I heard very little about Mr. Baker after that— his name would come up on rare occasions, and it seemed to me all was appropriate.

Andrea went off to college, and I truly thought Mr. Baker was behind us. So wrong. If I had only known the distress and pain she was going through.

It was several years later that I met with Andrea and her counselor so she could finally tell me that she had stayed involved all those years. This was such a blow and all the guilt and remorse came flooding back. It still weighs on me that I wish I had pursued the issue with the principal.

We were in California visiting Andrea's brother when she had finally been able to make a clean break from this man, and the freedom that glowed from her was wonderful but heartbreaking.

In conclusion, my advice to all parents who are feeling that something is "off" with a teacher—please, please don't ignore it. Your chances of being heard are so much better now. With your vigilance, you can prevent your daughter or son (as well as you, as a parent) from the pain and shame that Andrea and others have gone through."

—Linda Cieri

In 1996 I wrote my first song. *Ghost* describes the experience I had of returning to my childhood home as an adult, finally free and clear of all the abuse I had endured as a child, an adolescent, and young adult.

Ghost

Words and music by Andrea Clemens (1996)

This voice I hear all around me
Is something I heard long ago
It serves as a deep reminder
of something that I should know

It echoes through the rooms and the hallways
Through the attic and cellar down below
If I listen to that voice closely
Will it be someone who I should know

Ghost, it's all around me
Ghost, it's calling for me
Begging me not to go
Who belongs to this voice
I fear I have no choice
And yet . . . I don't want to know

I came to stay for a short while
Thought I could come and go with ease
Little did I know that your power
Would infect me and not let me breathe

Aimlessly walking in circles
Trying to rid you from my brain
Not even knowing who you were
You were with me just the same

INVISIBLE TARGET

Ghost, it's all around me
Ghost, it's calling for me
Begging me not to go
Who belongs to this voice
I fear I have no choice
And yet . . . I don't want to know

Now I have gone
Away from you, away from this
Cleansing my soul
Returning is my innocence

Soon I returned to that same
Hallway and cellar down below
I heard but a whisper
Just repeating, "I know . . . "

So now you think that you haunt me
With your actions from before
I think that you know those actions
Haunt you more

Ghost, it's all around me
Ghost, it's calling for me
Begging me not to go
Who belongs to this voice
I fear I have no choice
And now . . . I know

References

Chapter 3

Vermont Department of Children and Families. "The Grooming Process." http://dcf.vermont.gov/stepup/educate/how_it_happens/grooming. Accessed January 3, 2015.

Chapter 9

"School staff express dismay over colleague's arrest on rape charges." *Daily News Transcript.* Date of Issue: March 14, 2002.

Ellement, John. "Third student accuses teacher Norwood case seen expanding." *Boston Globe.* Date of Issue: March 15, 2002.

"Former Norwood teacher to be arraigned next week." *The Dedham Transcript.* Date of issue: June 3, 2002.

"Pupil reports affair with Norwood instructor." *The Boston Herald.* Date of Issue: March 15, 2002.

About the Author

———◄○►———

Andrea Clemens received her master's degree in clinical social work from Boston University and has spent the majority of her career working in higher education. Relating to her personal experience, she has been educating school faculty, students, parenting groups, administrators, and the general public about educator sexual abuse for over ten years.

She has participated in both local and national radio, news, and television programs. Andrea is a member of the speaker's bureau for S.E.S.A.M.E. (Stop Educator Sexual Abuse, Misconduct, and Exploitation), an organization dedicated to preventing sexual exploitation, abuse, and harassment of students by teachers and school staff. She is also an instructor with the nonprofit organization KidSafe Foundation. She is thrilled to educate parents, mentors, and teachers about different ways to protect children from abuse.

Although Andrea remains dedicated to being a single mother, a tri-athlete, and performing in various other roles, she continues to invest time and energy ensuring that schools can be safe environments for our children—free from harassment and abuse.